CITIZEN PARTICIPATION IN DECISION MAKING

CITIZEN PARTICIPATION IN DECISION MAKING

Towards Inclusive Development in Kenya

Edited by Kimani Njogu

TWAWEZA

COMMUNICATIONS

"Working Towards a Better World"

Published in 2013 by:
Twaweza Communications Ltd.
P.O. Box 66872 - 00800 Westlands
Twaweza House, Parklands Road
Mpesi Lane, Nairobi Kenya
website: www.twawezacommunications.org
Tel: +(254) 020 269 4409

Design and Layout: Catherine Bosire
Cover design: Apex Books and Publishers

With the support of The Ford Foundation

ISBN: **978-9966-028-43-3**

Printed by:
Franciscan Kolbe Press
P.O. Box 468, 00217 Limuru, Kenya
Email: press@ofmconvkenya.org

Dedication

This book is dedicated to the life of Mzee Geoffrey Njogu Kariuki (1924-September 8, 2013) for climbing the hills and breaking the rocks for a better Kenya.

Contents

Acknowledgements

This publication results from a series of knowledge sharing public forums organized by Twaweza Communications and which involved academicians, civil society actors, and the public. The forums were inspired by the recognition that academicians have little space to share their knowledge with members of the public yet they have so much to offer in the transformation of society. We are grateful to the Ford Foundation for giving us the opportunity to organize conversations on citizenship, governance and leadership. We are also grateful to all those who participated in the forums as presenters, discussants or audience members. By sharing your knowledge you are contributing in the construction of the Kenyan nation. A number of people have given important feedback towards this project and it is impossible to mention all of them. We thank you all. Special gratitude goes to Prof. Cege Gĩthiora, Dr. George Gona, Dr. Mbũgua wa Mũngai, Kakai Karani, Mueni Lundi, Dr. Cecilia Kĩmani, Athman Lali Omar and Thiong'o Ngũgĩ for comments on the papers and for continued support and guidance in this journey of enquiry. Twaweza Communications team deserves gratitude for organizing the public forums in Mombasa, Embu, Kisumu, Nakuru and Nairobi and coordinating various activities related to the social change project. I am also grateful to Catherine Bosire for designing this publication. Let us keep the flame of democratic practice alive.

Kĩmani Njogu
Nairobi.

Introduction

Citizen Participation in Decision Making: Towards Inclusive Development in Kenya is part of ongoing work at Twaweza Communications to strengthen citizen engagement in governance and contribute in creating resilient communities in Kenya. We believe strongly that if Kenya is going to move from a discourse of 'growth' to one of 'development', from a discourse of 'blame' to one of 'responsibility', leaders at all levels of society must devote their energies to a politics of inclusion, fairness and justice. We must all seek to create a society where each one of us feels at home. A life of excessive accumulation of material things, ethnic and political exclusion, marginalization of women and youth, poor delivery of services, corruption among public officers and unaccountable leadership is untenable and unsustainable. It can only lead to social insecurity, unhealthy lifestyles and political instability. Each one of us must take steps to reshape our country.

This book is a result of public dialogue forums organized by Twaweza Communications and with the support of Ford Foundation in pursuit of accountable and transparent governance in Kenya. From the dialogue forums held in Mombasa, Embu, Kisumu, Nakuru and Nairobi it was evident that the stability of Kenya will be driven by the extent to which citizens feel fully included in the development agenda. Quite often, political leaders see the role of citizens in governance as restricted to their participation in elections. This narrow view has led to arrogance and total disregard of citizens after poll results are announced. Under the new political dispensation heralded by the promulgation of the Constitution of Kenya on August 27, 2010 this trend must change and the sovereignty of the people, in theory and practice, must be reinscribed. The health of the Kenyan society was underlined constantly in our public conversations. But health is not the absence of disease; it is the well being of society at the political, economic, social, cultural, environment and technological levels. By creating a healthy and productive society, we lay a strong foundation for future generations.

The publication raises important issues worth serious reflection. It also suggests ways in which citizens can better participate in their own transformation. Case studies highlighted in the book exemplify the importance of consciously building the Kenyan nation by addressing patterns of exclusion and glaring inequalities.

Going back to the public dialogues, a number of avenues for citizen engagement in governance come to mind: They include how media can create space for divergent citizen voices to be heard and how political parties can be transformed so that they are become genuine channels for members' voices. The development of a media sector that is independent, plural and free from political and commercial interests is fundamental to democracy in Kenya. Realizing the power of media, the political elite have acquired radio and television stations in order to guide editorial decisions. But Kenya will need to wrestle itself from the shackles of unfreedoms perpetuated by a political class which seems totally blind to the dangers of exclusionary politics. This can be done by nurturing alternative media that courageously work in the public interest. Alternative media channels can be key cogs in the wheels of citizen participation in governance. Through these media citizens can share, learn and interrogate. They can monitor the performance of their leaders and bring them to account.

Within the political arena, citizens should contribute in building democratic, accountable and issue based political parties. They should demand that leaders who seek political office articulate the platforms on which they should be judged. By sharing with citizens their principles on a range of subjects around which they seek support, leaders will contribute to the entrenchment of inclusive and issue driven political engagement. But the articulation of principles is not enough if there are no clear strategies, approaches, channels and benchmarks that will be used to operationalize them. There is need to set higher benchmarks for the political class in Kenya and to move from uncritical support on the basis of blind ethnic loyalty to genuine engagement with issues at the heart of the people such as poverty eradication, respect for human rights, sustainable development, accountability and transparency in the conduct of national affairs, equality, justice and commitment to the realization of basic needs for all citizens.

Lacking in any form of ideological cohesion, political parties in Kenya, in their current form, are only peripherally instruments of genuine social change. As one politician said, parties in Kenya have become like 'matatus' into which one hops and alights at will! Yet political parties are vital organs of governance in the contemporary world. Citizens ought to join and start democratizing political parties in order to give them direction.

Essentially, a political party is a group of people who are formally organized with the aim of gaining the reins of governmental power in a country. Parties in Kenya are varied in terms of their visibility, resources and leadership. Some are economic ventures and others are ethnic enclaves; seeking to only protect local community interests. Political parties are ideally vehicles for orderly political competition in modern political systems. In a democracy, they serve as institutions of governance, and instruments of representation, mobilization and articulation of the interests of citizens. The principle of multi-partism is a critical prerequisite for democracy; it provides the electorate with a viable opportunity to determine their preference for rulers and policies to govern them, an issue that Musambayi Katumanga eloquently addresses in this volume.

The trouble with political parties in Kenya stems from the entrenched ethnic nature of the nation's politics as well as the opportunism that informs political action in the country. Parties lack clear ideological orientation and philosophy, and thus leaders retreat to ethnicity as the main organizing principle, as Felix Ngozi argues in his Chapter. Without doubt strong ethnic affiliation has greatly eroded the potential to entrench democratic culture. Just like in the colonial days when the state was used to open up opportunities for a clique and protect their interests, the post colonial state is also designed to entrench and consolidate sectarian and ethnic interests. As a result, access to political power translates to specific benefits for members of the ruling socio-economic class and individuals from the ethno-linguistic group in power. Significantly, however, the benefits do not trickle down to the broad masses of the people because, in the first instance, they are not active participants in the design of national politics as well as the often fluid philosophies against which they are governed.

These factors have led to low party discipline, patronage and the concept of "*wenye chama* "; that is, that political parties have their owners who, whether they are officials or not, have the right to run and manage the party as a private club.

Because they are ineffective, several arguments against political parties can be advanced. One, political parties can create conflicts in emerging nation-states because they are formed along ethnic, regional, and other sectarian interests and do not pay attention to the well-being of the citizens as a collective. Political parties are also capable of promoting violence as was evident in Rwanda, Burundi and Kenya in the 1990s by mobilizing members along ethno-regional lines and defining sections of the population as 'other.' In countries which have serious socio-economic inequalities, parties may be used to accentuate ethno-regional tensions by masking the class basis of the inequalities and instead attributing them to ethnic privilege and opportunity. Ethnicism, the negative manifestations of ethnic identity, becomes their hallmark.

Two, in most of Africa political parties are authoritarian, elitist and urban based. Due to absence of internal democracy in political parties, there is usually a tendency for parties to have the "big man's syndrome". A party cannot claim to champion democracy when the actions of its leaders are dictatorial and intolerant of alternative viewpoints. Also, a party cannot claim to uphold peaceful co-existence when its leaders support violence and insecurity. This tendency is evident in Kenya where members with alternative views have historically been subjected to embarrassing disciplinary action and at times expelled because they did not agree with the leader. They have been told to toe the line or else be kicked out. Again, the dictatorial tendency is a consequence of the internal systems in the parties and the leadership that is transitory and not inherent in parties *per se*. But, a well organized political party with clear ideological orientations can be an important institution to nurture the ideals of democracy among leaders and members. It can be humanizing if well utilized for the good of all.

Three, in the eyes of many, political parties are seen as corrupt and perpetuate the vice in society. Undoubtedly, this is a common phenomenon, since parties raise funds locally and internationally and never disclose their accounts for public (or even members) scrutiny. Rather, they award contracts and benefits to their benefactors once they get the reins of power. They are also engaged in manipulating poverty and the electoral process to ascend or maintain power. There is overwhelming evidence in Kenya to show that voting and identity cards are issued selectively in certain regions. In cases where the youth of a certain ethnic community are known to support a given political line, they may be denied identity and voting cards by the local administration and therefore denying them the right to vote. Violence in certain areas is also associated with differences in political alignments in order to deny citizens their right to vote. Parties could also be bought in the pursuit of power or for the formation of coalitions based on political survival and self interest and not principles or ideals. Moreover, lacking a steady funding base, political parties become personalized and are associated with individuals and not policies or platforms.

Four, political parties are said to kill individual creativity because members are expected to conform and toe the line drawn by their self-appointed leaders, who are often the founder members. In parliament, for example, members are expected to vote with their party on crucial motions, sometimes against their conscience.

The weaknesses associated with political parties in Kenya could be addressed by enforcing the right of citizens to choose their representatives without intimidation and to criminalize the purchase of voters' cards and other violations of the electoral process. It is also solved by examining how political parties can be funded by the state and encouraged to come up with political platforms. The platforms would have to be documents developed through consultations with members and citizens at large to provide a roadmap along which the leadership would be made accountable. This is an extremely important stage in political party organizing because the platform sets benchmarks against which leaders are judged. In essence, political parties have a huge potential in ensuring that democracy is consolidated.

But these are not the only avenues open for the entrenchment of democracy in Kenya. Reading through these Chapters points to a number of possibilities for citizen engagement at the national and county levels. But these openings will only bear fruit if pursued rigorously. Writing about the tensions at the Coastal region of Kenya, Rocha Chimerah draws from history to argue against the exclusion of Mijikenda communities, a matter that is followed up controversially by Halimu Shauri and Lusweti Sellah who challenge the communities to be more productive and embrace education.

In addressing gender inequalities in Nyanza region, David Omondi Okeyo discusses how women are vulnerable to HIV infections. An unhealthy public is unlikely to demand accountability from leadership and issues of democracy and transparency are viewed as abstract because the basic need of good health has not been met. In order for the public to effectively participate in governance, we must invest in quality health for all. That is not too much to ask, is it?

As Alexander Luchetu Likaka has shown, the growth of information technology has opened possibilities for the entrenchment of knowledge economy. To what extent can Africa harness the knowledge gained by youth to solve some of the Continent's problems? This requires a shift in mindset so that knowledge is seen as a resource. It is completely unacceptable that the people who live around Lake Victoria are not able to meet their basic needs despite being surrounded by masses of water and families with thousands of livestock die of hunger. This failure to solve basic problems is an indictment of the Kenyan leadership. But this can change if citizens become active participants in social transformation. The engagement of citizens as agents of change should not be tokenistic; it should, rather, be engrained in the national philosophy and psyche.

Kĩmani Njogu
Nairobi

Politics of Exclusion/Inclusion

Multi-Partism and the Political Economy of Exclusion in Kenya

Musambayi Katumanga

Introduction

This chapter recapitulates on the politics of multi-partism and exclusion in Kenya. It grapples with some core questions: *how does multi-partism engender exclusion? How does the media spawn this exclusion? What are the resultant security threats? What should be the mission of the state in the foregoing setting?* The chapter contends that exclusion is a function of leadership failure in its manifest mission of state building and that sustaining it (exclusion) through corruption, instrumentalization of ethnicity and violence strategies facilitates ruling elite protection of political power. The chapter calls for an alternative mode of organizing for politics outside the liberal construction of multipartism in favor of a developmentalist state to anchor the process of state consolidation. Critical here is the need to construct social citizenship and political pluralism to safeguard the society against careerism of political entrepreneurs.

Understanding what political parties are not: A Redundant Note

Political parties are voluntary entities set up by individuals who not only hold similar views with respect to public issues, but who also invest in their organizational structures with the view to using them to capture or negotiate for favorable values of power. Core elements here are that those constituting parties must at least share common principles with respect to certain values they seek to organize around. Secondly, there has to be an element of organization critical for the realization of party objectives. Parties must recruit and educate their members and the public on their programs with a view to generating the necessary numbers critical to winning political power.

More critical is the leadership variable which evolves party programs without which their very survival is doomed. To grow a party program that has an appeal to its prospective followers, leaders must seek social transformation of their objective context for the common good. The leadership must develop the requisite discipline and sense of mission as opposed to the mere search for self-aggrandizement and instead to passionately articulate a society transforming program. Where parties do not have the capacity to take power and implement their policy objectives, it is the duty of their leadership to articulate their policy options in contradistinction to the existing social order. The foregoing underpins the *raison d'être* for the existence of more than one party. The aim here is to provide voice to contending counter positions. This is what anchors pluralism as opposed to the mere presence of many entities, a factor that creates many or multiple parties.

Multi-partism is predicated on elite particularism instead of horizontal class differentiation. The dominant characteristics here are opportunism, indiscipline, low levels of trust, high levels of de-institutionalization tendencies and absence of organization and party program. Party differentiation is predicated mainly on the symbols espoused by their leadership. They become otherwise varied groups that provide labels under which candidates seek elections to governmental office (Greenstein and Polsby, 1975)[1]. The foregoing setting can only produce polarization and by inference; exclusion.

Underlying this are several factors. What are referred to as parties are essentially personalized outfits devoid of an organizing ideology, structures independent of their founders and internal democracy. They are basically individual enterprises for capturing power in the name of ethnic groups. Party constitutions do not get enacted subsequent to a popular participation process. Neither are they disseminated to the party members. Despite claims about existence of constitutions on which internal mechanism are supposed to be based, leaders and their senior colleagues often abuse most of these rules and regulations. Some parties are run like private fronts of party leaders who have no respect for membership participation in decision-making, perpetuating intolerance for fair dissent and divergent viewpoints. There is also an apparent streak of indiscipline among elected members who undermine their own parties with impunity. While few are in a position to articulate their party positions, most engage in banal politics that seek to fragment the society. The conflict resolution mechanisms and disciplinary clauses are weak in many political parties, a factor that has continued to engender fragmentations. No political party in Kenya has ever held free, fair and peaceful internal elections to the satisfaction of their members and the general public. Any such attempts have been characterized by conflicts as party rules and regulations espoused in the party constitution are flouted at party level nominations.

To date, parties in Kenya have no reliable records about their total membership or number of supporters. It is not surprising that most parties have not been able to sell their policy documents, manifestos, ideologies, visions, missions and programs to the public. Most entities are constructed in epiphenomena-logical conception. Here, a system of ideas which reflect and express interests of dominant individuals from the ruling class are constructed to represent class in illusory form. Here, ideas which compose the particularistic ideology are those that enhance the interests of these individuals to retain positions of domination. The conception is such that this reality is obscured and instead, interests of the dominant individuals are constructed so they seem to converge with those of the oppressed[2]. Parties are formed to fight for the "interest of the ethnic group" when in reality, individuals seek to assure themselves of a safe ticket as a reward for "fighting the we" interests. Lack of a participative culture with a high evaluative capacity ensures that these individuals are able to play the same games every five years. Lack of a political culture that calls for commitment, loyalty and commitment to one's party or organization ensures party-hopping. The culture of handouts and materialism, on the other hand, leads many electorates into ending up with multiple membership cards (most of these are distributed by party barons). Such cards are used for convenience, depending on which party is offering money[3].

Most parties are mono-ethnic or exist only on paper. Lack of visionary, program-oriented and organized leadership has confined these structures to entities for individual ascension to power through the logic of ethnic calculations. The core message of most political party leaders is that it is the turn of their ethnic group to rule. In a bid to camouflage this weakness, party entrepreneurs have sought to form alliances of parties (essentially alliances of ethnic notables). The speed with which Kenya African National Union (KANU)[4], Forum for Restoration of Democracy (FORD)[5,] National Rainbow Alliance Coalition (NARC)[6], Orange Democratic Movement (ODM)[7] and Party of National Unity (PNU)[8] have fragmented over time in space points to the fact that the key drive of these coalitions is raw power that can hardly hold in the context of low levels of trust among elite and de-institutionalization tendencies.

Ake's remarks may have had Kenya in mind when he notes that the African state has emerged as a contested terrain peopled by strangers with little in common except endless struggles for power that have transformed politics into Hobbesian experience. Underlying the reproduction of this politics is the political competition that always ends up in either the survival of the incumbent Leviathan or in the enthronement of a new one, without diminishing the premium on power or changing the dynamics of political competition.

Such political dynamics preclude liberal democracy which demands the rule of law, not only in government, but also in the course of political competition. While liberal democracy would have been useful given the egocentric nature of political actors and their constantly clashing interests that need to be negotiated, it instead is highly problematic, if not impossible. Notably in the localized informal politics which are tamer and lawful, liberal democracy becomes largely irrelevant[9]. It is not a surprise that the state has tended to remain unable to penetrate society at structural and social levels to create a political community. The existence of a political community emerges with certain prior constants. These include constitutionally engineered institutions that mediate relations among groups, and those between them and institutions. There is also the critical role that has to be played by institution-friendly leadership. Its ethos has to allow for rationalized deployment in institutions to ensure a balance between societal needs and institutional prerequisites is struck. The end state of this should be high levels of institutionalization, predictability of behavior and value provisioning. There is equally the need for the state to pursue the project of transforming the Polis into an ideal environment for nurturing happy and good citizens[10]. The assumption here is that only good citizens endowed with civic competence can anchor a strong state. A virtuous state begets a virtuous citizenry. Virtue here is that inherent inclination to seek good for others[11]. Such citizenry has to seek justice for their fellow citizens and common interest.

A State leadership has to seek equity, justice and fairness while provisioning values that secure the individual and by inference the state. There has to be respect of rights and equality before the law. Equally salient is the right to participation. In such a setting it is not multi-partism that emerges but rather pluralism. Where this becomes the agenda of the state, then the negative tendencies such as ethnicity and corruption are eschewed. The push and pressure for good governance becomes a collectivized desire for all, thus a basis for negating self-serving elite. Unfortunately for Kenya, the state is characterized by high levels of inequality, insecurity, corruption, factionalism and instrumentalization of violence and ethnicity. The media has not helped things either by giving voice to certain elements without subjecting their positions to a critical contextual appreciation with a view to exposing their falsehoods for the common good. This is despite its claim to the right to inform, educate and expose falsehoods. Where a government fails in its duty to create a political community, it is the responsibility of the media going by its self-declared mission, to step in to expose false narratives and provide different perspectives to the public around which decisions can be made. It is also its duty to provide voice to the excluded by exposing dangers inherent in marginalization.

Such a role is predicted on the assumption that the media seeks to pursue the logic of virtue, has morally competent managers, that is, those who know what is right and seek to ensure its operationalization. There also has to exist a high level of instrumental capacity predicated on the assumption that there is an appreciation of what needs to be done[12]. Where the foregoing is absent, the media becomes a valve through which banal ideas are circulated to the society given its ability to facilitate fixation, reproduction, and participation. The fact that as an institution it facilitates decoding, encoding, select censorship, design and exclusion of certain texts implies it can either negatively spawn exclusion or engender inclusion. Exclusion or inclusion may result from how it manages the dynamics of space and time distanciation in terms of content and extension of availability[13].

Reinvention of and Appropriation of Ubuntu[14] Communalism and Ethnic Politics

Ethnically defined politics in Kenya have their roots in colonial social engineering. Informing subsequent ethnic differentiations, polarizations and exclusion is what Brett[15]calls capitalist penetration of traditional socio-economic structures. This process, he notes, resulted in the creation of "islands of capitalist modernity co-existing with great seas of pre-capitalist traditionalism". Accordingly, persisting peasant forms of production in agriculture was a factor that hampered capitalist accumulation and by inference the evolution of a working class critical for anchoring both plural politics and constriction of ethnically defined social polarization.

To Brett, this social evolution was in line with the colonial State's policies whose central objective was to control and maintain a balance of social forces to ensure its exclusive access to economic resources. The resultant differentiated development was deemed imperative for unequal economic exchanges between the colonial state and local ethnic groups. This had a net effect of engendering differentiated socio-economic development that would later serve as a basis for animating ethnic polarization. The evolution of cash crop and socio-economic infrastructure falls in this logic. While the former was differentiated in time and space, a factor that advantaged certain communities by integrating them in the cash crop economy faster, the latter had a net effect of distancing large parts of the Kenyan territory. It denied them the ability to move goods and services, in effect locking inhabitants out of the socio-economic and political system. It is not a surprise that the first post-independence leadership, as Kipkorir[16] notes, had its roots in this differentiated development. These leaders belonged to communities living close to missionary activities and families that had collaborated with the colonial State, a factor that had enabled them to access education. Their subsequent success was dependent on their links with the colonial regime. Their main failure lay in their inability to enhance institutional penetration at economic, social and political levels that would have enhanced internal articulation while spawning equitable economic reproduction.

The fact that the colonial regime would not allow cross ethnic associations meant that their maturation in politics as articulators of social interests would reflect essentially the interests of their ethnic groups. This in turn ended up animating social distance decay among groups that were increasingly constructed to believe they were rivals over state political power. In any case, ethnic politics were part of the colonial state's strategy of "divide and rule" and indeed for the preparation of the successor elite. These elite were meant to be polarized and to facilitate their dependence on the colonial powers (even after the latter had handed over formal power). Formation and legalization of ethnically-based associations for interest articulation ensured that political consciousness evolved as ethnic consciousness.

Mwalimu Nyerere is right to note that parties were founded as nationalist movements for freeing the whole Nation from colonial domination. Their differences were not anchored in any socio-economically defined interests as is the case in the West. To the extent that this was not the case, parties would be reduced to the level of a football game or a game of groups rather than differentiated policies.[17] What Nyerere seems to be advancing here is the argument that the success of pluralism is predicated on the existing sub-structural conditions and the objective leadership factor. The converse engenders the current ethnically defined politics. Yet the prevailing socio-economic conditions offered a veritable challenge for building ideologically-based parties whose main divide would have a commitment to the idea of how best to deliver citizens from the thralldom of poverty and underdevelopment with the help of a developmental state. This orientation would have presupposed the presence of a leadership committed to equal development of the entire state rather than the mere replacement of the colonial elite and consolidation of power. Such an orientation would have presupposed what state building is all about.

The State, as Max Weber (1946) notes, is a compulsory association that successfully claims the monopoly of the use of physical force in a given territory. The essence of Stateness is in effect not only about the ability to demonstrate and enforce compliance with respect to the laws but also the mediation of social relations within established realms. These tasks demand the enhancement of institutional capacity of the state to provision values, and thus contain insecurities to the citizen. When they emerge, institutions facilitate interactions within the field and access to values. They give shape to pre-existing fields of interactions while creating a new set of positions and possible trajectories. When not well mediated, institutions animate contestations as groups seek to reverse what they consider as asymmetrical positions for advantageous ones. These may range from new forms of resistance aimed at seeking to reconfigure the fields, to new alliance formations. They may also include the construction of new symbolic forms through which meaning is reconstituted and conveyed in a bid to sustain and reproduce new forms of power conservation.

Together with the physical base, and ideas, institutions[18] form the triage that makes up and either sustains or disintegrates the state. Institutions are the arteries through which regulatory functions and welfare goals are undertaken. These have to be perceived at two levels; the human resource level that provides actors who operationalize objectives for which institutions are developed, and the infrastructure component. Both demand investment in ideas, organization and sustenance. Success in this leads to the enhancement of stateness. This becomes apparent through functions such as defense and security, enhancement of property rights, law and order, macroeconomic management, public health, and infrastructure constructions. The failure to perform these foregoing, not only undermine the state's legitimacy but also increases societal distanciation.

While economic and political institutions can animate insecurity (especially if the ideas around which they are organized are particularistic), nothing brings the state quickly to its knees like the failure to manage its instruments of violence. These become problematic when the elite, due to rationalities of power, opt to "capture" security institutions for their self-interests. Such capture includes speeded upward mobility of incompetent elements who in turn saddle institutions with corrupt elements. The net effect is that instead of security institutions being at the core of state building, they spawn collapse once they are dragged into strategies for elite regime consolidation processes. State building demands competent actors operating within an institutional framework defined by laws and backed by oversight institutions of accountability that can control security expenditure and procurement, recruitment and promotions, deployment and use. Failure in these processes produces threats of coup d'états, the emergence of unaccountable governments, insecurity impunity by way of abuses of human rights, power, corruption, waste of resources on worthless and overpriced equipment and the inability to control resultant multiplicity of security institutions. This situation is compounded by the crisis of ideas.

A State is secure to the extent that it is organized around correct ideas. This revolves around what the state leadership defines as the common interest or reason for existence of state. It is about what binds its people together within a socio-political and territorial entity. It is reinforced by the governing functions of its institutions, more specifically, the value provisioning roles, such as the defense of societal interests from external aggression, internal insurgency and provision of collective common public goods. To the extent that state leadership and institutions are able to evolve rationalized mechanisms for resource distribution and allocation, they engender a sense of belonging and nationhood among various social formations. While the notion of a nation has its roots in the logic of homogenization, in the case of

Africa, the nation state was expected to evolve out of the ability of a state to evolve ideas, institutions that enable value addition on its physical base to the extent of addressing vertical and horizontal differences among groups and identities. This was expected to lead to the construction of a new man capable of submerging his ethnic identity within a wider collective good. To the extent that citizens find themselves besieged by a competition between the state and the ethnic, the notion of the nation state is said to be in a recession mode.

The physical base of the state on the other hand has to do with its population, territory and natural resources. How value is added to the population which is the first core resource, how infrastructure is developed to facilitate territorial penetration and integration ensures that the natural resources of the state become the basis for state building and evolution of a political community. Without an organized security sector, to guarantee order, the state must bear with insecurity that compounds poverty and by inference, animates conflicts. McNamara Robert is apt when he notes:

> There is a direct and constant relationship between the incidence of violence and economic status of the countries afflicted. There is a relationship between violence and economic backwardness and the trend of such violence is up, not down. If security implies anything, it implies a minimal degree of order and stability. Without internal development of at least a minimal degree, order and stability are impossible. They are impossible because human nature cannot be frustrated indefinitely. It reacts because it must[19].

Where the political elite fail in the mission of consolidating the trinity of the state, they begin to generate the elements of state insecurities. The notion of national security is rooted in the assumption that collective experiences and institutions over time shape and mould people into seeing themselves as one. While security here can be conceptualized as that ability of the state to assure its citizens' right to core values, a threat to national security would refer to a sequence of events that threaten drastically and over a relatively brief span of time, to degrade the quality of life of inhabitants of a given state.

While national security would be expected to be about the protection and sustainability of certain core values critical to a state's survival, in Africa it tends to become synonymous with regime consolidation, a factor that generates insecurity. State insecurity in this sense can be internally generated through negative ideas of the state, poor institutional organizational logic, and mismanagement of its resource base. When these are used to promote self-interest, certain negative values emerge, such as instrumentalization of ethnicity, corruption that undermines the competence of state institutions and resource distribution. The net result is marginalization. To maintain themselves in power the elite resort to regime consolidation security measures such as ethnicization of institutions, corruption and violence. These in turn spawn further resistance generating what is referred to as insecurity dilemma[20] that animates weakness and eventual collapse of the state. This orientation is the very antithesis of the organic essence of a state. As a system, all parts have to be treated equitably if stability has to be maintained.

As Foucault notes, "the government within the large state should ultimately think of its territory as the model of the city. This is not perceived as a place of privilege but models of governmental rationality that can be applied to the entire state will be well organized when a system of policing as tight and efficient as that of cities extends over the entire territory".[21] The import of this is the need for state managers to eschew intentional differentiations while enhancing ability to control through the process of reduction of distance decay. For this to be a reality, the government needs vigilant and virtuous citizens and organizations. Core here are political entities. Unfortunately what exists are political entities that articulate and celebrate marginalization and members of the state who celebrate the mediocrity, corruption and impunity of individuals they deem to be members of their ethnic cluster. Majority of Kenyans are less virtuous, their predisposition is to seek ethnic good even if it hurts others to the extent that it is constructed for them as good for the "we", despite the fact that on the overall, this logic is against the organic good of the entire state. The net consequence of this is the increase in distance decay at economic, political and social levels.

Part of the process of achieving control is the production and organization of knowledge. For states like Kenya, rationalities for drawing maps were geared towards sustaining colonial extraction and the securitization of the colonial state. Notably, maps outline spaces identified with certain nationalities, ethnic groups and religious identities. They were designed to respond to colonial rationalities of effective native control for resource extraction. This was mediated through violence and the divide and rule tactics. The net effect was the skewed resource distribution and allocation processes, legal instrumentalization that arrested the then evolving ethnic fusion. Without meaningful attempts to enhance institutional penetration in the society, the colonial state produced and mediated the closure of spaces.

Closed spaces and Politics of Marginalization

Closed spaces here imply spaces that are constructed in discourses and behavior of state institutions and citizens to belong to certain groups either on ethnic, racial or religious reasons. Consequent results are that core values obtained in these spaces are assumed to belong to those of the constructed identity. The task of those who inherited the state should have been to redraw internal maps to objectify and make visible several socio-economic and political variables at a single glance. The aim here should have been that of facilitating the production of convictions among people, through variables that can be influenced through technology and those that are evolved through the means of responding to the needs of the populations in the process facilitating value addition and securitization. The failure of the successor elite on this merely anchors the current identity crisis. Maps now reinforce perceptions about what people perceive as their spaces which they think need to be protected. It is this that produces current challenges of multi-partism and state security architecture.

Due to slanted resource distribution and allocation and differentiated development, spaces created on maps soon denote identity of persons, who they are and their relationship with the state. They become critical to control of political power. In Kenya's case this process was consolidated by the legal changes that transformed provinces into constituencies. There was an additional requirement that presidential candidates garner 25% in at least five provinces in addition to total vote cast. This phenomenon affirmed the colonial ethnic mapping. They were now reinvented and appropriated as spaces of indigenity. As one of the three categories of spaces, access to citizenship rights such as participation here was, and remains a function of one's willingness to accept the dominant political orientation of the ethnic group in space. Right of representation is limited to members of the ethnic group. Those who do not accept this proposition are usually expelled. This space is ideal for elite preferred ethnic instrumentalization critical for regime consolidation. This type of politics finds appeal in the nature of African societies in the rural areas whose culture remains predominantly parochial and/or subjective. Emphasis here is on hospitality, friendliness and consensus along the principle of ubuntu with emphasis on the community rather than the individual. The individual and self are expected to be dependent on, and indeed to be subordinate to the social entity and the cultural process[22]. The community is presumed, and is indeed expected to provide security.

Politicians seeking power fall back on ethnic mobilization. Using latent modes of ideological conception, ethnicity is instrumentalized taking advantage of poverty and lack of critical analysis of the objective realities. Under this conception, ideology is used as a system of representation, "which serves to sustain existing relations of domination by orienting individuals towards the past rather than the future, or towards images and ideals which conceal class relations and detract from collective pursuit of social[23]. Ethnicity in this sense is an instrument used to camouflage and conceal elite domination and control over political power. Politics are symbolically constructed in a manner that they are able to appeal to the ethnic sentiments about its common origins, destiny, collectivity and social responsibility[24]. Politics that appeal to people are those that invoke solidarity and the mythic of "protection" of the interests of the ethnic group from its elite constructed 'enemies''. This appeals find resonance in the ethnic group's collective consciousness and perceptions about values of a " good family'' (as being one where everyone is also every ones business and each gives according to capacity and receives according to need).

This communal existence of majority peasants remains un-comfortable with the whole notion of privatization of collective interests. It is seen to be pernicious given that it implies disassociation of person from the context in which morality and integrity are possible[25.] Here freedom is embedded in the reality of communal life; people are less inclined to the pursuit of rights and contestations for the individual self. Indeed that is why even the elite who loot the state do it in the name of their ethnic groups. Likewise, the ethnic group is mobilized to defend its own who are accused of corruptive activities not because it has benefited from the same but mainly because the moral ethnicity demands that it defends its own from outsiders. The Kenyan peasant is not a negative ethnist by choice; he expresses support for elite from his ethnic group because this is the only logical way he is able to interpret social reality and how best he can extract benefits.

Rights are acquired on the basis of one's station in society and duty to the collectivity. Freedom is not acquirable outside the context of the collective[26]. Here tensions between an individual and the collectivity in pursuit for self are frowned at. Freedom is not perceived in terms of opposition or autonomy but rather the organic whole. Emphasis is on participation with others and not contestation against them. As Ake notes, people participate not because they are individuals whose interests need to be asserted and protected but because they are part of an inter-connected whole. Participation rests not on the assumption of individuality but on the social nature of being and the organic character of the society.[27] It is a question of sharing burdens and rewards of community membership. Participation denotes citizenship and it is about deciding on and setting goals, making decisions about the wellbeing of the society and in the process the individual is safe because the whole is safe. Socialization in this form of setting finds liberal constructions of participation through representation alienating and disempowering. Underlying this is the fact that power is alienated to power wielders except during the election periods.

Most Kenyan elite is constantly nested in two strategies, the maximum and the minimum. While the former entails attempts at grabbing power, if this fails, then they tend to have no problem in relapsing into the latter which entails retaining control over their ethnic groups. This way, they can negotiate deals with others. It is the foregoing that continues to reproduce politics of accumulation and exclusion in the process making politics a zero sum and exclusive game. Political competition ends up reproducing the predatory leviathan except for changes in guard. On the other hand, disagreements and quarrels among elite immediately find their expressions along ethnic lines.

The second categories of spaces to emerge are those of gerontocracy, where the old elite struggled for control with the youth who deployed instruments of violence to gain political power. Here, recruitment and use of youth has transformed spaces into critical assets for access and consolidation of power. Those excluded from power seek it by instrumentalizing their core ethnic base engendering tension, and extreme ethnic mobilization. While those in power seek to mobilize their core base on the basis of the need to "fight" to retain power. This engenders measures that are interpreted to imply the process of vertically fencing off the center while "encouraging horizontal push into other State places "perceived" to belong to other ethnic groups. Their "hidden" discourse is that of constructions that seek to give an impression that survival of the ethnic group is inherent in their clinching together and retaining power. Underlying this is a laborious ideological symbolic construction that seeks to fragment before unifying groups in a bid to conserve political power. This process produces a counter-reaction. It is this process that engenders the dual process of closing spaces as groups are mobilized to protect one of their own. Metal maps evolve in this sense as a rallying point structuring out the frontiers to be protected. In Kenya, this process encompasses the tendency to use violence on the un-wanted "outsiders". The entire phenomenon has produced the logic of politically closed spaces.

Within this gerontocratic space are contestations pitying the old against the youth. The latter maximize on their numbers and ability to organize for violence which they sell to the highest bidders among the political class. Since the re-introduction of multi-partism, their role and indeed the instrumentalization of violence have animated two elite strategies. They include the expropriation of private violence and the privatization of public violence. By 2007, among groups categorized as hard core militias, there were a total of 11 overtly armed groups, two pseudo militarized groups and six ethno-regionally organized groups in Kenya[28]. There were other groups that were constituted on need basis to offer violence and extract resources. These groups emerged demystifying the state's dominance over instruments of violence. In this sense, spaces of gerontocracy have become sites of resource extraction. Here, resources whether diffused or proximate, meaning that they are closer to the centers of power, or diffused and spatially spread out, have been used to facilitate access to power and in the process spawning marginalization. How groups maximize on these resources in space over time has an impact in the modes and forms of contestations. The nature of the resources not only explains relations among and within groups, and between groups, but also their relations with the state, the security architecture and actor behavior.

Diffused and distant resources found in rural frontiers such as cattle rustling have been facilitated by the mode of structure of the security architecture and the ideas that inform its design. What is interesting is the emerging influence facilitating capture of political power. Core here is the paid-for displacements that impact electoral outcomes. It is notable that in 2007, ethnic spaces saw the convergence of prevailing dominant political entities and bandit groups with the latter appearing more as ethnic "armies" engaged in "liberation" of the so-called ethnic spaces. In this sense such convergence has created a situation where "armed" multi-party entities are causing displacements, marginalization, individual, group, and state insecurities.

The third category of space is what can be described as National spaces where all citizens are expected to access their rights under the protection of the constitution. As elite de-institutionalization tendencies and corruption have taken root parallel to low levels of trust, they have directly spawned decrease of the felt sense of political community. The resultant informalization of politics has not only produced a multiple identity crisis as individuals grapple with the notion of which of the two, state and ethnic identity, they should extend their loyalty to. As informalization of politics has taken root, individual confidence in state institutional frameworks to access values equitably, has continued to diminish, causing ones decision to negate formal order for the informal one. This provides the basis for emergence of informal groups that seek to substitute the state in value provision including security. Parallel to this process is the intentional actions of the elite in power to undermine institutional rationalities eroding their competence and probity. The net effect has been that since the 1990s, this capacity has been diminishing the state's monopoly over the instruments of violence.

The Leviathan: Closed Spaces and Conflicts

The phenomenon of closed spaces is enhanced consequent to poor penetrative infrastructure and limited transformation of existing dead capital through application of technology and capital. This factor in turn spawns what Mukandawire calls termite economies. These termite economies reinforce identity polarities. Identity here is formed through a combination of the individual as an agent, and his relationship with emerging structures. How structures either include or exclude facilitates the process that Louis Althuser (1971) calls interpellation. As people continue to answer the question "who am I with?", the focus revolving essentially on similarities and differences between groups that they interpelled through constructed symbols and images that rally them about themselves, about their origins. Effects of structural exclusion or inclusion are made to provide an explanation about their experiences as opposed to those of others, thus underpinning reasons why they should rally behind or oppose. This process is undertaken through what Goffman Erving calls the dramaturgical approach. Here, the social world is constructed and received through a drama of performances. A play enacted to convince others about who we are, and what we are. In Kenya, this process gets animated as elite seek political power. Those seeking positions begin by constructing themselves as representing the interest of the ethnic group, this is followed by the process of reinventing the traditions through public ceremonies paid for by political actors and led by carefully selected old men who "anoint" the actor as the leader of the "ethnic group" with powers to negotiate with others from other ethnic groups. By mid-2000, this logic had become institutionalized to the extent that structures of old men merged to take up the role of mediating inter-ethnic relations. These dynamics operating within gerontocractic spaces have a net effect of weakening the role of political parties as mediators of political processes and instead end up informalizing politics.

Indeed, they tend to sustain the construction of subjective identities. The same increases thanks to the limited industrialization and poor planning of urban and rural spaces to access social values to all individuals equally. The dominant orientation becomes that of a false defense of the ethnic interest in total disregard of others. The net effect is the production of tensions among groups as spaces get transformed into sites of protests and imaginations of insecurities.

Implicit support to these groups from political elite and the society which they predate, continues to spawn the growth of these groups and their ability to embed themselves within the society. There is also another consequence of threat from their growth. This is rooted in the economic impact. Non-state actor groups seeking to maximize on such spaces with limited state presence have been able to maximize on space to create time and in the process, consolidate their spaces of accumulation. Their objective in the short run is the extension of the spaces of accumulation. The net effect is that most control peri-urban spaces and transport fields that host small and medium enterprises. Their activities and insecurities continue to contribute to the death of Small and Medium Enterprises (SMEs), a factor that anchors marginalization, poverty and the reinforcement of the social context that under-gird instrumentalization of ethnicity and violence. For instance, it is estimated that criminal gangs and other illegal groups make an average Ksh 7.6b from the transport sector alone[29.] According to the parliamentary budget office Ksh 835b is under the control of bandit economy and denies the state Kshs 275b as uncollected tax. According to estimates, the national economy is actually twice its current estimate of Ksh1.6 trillion[30.]

If extraction from SMEs is a mode of daily occupation, their role in "protecting the ethnic agenda" is an activity engaged in during the electoral period. While politicians voice the concern of the ethnic groups calling on those they call settlers to "respect the natives or else?" The "or else" is actualized by threats and actual violence on the imagined occupiers. This process also produces imagined fear among all groups with the settlers seeing their survival in the need for one of their own to control power, while the "natives" seek liberation through expulsion from spaces. The net effect is violence in spaces as fears and competition converge to instrumentalize ethnicity. The need to accumulate and consolidate control by political elite produces banditism on different scales due to the rentier effect producing corruption, high taxes and patronage. It is the foregoing that produces repression and closed spaces. These are characterized by a vertical push towards the centre by elites excluded from power and an opposite and equal resistance by those in power through the mobilization of their ethnic power base by instrumentalization of ethnicity. Here, constructions such as the need to protect the presidency as a means of collective survival come in hand.

There is also that economic and political horizontal push into what the ruling elite perceive as the frontiers. This is resisted by excluded elite who mobilize their ethnic spaces into resistance by invoking ethnic solidarity and ethnic civic citizenship. These two processes not only produce polarities but also dualities of closed spaces of insecurities (See Schema below). Security organs operating in this setting find themselves constantly challenged by lack of cohesion, ethnicization, corruption, crisis of command and control which reduces their capacity, probity, and competence. The net effect is their inability to guarantee security, the very *raison d'être* for the existence of the leviathan. Instead, individuals opt to either arm themselves or seek protection from organic soft and hard core security providers. This factor engenders the gradual degeneration into a near chaotic state of nature as exemplified by election moments such as 1992, 1997, 2007-8. In all these moments thousands were killed, displaced and property destroyed. The said years account for more than 1,000,000 people displaced.

Insecurity is also a function of evolved methods used by actors to consolidate control over their resources. This includes the appropriation of private violence and the privatization of public violence. The operationalization of these twin strategies have the negative effect of reducing the forms of visibility (which has more to do with the picturing and constituting objects), the techno of government (which is about what means, mechanisms, tactics and technologies are sin qua non for the constitution of authority to facilitate the accomplishment of rule, in the administrative, political, social and political realms), the episteme of government (what forms of thought, knowledge, expertise, calculations employed in governing and how form is given to what is governable); and the forms of identification (the forming of subjects, agents, actors, and the production of governable subjects).[31]

It is the foregoing that makes it hard for liberal democracy, a prerequisite for multi-partism, to take root. Liberal democracy is contingent to historical contestations in Europe. It was not only influenced by this context, but is also specific to each State. Its political specifics pre-suppose a society of equals organized around contractual social relations, formal freedom, respect for private property, rule of law and government by consent. Its economic logic revolves around emergence of markets that scorn mutual dependence and instead spawn self-aggrandizement. This in the process spawns social automation of individuals as opposed to solidarity.

Here, people pursue individualism to its limit thus facilitating the perception and definition of freedom in terms of individual right to privacy, autonomy, absence of constraint and guaranties against collectivities[32]. Indeed every man is on his own and the state is there for those who cannot manage. The rule of law here is dependent on the market economy- where people are perceived to be sellers and buyers on a long contractual basis[33]. It is this that reinforces the logic of representation and negotiated consensus. Indeed as social contract theorist in particular Locke, Hobbes and Rousseau have shown a market society:

> A society of commodity bearers who are formerly free and equal and whose social relations are essentially and pervasively contractual, will (provided they act voluntarily) constitute political society only as a liberal democracy, a government whose organizing principles are formal freedom, formal equality, respect of private property, the rule of Law and government by consent[34.]

Towards a New Alternative politics for state reconstruction

Decades after independence, most political elite in Kenya still derive motivation mainly from a mélange of the negative aspects of the traditional society and colonialism (such as intolerance, misconceived absolute monopoly to knowledge, political exclusion and violence). They have remained incapable of forging national alliances informed by ideology. As a result, conduct of politics has at best remained an ethnic affair. So-called political parties are more of unions of tribal chiefs and their quislings with each politician seeking ethnic alliances than coalescing around a shared vision, principle and ideology. For most of the elite in Kenya, modernity in politics is merely a veneer. Rarely does the concept of a political community go beyond the epidermis and indeed political parties have tended to remain ethnic clubs donning colors of nationhood.

Attempts at multipartism have remained stunted even 20 years after pluralism was reintroduced. Party democracy is perceived as a means through which the successor elite can establish their control and demands over the rest of the society. Apart from reducing everything else to elections and representation devoid of voice and content for the masses, they have become the means through which the majority legitimizes the decisions of a few. Those defeated in elections opt to abandon any pretense they may have had about nationalism and instead opt to play the ethnic card forgetting completely the real problems facing the society. As Lawino, Okot p'Bitek's character in Song of Lawino in reference to the polarized animosities between the Democratic and Congress parties in Uganda observes:

> And while the Pythons of sickness swallow children and buffaloes of poverty knock the people down and ignorance stands there like an elephant, the war leaders are tightly locked in bloody feuds eating each other's liver as if the DP was leprosy and Congress the yaws: If only the parties would fight poverty with the fury with which they fight each other, if diseases and ignorance were assaulted with the deadly vengeance with which Okol assaults his mother's son, the enemies would have been greatly reduced now[35].

The main obstacle to pluralism in Africa is the predatory State and the convoluted ruling elite. Both must be contained by being restructured and re-socialized respectively. There is need for evolving broad-based structures that animate national unity through productive organization of masses from below.

The coming together of parties under the framework of NARC, ODM and PNU is in itself an acknowledgement that multi-partism has remained stunted ten years after birth. The structures are an afterthought realization that a "winner takes it all" logic of liberalism was not practicable among self-centered elite organizing within the setting of an ethnic ideology. Indeed in 2008, parliament had to legislate a Bill setting into motion a shared government after election chaos of 2007. Despite the enactment of the new constitution that sets out to end state politics of exclusion and predation in favor of new structures and politics that seek to engender integration and democratic participation, the old practices continue to prevail. Underlying this is the fact that majority of the political actors are seeking political power for the sake of power and not State building. They are interested in raw power. So anything that can facilitate this is considered worth trying. Lack of commitment to any serious State building around which a binding ideology could evolve, means that particularism which brings them together takes a toll on the organization.

NARC, ODM or PNU for that matter have had no broad-based values on the basis of which they could filter their core membership. Indeed anybody who was willing to opportunistically ditch one faction seeking to consolidate control over power for the other seeking to capture power fast enough, was welcome. The many years of KANU seemed to affirm the imaginations of Moi that KANU would rule for 100 years. As a progenitor, its genes in their mutated form are dominant in the current progenies to the extent to which party structures are a mirror images of the dinosaur Alfa male. It is this differentiated value system and past carriers that have literally grounded NARC's attempt to fight corruption, and deal with past human rights violations. The current regime has become a continuity of the past and thus incapable of investigating itself. While approach to national politics is through an ethnic matrix, elite continue to share common economic interests. A large part is rooted in land. It is also consumerist in nature and thus dependent on the state for political and economic nourishment. Its attempts to appear in defense of ethnic interest thus is an ideological construction whose main objective is that of using representations that serve to sustain existing relations of class domination by orienting individuals towards the past rather than a common future, or towards ethnic images and ideals that conceal class relations and in the process, detract the peasantry and urban lumpen from a collective pursuit of social change[36.]

For structures like NARC and ODM to succeed, they need the existence of a faction committed to a developmental state, with a requisite political will built around this core interest and willing to establish consensus on this by domination. Such a faction has to entail the presence of common values and a committed leadership willing to remain close to and to listen to the views of the people it seeks to lead, operate along the principle of frank and open discussion, sacrifice for the general good and evolve solutions to problems confronting the society rather than implementation of prescriptions ex-ante to the social reality. Energy has to be mobilized to evolve innovative options to deal with the supply side of contemporary insecurities borne out of economic marginalization. This physical base of the state has to be put on socio-economic infrastructure constructions such as road, market and school works to reduce distance decay at economic political and social levels. The foregoing elements constitute democratic capital without which national cohesion and economic growth cannot be achieved.

The failure of the NARC experiment demands a rethink of the logic informing institutional designs, in Africa. It is imperative that these are society-specific. Solutions to problems should not only be context specific but that if they have to be replicated elsewhere, then they have to be adjusted to enable them to adapt to existing social conditions. The fact of the matter is that multi-partism in Kenya is in danger of being derailed by polarization created by the political class. The net consequence is the increasing levels of nation state crisis. This is manifested by the crisis of identity, resource distribution and allocation, participation, conflict management and resolution, and absence of penetrative institutions in the society. There is need to argue for serious broad-based politics that can offer the possibility of guarding against relapsing into chaos. These must be geared towards evolving political consensus on common rules of political engagement, an agenda for national unity and reconciliation in fragmented societies, pursuit of a developmentalist state program pending the maturation of institutions, evolution of a political community and a political context that will under gird political competition.

Inherent in this form of politics is the need to encourage citizens to put pressure on political entities to emphasize individual merit. The logic of individual merit carries with it a certain judgment on the moral rectitude (for instance those involved in criminal acts such as corruption and negative ethnicity should be automatically disqualified). This should be enhanced by insistence on moral competence and instrumental competence (individual capacity to perform certain tasks that go with the position one is seeking). This will engender the emergence of politically competent[37] individuals capable of moving the polity forward.

There is equally need to enhance positive participation by creating real devolution. Efforts have to be made to facilitate economic reproduction from the new counties. Yet this is only tenable if an innovative curving base on rationalities of economic reproduction is undertaken as opposed to the current ethnic based design. It would have made sense to anticipate their reproduction logic by curving them in zones while anticipating the regional federation. This would have allowed the new counties to undertake their planning with regional spaces in mind. Critical to this is the need to evolve strong structures of horizontal accountability. These will allow socio-economic groups to directly bring accountability among local councils. Given that parties are largely absent in policy debates, there is need to enhance social pluralism. This entails strengthening of other social forms of representation and interest articulation. Core in this process are trade unions, professional associations and co-operative unions. These types of groups have the potential to force political parties to become drivers of pro-poor change.

Serious efforts should be made to facilitate the access of citizenship to means of livelihood to facilitate what Roche calls social citizenship[38] to all members of society. This calls for a developmental state that can access education, infrastructure, security, jobs, and other means of production to its citizens. Means of production such as land must be accessed to the majority poor. In its core, there is the necessity to reverse the adverse effects of the IMF and the World Bank structural adjustment programs that continue to weaken the state. As Adam Przeworski *etal* note, a level of improved standards of living is necessary to safeguard democracy.[39]

Broad-based politics can enhance participation of ordinary citizens, more so, in deliberating issues that directly concern their lives.[40] As Pateman[41] notes, views cannot be adequately delegated and represented in a multi-cultural setting. The danger of parties' politics is that tendency to distort citizen preferences while minimizing individual equality in influencing outcomes.

Here, the right kind of institutional reconstruction must seek to respond to and negotiate with social forces. There are no outright thought-out solutions and indeed there should not be. What is imperative is the evolution of a shared vision as to where the society should be headed, followed by concerted attempts at evolving strategy aimed at ensuring that this vision is attained through evolution of the requisite institutional infrastructure and manpower.

At institutional level experiences of post-independence plural politics point to the fact that political pluralism is only likely to take root in the context of what Mamdani calls social pluralism[42]. The objective should be that of building a multi-cultural political community. It will entail the evolution of multiplicity of associations from trade unions to student, farmers unions to religious and other social organizations. Not only will this provide a vanguard against errant politicians, but will also force them to make themselves relevant through provision of alternative organizing ideology and programs. Secondly, this will provide not only room for alternative sites for contestation, but also position for elite a way from power at the center of the State.

A combination of social pluralism, social citizenship and respect for institutional norms is bound to increase citizen participation in political process, state penetration in society, while minimizing conflicts emergent out of the process of resource distribution and allocation. While enhancing institutional capacity, the foregoing retain the chance of facilitating emancipation of political structures from society, thus taking the state beyond the Marxist approaches that sees it merely as an instrument for mediating violence by the ruling elite. Both states point to the fact that institutionalization is neither basically the gradual acquisition of monopoly of legitimate violence (Weberian construction finds this as an acceptable necessity[43]) nor the mere evolution of an independent bureaucracy. It is instead a function of increased levels of alternative participation and the deconstruction of the neo-colonial state and its forms of indirect rule. The crystallization of the foregoing is at the heart of state construction. Construction here denotes the process of enabling the state to perform functions required of it to pass as one.[44] These functions revolve around state as an accepted source of identity in the arena of politics. State as an institution – a tangible organization of decision-making and an intangible symbol of identity, state as a security guarantor for a populated territory. Construction implies that a state's basic functions such as governmental decision-making process are undertaken and rendered operative. Laws are made as order and societal cohesion is preserved and enhanced.[45] Underlying the foregoing is institutional functionality, which manifests itself in the enhanced state penetration of society and the putting into place of institutions and mechanisms for handling resource distribution and allocation, and participation processes (usually sources of conflict).

Notes

[1] See Greenstein F and Polsby. (ed). *Non-Governmental Politics*, Massachusetts, Addison-Wesley, 1975. P 175

[2] See Thompson J.P. *Ideology and Modern Culture*, Stanford University Press, Stanford California 1990 p. 39

[3] See NDI reports on political parties' capacity building workshops between November and December 2001 and between March and   May 2002

[4] Mass party for mobilization brought together the 'dominant Kikuyu and Luo during the fight for independence. It was opposed by KADU (a counter force made up of the Luhya and other 'smaller groups afraid of this domination.

[5] FORD was a broad movement that emerged to counter KANU's one party dictatorship. It brought together   a set of notables from groups that had felt marginalized by the party. They included Kenneth   Matiba (Kikuyu), Martin   Shikuku (Luhya), Jaramogi Odinga(Luo), Ahmed Bamariz (Coastal), George Nthenge (Kamba).

[6] An alliance of "major" ethnic notables Raila Odinga (Luo), Wamalwa Kijana (Luhya), Charity Ngilu and Kalonzo Musyoka (Kamba), Mwai Kibaki (Kikuyu) who aligned around Mwai Kibaki and by inference brought with them their ethnic groups to vote for Kibaki

[7] Raila Odinga (Luo) Musalia Mudavadi (Luhya), Najib Balala (Coastal), William Ruto (Kalenjin), Charity Ngilu (Kamba), Nyagah (Embu)

[8] Mwai Kibaki (Kikuyu) and other Gema notables

[9] Ake C. Democratization of Disempowerment op cit p. 8

[10] See Dahl Robert A. *Democracy and Its Critiques*. Yale University Press, New Haven. 1989. P13-14

[11] Dahl ibid

[12] Dahl ibid

[13] see Thompson J. p 216-225

[14] Concept is borrowed from Makgoba M.W 1997. *MOKOKO the Makgoba Affair: A Reflection on Transformation.*Florida hills Vivlia Publishersp197-198. It refers to a common inclination towards emphasizing values of communality rather than individual, hospitality, friendliness, consensus that he argues are common to all people of African descent.

[15] BRETT E. Colonialism And Underdevelopment in East Africa: The Politics Of Economic Change 1919-1993 (London Heinemann Education Books, 1973)

[16] Kipkorir B. *The Alliance High School and the Origins of the Kenyan African Elite 1926- 62* . (Ph.D thesis St Johns College, Cambridge university, 1969)

[17] See Nyerere J.K *Freedom and Unity*. Oxford University Press Dar-es-Salaam, 1966.

[18] Buzan B (1991), *People, States and Fear*, 2nd edition, An Agenda for International Security Studies in the Post war Era, Harvester Whitshiaf, New York.

[19] McNamara R.S. "The Essence of security: Reflections in Office". New York. Harper and Raw, 1968, p145-9

[20] Jackson Richard: Regime Security. In Alan Collins (ed) *Contemporary Security Studies*. Oxford University Press2007 p149

[21]Robinow P. (1984), *The Foucault Reader: An Introduction to Foucault's thought*, Penguin Books, London P241

[22] See John S Mbiti. *African Religions and Philosophy* . New York Praeger Publishers see also Mbiti S.J 1992 *Introduction to African Religio*n second ed Nairobi East African Educational Publishers Ltd

[23] See Thompson J P. P41

[24] See Thompson JP for these forms of constructions. Thompson p40

[25] Ake C . *Democratization of Disempowerment* opcit pp4

[26] On this perspective of citizenship, see Musambayi Katumanga « Banditisme D'Etat, Brigandage Social et Economie de la violence: Problèmes de Citoyenneté aux Frontières du Berceau de l'humanité Sous la direction De Claude Fievet invention et réinvention de la citoyenneté » editionsjoellesampy UPPA 2000

[27] Ake C. *Democratization of Disempowerment* opcit pp6

[28] See Ngunyi M and Katumanga M: *From Monopoly to Oligopoly of Violence:* Exploration of Four Point Hypothesis regarding organized and Organic Militia in Kenya. TCH 2011

[29] Kenya Private Sector Alliance. Cited in Ngunyi M and Katumanga M: *From Monopoly to Oligopoly of Violence* Op cit 2011.

[30] Ngunyi M and Katumanga M Ibid

[31] We pick up from Dean's outline's four dimensions through which government is construed to note that these have mutated and diminished into a crisis of sorts over time. Dean M. *Governmentality*, London: Sage 1999.

[32] Ake Claude .Democratization of disempowerment op cit p5

[33] Peter Gibon, "State-Civil Society Relations with Specific reference to Developmentalist States in Africa", Paper Given In Workshop on Experiences of Political Liberalization in Africa, Copenhagen May 1993

[34] As cited in Ake C. *Democratization of Disempowerment in Africa.* CASS Occasional Monograph No Malthouse Press UK 1994p4

[35] Reference of Ocol's hatred for his Mother's son is in Reference to divisions engendered by political parties in Uganda . see P'Bitek(O) Song of Lawino, East African Publishers Nairobi, 1993 p89

[36] See Thompson JP: on these modes of constructions. Thompson J.P: op.cit *Ideology and Modern Culture* p 40-41

[37] On political competence, see Robert Dahl. *Democracy and its Critiques* opcit p 52-64

[38] Roche M 1992 Rethinking Citizenship: Welfare, Ideology and change in the modern society London polity press

[39] Adam Przeworski, Michael Alvarez, José Antonio Cheibub and Fernando Limongi, *What makes Democracies Endure?* In Larry Diamond et al eds *Consolidating the Third Wave Democracies"*, Themes and Perspectives Baltimore John Hopkins University Press, 1997: 297

[40] Yoweri Museveni, *Sowing the Mustard Seed: The Struggle for Freedom and Democracy in Uganda*, London Macmillan 997: 134

[41] See Carole Pateman, *Participation and Democratic Theory*, Cambridge University Press 1970

[42] Position adopted from post Seminar discussions of my proposal with Mamdani at CBR August 12/1999

[43] See Weber Max 1958 essays in Sociology H.H. Gerth and C Wright mills (ed) New Galaxy

[44] DawishaAideed and Zaartman William (ed) Beyond Coercion, the Durability of the Arab State, Groom Helm London, 1988.

[45] Weber Marx, Essays in Sociology: H H Garth and C. Wright Mills, (ed.) New York Galaxy.

References

Adam, P,, Michael. A, José, A. Cheibub and Fernando, L. (1997). *What makes Democracies Endure?* In Larry Diamond *et al* eds *Consolidating the Third Wave Democracies"*, Themes and Perspectives. Baltimore: John Hopkins University Press, p 297.

Ake, C. (1994). *Democratization of Disempowerment in Africa,* CASS Occasional Monograph No Malthouse Press UK p4.

Brett, E. (1973). *Colonialism and Underdevelopment in East Africa: The Politics of Economic Change 1919-1993.* London: Heinemann Education Books.

Buzan, B. (1991). *People, States and Fear, 2nd edition, An Agenda for International Security Studies in the Post war Era.* New York: Harvester Whitshiaf.

Carole Pateman (1970). *Participation and Democratic Theory.* Cambridge University Press.

Dahl Robert, A. (1989). *Democracy and its Critiques.* New Haven: Yale University Press, P13-14.

Dawisha, A. and Z. William (ed) (1988). *Beyond Coercion, the Durability of the Arab State.* London: Groom Helm.

Gibon, P. (1993), "State - Civil Society Relations with Specific reference the Developmentalist States in Africa", Paper Given In Workshop on experiences of Political Liberalization in Africa, Copenhagen May 1993.

Greenstein, F. and Polsby (ed) (1975). *Non-governmental Politics.* Massachusetts: Addison-Wesley, p175.

Kipkorir, B. (1969). "The Alliance High School and the Origins of the Kenyan African elite 1926- 62" (PhD thesis St. John's College Cambridge University.

Mbiti, S.J (1992). *African Religions and Philosophy* New York Praeger Publishers see also Mbiti, S.J. 1992 introduction to African religion second ed. Nairobi: East African Educational Publishers Ltd.

McNamara, R.S (1968). *The Essence of security: Reflections in Office.* New York: Harper and Raw, pp145-9.

Museveni, Y. (1997). *Sowing the Mustard Seed: The Struggle for Freedom and Democracy in Uganda*, London Macmillan: 134.

Nyerere, J. K (1966), *Freedom and Unity.* Dar-es-Salaam: Oxford University Press.

P'Bitek, O. (1993). *Song of Lawino.* Nairobi: East African Publishers, p89.

Robinow, P. (1984). *The Foucault Reader: An Introduction to Foucault's thought.* London: Penguin Books, p241.

Roche, M. (1992). Rethinking Citizenship: Welfare, Ideology and change in the Modern Society London polity press.

Thompson, J.P (1990). *Ideology and Modern Culture.* Stanford California: Stanford University Press.

Weber, Marx (1958). *Essays in Sociology*: H.H. Garth and C. Wright Mills, (ed) New York: Galaxy.

Natural Resource Governance and Multi-stakeholder Dialogue

Kimani Njogu

'Buy land. They're not making it any more' – Mark Twain

Introduction

The vision of all leaders in Africa must to devote their energies to eradicate extreme poverty from the continent. This can be done if they reconconsider the direction that development initiatives have tended to take in the past fifty years. Most development efforts have been narrow, urban targeted, focused mainly on 'growth' not 'the people and excluded majority of citizens. In the process, they have created an economic elite defined by its attraction to consumerism and 'primitive accumulation' of property even as the majority languish in abject poverty. Reorienting development to focus on people means addressing access to clean water, sanitation, education, and healthcare and reaching the most vulnerable populations. Even more significantly, a ' people centred' development which must now be adopted will need to be conflict sensitive and entrench good governance and accountable leadership and institutions guided by the rule of law, freedom of speech, protection of the environment, and transparency in the performance of public duties.

A major player in the eradication of extreme poverty will be natural resource management and use. We are witnesses to the new scramble for the continent's resources being undertaken by Western and Eastern nations. Africa is endowed with enormous natural resources and the continent's global share of platinum stands at 77 percent, diamonds 55 percent, chromium 46 percent, gold 22 percent and uranium 19 percent. Recent discoveries of mineral deposits in the East African region including oil, coal, gold and natural gas are likely to substantially increase these percentages. Sadly, the bulk of the people of Africa languish in hunger and poverty despite the global recognition of the place of natural resources in improving the lives of people, accelerating economic growth and transforming societies. The potential available on the continent has led into the 21st scramble for Africa and 'land grabbing' (Pearce, 2012) by Asian, American and European commercial interests in the pursuit of minerals, forests, fisheries and large scale agricultural activities. The people of Africa, who have served as the custodians of these resources disproportionally bear the cost of the land acquisitions and participate minimally, if at all, in determining the process and direction of this global rush. Furthermore, where there are abundant reserves of minerals and petroleum as has occurred in Sierra Leone, the Democratic Republic of Congo and Sudan, and in the context of weak governance institutions, local communities have been subjected to violent conflict as well as devastating social and environmental effects resulting from massive extraction operations. The urgency of addressing natural resource governance is compounded by national inequalities, ethnic mistrust and corruption among political leaders.

How can the growing interest in natural resources in Africa contribute in eradicating poverty and enhancing the quality of life on the continent? One way of doing this is through committed and consistent multi-stakeholder dialogue in governance. Multistakeholder partnerships bring together different levels of government, civil society organizations, experts, business, universities and local communities to dialogue and work together in achieving a shared vision. In the process they inject accountability in the conduct of public affairs. Accountability is only possible if people have the right information which is easily accessible and easy to use. A key principle in multistakeholder dialogue is the right to information. With the growth of information technology, especially mobile telephony in Africa, it is possible to increase access to information and ensure accountability in the extraction and utilization of natural resources. Technology can help increase transparency and inclusivity in natural resource governance but only if the leaders of Africa truly care about the children of the continent.

West and East have landed on the continent, hungry for a piece of the resources. More than any other continent in the world, the global rush for acquisition of natural resources has targeted Africa which accounts for 134 million hectares of reported land deals. The rush is for agricultural production (mainly for biofuels), mineral extraction, industry, tourism, and forest conversion (Anseeuw et al 2011). In this process, just was the case at the onset of colonialism, the best land that is irrigable and close to infrastructure, is acquired; contributing to conflict among communities as happened in August and September 2012 in the Tana Delta of Kenya. According to a 2011 International Land Coalition Report, *'the high levels of interest in acquiring land in Africa appear to be driven by a perception that large tracts of land can be acquired from governments with little or no payment.'* This perception may be a consequence of endemic corruption and poor governance structures on the continent. Furthermore, there is a feeling that much land in Africa is empty and available; yet the unfarmed forests, grasslands and marshlands are communal assets, traditionally owned and used collectively.

It is not just international players that are involved in the rush for natural resources: national political and economic elite are involved and through corrupt practices and use of gaps in policy and legal framework are contributing in the marginalization, dispossession and displacement of the poor people in rural areas. Women and children are especially affected by this process because of their exclusion from power and decision making. Moreover, global trade and investment trends which protect international investors and acquirers of resources, with little protection for the poor, coupled with national laws that do not recognize customary ownership of land provide little room for meaningful compensation of the affected. Additionally, there is very little consultation among stakeholders in natural resource governance.

Stakeholder Involvement and Governance

Because stakeholders in natural resources are interested parties, they ought to be involved in the design, delivery, monitoring, and improvement of products and services, including those that have political, economic, social and environmental ramifications. Their involvement is informed by a systematic and continuous stakeholder dialogue - an interactive two-way communication process between all actors towards a shared vision. By bringing on board, multiple stakeholders we guarantee sustainability of services and broaden 'ownership' and engagement. The multi-stakeholder dialogue in natural resource management which we have in mind is not ornamental or tokenistic: it is a *participatory, inclusive, open, multi-voiced, non-patronizing, non-dominating, transparent and genuine engagement with communities and civil society actors.* It is a dialogue driven by human rights, good governance practices and commitment to a sustainable environment.

If governance refers to the interactions among structures, processes and practices that determine how power and responsibilities are exercised, how decisions are taken and how citizens and other stake holders have their say (Graham et al, 2003), then it central to the management of natural resources. In the contemporary world, it is no longer tenable that only a small group of actors make decisions about livelihoods on behalf of the majority; decision making must of necessity be consultative and collaborative.

The development of Natural Governance and Dialogue in Africa

Broadly speaking, most of African countries have undergone three major phases of governance systems in natural resource management: *pre-colonial, colonial* and *post colonial*. In the three phases, land governance has been dictated by political governance with its consequences on access, management and use. In the pre-colonial period land tenure was communal and based on unwritten laws about access, management and use. Knowledge about individual and collective responsibility was passed inter-generationally through family members. Natural resource governance practices in pre-colonial Africa were bottom-up, dialogic, consultative and adaptive to environmental conditions and cultural practices. But with the onset of colonialism, the system changed drastically and became monologic, dictatorial, oppressive, destructive, non-consultative and top-down. Local communities were not consulted by colonial regimes and foreign policies and assumptions about ownership, management, and revenue allocation were imposed on customary institutions. There was hardly a significant local elite to facilitate extraction of natural resources, or determine their management and use and the colonial regime had a field day. The governance of natural resources during the colonial era was top-down.

Whereas one would have expected that at independence, the new African states would dismantle the ideology of exclusion perpetuated under colonialism, they did not. Instead, the majority of the emergent leadership embraced colonial policies of dehumanization, exclusion of communities in decision making and utilization of natural resources for individual interests. Dictatorial tendencies in access, management and use of natural resources were enhanced and the political and economic elite continue to pay little attention to the needs of communities. The governance structure in the post colonial era has been top-down and 'mixed' at best: archaic policies are still in place, good policies remain unimplemented, there is little community participation, and evictions and corruption abound.

This approach is clearly untenable. In the words of Noam Chomsky:

> "We are coming close to the edge of a precipice of environmental destruction. If growth is understood and accepted to include constant attack on the physical environment that sustains life – like for example greenhouse emissions, destruction of agricultural land, and so forth – if that is what it means, then we are like lemmings walking over a cliff. This isn't what growth has to mean. For example, growth can mean simpler lives and more livable communities." (Chomsky in *Occupy,* 2012: 84).

The growth that Africa should pursue is one driven by a people-centred dialogue. This requires a paradigm shift with a focus on genuine community participation for sustainable utilization of natural resources; dynamic application of participatory approaches to resource governance; and rigorous dialogue involving all stakeholders in the determination of how natural resources should be managed. In order to ensure compliance, this paradigm shift might require enactment and implementation of people-centered constitutions across Africa, review of bad contracts and the introduction of taxation regimes that benefit communities.

Natural resources belong to current and future generations and must therefore be protected, conserved and managed prudently. They are finite assets and therefore all ecosystems must be managed in an integrated manner even as people benefit from them. In the case of Kenya, the management of natural resources- especially wildlife, forests, water and minerals – has been the preserve of the central government leading to a near collapse of traditional management systems. There has not been any systematic process of involving stakeholders in decision making and the central government has tended to rely on ad hoc decisions captured through Five Year Development Plans, Presidential Decrees and Declarations by Chiefs. An attempt was made in 1999 to bring order with the enactment of the Environment Management and Coordination Act whose aim was to superintend the management, protection and conservation of natural resources. In really though the Act focused on the Environment and pieces of legislation that have been scattered and used to address natural resource issues have related to water, forests, wildlife, mineral, agriculture, minerals, fisheries and petroleum. Although natural resources are interconnected, the Kenyan State has addressed natural resource needs through separate and independent bodies.

With the enactment and promulgation of a people driven Constitution in 2010, Kenya has embarked on a dynamic and robust path towards management of natural resources in a sustainable manner. Recognizing that in the past, the acquisition, management and use of natural resources have been shrouded in mystery, the Constitution of Kenya has provided a framework for addressing land, environment and natural resources (Articles 60 – 72). A key institution in this regard is the National Land Commission (NLC). Among other functions, the NLC shall 'initiate investigations, on its own initiative or on a complaint, into present or historical land injustices, and recommend appropriate redress' (Aricle 67 (e)). In addition, the State is mandated to 'ensure sustainable exploitation , utilization, management and conservation of the environment and natural resources, and ensure the equitable sharing of the accruing benefits' (Aricle 69).

In undertaking its task, the NLC will need to appreciate the rapid population growth, climate change and declining forest cover. The population of Kenya now stands at over 40 million people and growing at 2.6%. This population is served by a total land size of 582,647 square kilometers. Land is a key feature of production and 80% of the population relies on 20% of land surface area of high-medium potential agricultural space and 20% of the population is supported by 80% of land surface area that is arid or semi-arid. Over 80% of wildlife and 50% of livestock are found in the sparsely populated arid and semi-arid areas.

With the discovery of oil deposits, gas, gold, and other minerals it is crucially important that the State provides reliable, correct and updated information related to the exploitation, production and commercial value of Kenya's natural resources. This right to information is constitutionally guaranteed as follows:

Article 35 (1): Every citizen has the right of access to –

(a) Information held by the State; and

(b) Information held by another person and required for the exercise or protection of any right or fundamental freedom.

The State can state by sharing information on the mapping of Kenya's natural resources including value, type, location and value of investment. Other crucial information that should be shared urgently related to the sedimentary basin including Lamu Basin, Mandera Basin, Anza Basin and Tertiary Rift (Lotikipi, Turkana, Lokichar, Suguta, South Kerio, Magadi and Nyanza Trough).

It is no longer tenable for the Kenyan State to exclude citizens from decision making in national matters including the management, protection and conservation of natural resources. The new approach in which the public participate meaningfully in development is humanizing and sustainable. It will ensure that certain sector are not left behind in the struggle to end extreme poverty in Africa.

Areas for Multi-Stakeholder Dialogue

There are three areas of dialogue for natural resource governance that are worth consideration:

(a) *Ownership of natural resources:* There is need to develop clarity about the nature and limitations of private ownership, community and customary rights and state ownership. Domestic and international investors will feel confident to participate if they know precisely what is expected of them. Ambiguity about rights breeds corruption. But in the pursuit of clarity, ownership should not be seen as license for unfettered management and use of natural resources. The interests of the people should be at the centre of all dialogue on ownership and there is need for precise legislation about this.

(b) *The power to manage and develop natural resources:* Recent constitutions in Africa provide guidance on the enactment and administration of laws for the development and exploitation of natural resources. In other words, there should be dialogue on who should pass laws relating to natural resources, who administers the laws and which courts resolve disputes under them. Some of the areas of engagement might include contracting authority and procedures; licensing; taxation and royalty regimes; employment practices; safety and environmental standards; transportation networks; labour laws;

import and export permits and tariffs and so forth. But the existence of constitutional powers to control, regulate and manage natural resources is insufficient without a leadership committed to the genuine transformation of our societies. A dialogue on constitutional mandates should go hand in hand with a conversation on leadership and the tenets of good governance practices, including accountability and equity.

(c) *Sharing of natural resource revenues:* If we are serious about transforming societies, we must engage the state and international players on the transparent and fair extraction, collection and sharing of the benefits of natural resource revenue. Clear, specific and well monitored rules to govern the process of revenue sharing are key in ensuring that communities benefit from the resources around them

The deliberate exclusion of communities in decisions on resource management and use coupled with incessant corruption among public officers, lack of transparency and accountability within institutions of governance and limited skills in engaging global players have meant that the African people do not benefit from the resources around them. It is only through genuine multi-stakeholder dialogue, people-oriented leadership at national and local levels and the transparent and accountable systems of natural resource governance that the lives of the African people can be transformed.

Conclusion

Without doubt, one of the ways of ensuring that the natural resources benefit the people of Africa is the deliberate inclusion of relevant stakeholders including local communities, grassroots organizations and civil society, in decision making processes from conceptualization, design and formative research to implementation, monitoring, impact evaluation, closure and exit. Participation in constructive dialogue, transparency in contractual arrangements and people-centered utilization of the resources will build trust and confidence in communities that there is value in supporting the venture. But trust is not enough: communities must see *real benefits* from the exploitation of the resources around them. In addition, good governance in natural resource management cannot be delinked from governance practices at the national level. Again, citizen participation in determining governance practices is vitally important because it ensures sustainable and efficient service delivery by public officers.

In natural resource management, the range of actors or stakeholders is mainly wide due to the common nature of the resources. Consequently, the process of decision-making and implementation is complex. Despite the complexity, governance in natural resources must be participatory, consensus oriented, accountable, transparent, responsive, effective and efficient, equitable and inclusive and follow the rule of law. It also has to ensure that corruption is minimized, the views of minorities are taken into account and that the voices of the most vulnerable in society are heard in decision-making. It should be responsive to the present and future needs of a society.

Whereas the multi-stakeholder nature of natural resource ownership is not debatable, the link between governance and stakeholder dialogue is not explicit. Ideally, in my view, dialogue should determine the nature of resource governance to be adopted. In other words, the determination of the structures, power relations and responsibilities in resource management should be a consequence of multi-stake holder engagement. Thus constructive dialogue will result to a well thought out governance system which addresses the needs of all those with a stake in the resource in question. Lack of dialogue on the other hand results to a governance system that does not ensure equity and sustainability.

Moving forward, some policy considerations by states may include the following:

1. *Develop and implement national and regional communication strategies on natural resources* in order to increase knowledge and facilitate informed decision making among communities. As much as possible, the strategies should be implemented through local languages and should use community based channels of communication.

2. *Acknowledge and uphold the existence of and respect for the rights of rural communities whenever large scale acquisitions are being undertaken.* All land is used by communities for their livelihoods; no land is 'idle' and 'unoccupied' *per se*. These users of land have a moral right of possession and must be engaged and their informed

consent sought, preferably in the local language, before any acquisitions are made.

3. *Constitutionally recognize the rights of communities in natural resource governance*. This can be done by legally protecting customary community property rights to land, even if that land appears underused.

4. *Draw on international human rights law to protect the poor in Africa*. This is especially important where national laws fall short of international standards.

5. *Ensure transparent, accountable and inclusive multi-stakeholder dialogue on natural resources*. The acquisition of large scale land cannot be left to international players and the national elite. Local communities and civil society actors must be part and parcel of this process.

6. *Introduce revenue-sharing processes* that benefit local communities. These arrangements should be precise and legally protected.

7. *Entrench environmental sustainability in all decisions related to natural resources*. This can be done through rigorous Environment Impact Assessments and people-sensitive and environment friendly contracts

References

Anseeuw, W, Liz Alden, W., L. Cotulo and M. Taylor. (2011). 'Land Rights and the Rush for Land: Findings of the Global Commercial Pressures on Land Research Project.' ILC, Rome.

Chomsky, N. (2012). *Occupy*. New York: Penguin.

Davidson, J., M. Lockwood, A. Curtis, E. Stratford & R. Griffith. (2006). 'Governance Principles for Regional Natural Resource Management'. Pathways to Good Practice in Regional NRM Governance.

Graham, J., Amos, B & Plumptre, T. (2003). 'Governance Principles for Protected Areas in the 21st Century'. Durban: The Fifth World Parks Congress.

Pearce, F. (2012). *The Land Grabbers*. London: Transworld Publishers.

The Story of Coastal Kenya: More than Five Centuries of Externally Crafted and Internally Inflicted Marginalization

Rocha Chimerah

Historical Background

Before delving into the rather controversial topic of marginalization of the indigenous people of present day sea-shore coastal Kenya, it is worth mentioning that almost all of them trace their beginnings at a place known as Shungwaya. This is a place located by several studies as having been somewhere in the south of present-day Somalia. However, the Chapter will not dwell so much on that part of history as it does not add much to the topics core theme of marginalization. At this juncture, it is worth mentioning that the people referred to as sea-shore coastal indigenous communities here are the Mijikenda, Swahili, Pokomo (all Bantu) as well as a number of Cushitic peoples such as the Gabra, Waata, Dahalo, Langulo, Borana, Boni and Sanye.

The historical periods that are the focus of this Chapter are, first, the actual occupation of the Kenyan Coast by the Shungwaya Bantus from around the 7th Century to the 16th Century and, second, the advent of the first significant group of settlers from Oman in the 12th Century. These Arab immigrants settled in Pate area; an area that later came to be known as Uswahilini (i.e. Swahili land). During this time, the form of marginalization that took place may be described as an intense 'arabization' of Bantus, particularly the Swahili. The Swahili referred to here belonged to the sub-tribes: Wapate, Wasiu, Wafaza, Wagunya (Bajuni) and the Waamu of Lamu.

At a second remove, such *arabization* also influenced other Bantu neighboring ethnicities such as the Pokomo and, to some extent, the Mijikenda. On the other hand, the reverse also happened; that is, the incoming Arabs also got *bantuized* by their African hosts. Nevertheless, it was the *arabization* of the Africans that registered the most pervasive influence. So much was the influence that within a brief passage of years, political, religious, and educational, and even some important aspects of the cultural leadership was vested in the hands of the Arab immigrants.

Thirdly, at a critical period during the 15th century, Vasco da Gama arrived, having travelled all the way from the King's court in Portugal. This seafarer, who was heading to India, ushered not only the unfettered flocking in of more Portuguese adventurers to coastal Kenya, but even more significantly, his visit heralded the introduction of Portuguese rule in these parts. During that rule, marginalization of the indigenous people was effected with a vengeance and any resistance was brutally crushed. It is in this context that Mombasa and Faza were razed to the ground, not once but severally; whereas Malindi was treated as a launching pad against recalcitrant city states (such as Mombasa). The Portuguese Viceroys Francisco De Almeida and Alfonso de Albuquerque, based in Goa, India, are particularly remembered for the inhuman acts against the Swahili people.

The defeat of the Portuguese

Early in the 16th century, Arabs in Oman defeated their Portuguese overlords, kicking them out of their country in the process. That event led to Omanis regaining their full sovereignty and pride. There was jubilation not only in Oman but also in Swahililand. Unfortunately for the Swahili at this time in history, things did not quite work out in accordance with their expectations. In no time, the Omanis were looking abroad to East Africa not for diplomatic relations on equal terms but for colonies. The very first expedition of the newly liberated Omanis to the Swahili Coast was not aimed at forging any friendly political bonding with the natives, but rather, to conquer and pacify the Swahili nations. Unknown to the Omanis, the Swahili people had an understanding with their neighbours, the Mijikenda, that in case one of them was attacked by an external force, the neighbours would come to the aid of the one under attack. It is in this context that the Omanis found the going very rough when they attacked the Swahili people. Frustrated, the aggressors went back to Oman to regroup and strategize afresh. Back home, a second attack was planned, but this time round the target people were the Mijikenda. The aim was to not only punish them for supporting the Swahili, but to completely vanquish them. It is in this regard that Omani troops were sent to Mijikendaland, just a stone's throw away from the Swahili Coast. In the battle that ensued, as many as four hundred (400) Arab fighters were killed. This expedition ended miserably for the invaders who incurred heavy losses, forcing them to retreat in haste after the routing. From the two experiences, Mombasa Swahilis decided to change tact, seeking foreign allies elsewhere. They did not have to look far, for the Turks were stationed somewhere in the Horn of Africa and the Red sea, guarding their interests. Thus, it is to the Turks that they turned for help and their request was readily granted. The Turks dispatched Amir Ali Bey to spearhead the Swahili resistance against both the Arab aggression and Portuguese tyranny. On their part, the Portuguese enlisted the help of the incoming Zimba from Southern Africa to put the Swahilis in their place. The Zimbas used unorthodox tactics in the war against Swahilis; tactics that caused fear and completely shocked the embattled natives. This occasioned a state of complete chaos in Mombasa in which the Swahili people were temporarily subdued.

Content with the results, the Portuguese let the Zimba proceed northwards where it was expected that stubborn northern Swahili would meet the same fate as their southern kindred. However, the Zimbas' ferocity had run out of steam. On their way to Malindi, they tried their vicious tactics against a more ferocious people, the indigenous Segeju who stood their ground; fighting back furiously. In that encounter, the Segeju utterly decimated the feared Zimbas. Thus the Zimba advance was completely put to an end.

Malindis in Mombasa

Despite the routing of their Zimba allies, the Portuguese emerged stronger. Circumstances being thus, the colonialists grabbed the opportunity to completely humiliate the Mombasa people by imposing the Malindi dynasty upon them. To succeed in doing that, they killed the native Mombasa King, thus clearing the way for the imposition of a foreign ruler. For a while, the Mombasa people resisted the humiliation but eventually accepted the Malindi King, Hassan, as their legitimate ruler. For a while, things worked according to the wishes of the Portuguese overlords, but differences in culture were too many. One major difference was religion since the Portuguese were Christians of the Catholic denomination whereas the (Malindi) King and his Swahili subjects were Moslems. Therefore, when the Portuguese tried to force the King to change religions and help convert his subjects into Christianity, the latter flatly refused and rebelled. Whereupon a plan was hatched to arrest and punish him; he sought asylum among the Mijikenda, the traditional allies of his people.

Faced with this new challenge, the shrewd Portuguese Captain of Fort Jesus and Mombasa city state, Simao, hatched a plot that would lead to the king's capture. He bribed the Mijikenda (Rabai) elders in charge of the King with rolls of cloth. On their part, the elders arranged to capture the King and his queen and thereafter put them to death. The severed heads of the murdered royal couple were then sent to the Portuguese captain as proof of sealing of the deal.

Religious Marginalization

The treachery took a paradoxical twist when Yusuf bin Hassan, the son and heir of the murdered king returned to Mombasa from Goa, where he had been taken to by the Portuguese whose goal was to indoctrinate the young prince into the Catholic doctrine and way of thinking. As a boy, the prince had been removed from his familiar native setting, Mombasa, and native religion, Islam, at the tender age of only seven years, with the express aim of alienating him from those two cultural pillars, in order to have him embrace the alien beliefs and practices of the Portuguese. In this, they succeeded, for when as a mature young adult he was sent back to Mombasa and put in his dead father's throne, he was the one who terrorized Moslem adherents and followers of the religion considered indigenous by many of his subjects. In that regard, he was viewed by many of the subjects as a black Portuguese subjecting them to worse treatment than the white Portuguese had ever done. He was ruthless.

As he settled in, however, and with the passage of years, he recollected what the Portuguese had done to his father and mother, and the reasons behind that action as well as others of a similar nature. He began resenting the Portuguese once again. When the resentment reached its peak, he secretly began praying in the Moslem manner. And when one day, he was found doing so by a Portuguese gentleman known as Perez, the king killed the 'spy.' Fearing arrest and the prospect of getting committed to the Inquisition in Rome, he rallied his subjects in Mombasa against the latest Portuguese Captain Leitao de Gomboa and every other Portuguese in town. In no time, a great number of the Europeans were put to death. That gory event accomplished, the city state was thus liberated from the Portuguese colonial yoke by the King and his Swahili subjects, aided only by their loyal Mijikenda neighbours and allies.

The King, nonetheless, wanted the Mombasa people to go after the Portuguese wherever they were to be found and put them to death, failure to which he was certain they would face the wrath of the much hated colonialists when the latter came back for revenge. When the Mombasans refused to go along with their King's suggestion, he got extremely annoyed and decided to burn the city himself rather than wait for the Portuguese to do it.

After a long while, the residents rebuilt the town with the help of the Portuguese who came back – just as King Yusuf bin Hassan (christened Jeronimo Chingulia by the Portuguese) – had predicted. Hence the Portuguese ruled Mombasa once more, as tyrannically as they had done before. Yet again the people of Mombasa revolted; and for the umpteenth time, war was declared against the tyranny and misrule of the foreign power. This time around when the Portuguese were defeated, it was to be the last time they would ever rule coastal Kenya.

Fearing that the Portuguese would make it back once again, the Swahili and their Mijikenda allies sent their delegations to Oman to seek military assistance in case of any future Portuguese attack. The Sultan of Oman at the time decided to send members of the Maamiry and Mazrui clans to Mombasa for the purpose of supporting the coastal people against any future foreign aggression. That was in 1728 (Strandes, 1961).

Political Marginalization

From the onset, Governorship in Mombasa was the preserve of Omani Arabs, particularly the Mazrui (Kindy 1972). The Arabs also led in all matters pertaining to religion and education, as was the case in Pate. This resulted in overt political marginalization of the coastal peoples, which survived stubbornly for decades and centuries.

Busaidy Dynasty

Soon after Seyyid Said bin Sultan took over the royal reigns as the Supreme Ruler of the Sultanate of Oman, he annexed Zanzibar in East Africa and proceeded to make claims on much wider territory in the region. Meanwhile, the French and the English were making similar claims in the same region and representatives of these two European states, acting together as well as separately, disagreed with the Sultan on the extent of his legitimate territory.

The Sultan eventually confined his claims to the ten mile coastal strip from all the way south in Tanganyika (Tanzania) to northernmost coast of Kenya. Except for Zanzibar and Pemba, which were ruled directly by the Sultan, the rest of the territory became loosely recognized as part of the Sultan's East Africa possessions, and was later ruled indirectly by the British as a protectorate on behalf of the Zanzibar ruler.

Challenged

No sooner had the Sultan made those claims and gotten support from the British than was his overlordship of the ten mile strip challenged by the Mombasa Arabs led first by Mbaruk bin Rashid Mazrui who was later joined by his cousin Mbarak Mazrui, 1975. The British received the support of other Arab notables such as Ali bin Salim and his brother, Seif bin Salim. On the other hand, Mbaruk and Mbarak were supported by the erstwhile supporters of Swahili cause, the Mijikenda, this time led by Ngonyo wa Mwavuo. The significance of this is the fact that the most vicious battle was fought in Mijikenda country, Buni in Rabai to be precise, which speaks volumes about the enduring relationship between the Mijikenda people and their neighbours, the Mombasans.

This rebellion against the Sultan of Zanzibar and his British overlords was not just a Mombasa-Mijikenda affair as were the earlier ones against the Portuguese. This was a war that involved all the coast people at that time, and its leadership reflected that backdrop. For example, apart from the Mbaruk/Mbarak axis (Arab) and Ngonyo Mwavuo (Mijikenda), it had at its helm such leaders as Hamisi Kombo and Mwinyijaka, and Swahilis of the Tangana and Changamwe sub-tribes (Kindly, 1972; Salim, 1973). This combined force was defeated, eventually. The defeat saw Mbaruk, Mbarak, Hamisi Kombo and Mwinyijaka seek asylum in German East Africa (Tanganyika) where they lived to old age and died.

Land Alienation

As a result of the war, marginalization now took its most emotive form; to wit, the alienation of non-conformist people from the fertile ten-mile strip. The land policy after the crushing of the latest rebellion against foreign powers by sea-shore coastals changed drastically. From then on, communal ownership of the land was not honored by both the British and the Sultan of Zanzibar. This immediately alienated the Bantu Swahili and Mijikenda whose system of land ownership had always been communal.

Secondly, loyalists such as Ali bin Salim and Seif bin Salim were rewarded with large tracts of land. In addition, non-rebellious Mazrui were also given many hectares of land to be owned as *wakf* (i.e. in trust) for the entire clan, especially the branches of that family that had remained loyal as the war raged. On the other hand, the Sultan was allowed ample space by his British overlords, to dish out chunks of land to whomever he wanted, according to his own wishes. It is in this manner that those who completely lost out in the sharing of the bounty were the communalist Mijikenda and their cousins, the Swahili.

This skewed awarding of the spoils of war inevitably led to a lot of friction and resentment. This is what resulted in the Mekatilili-led rebellion, or the so called Giryama war of 1914. In reality, this war was simply a continuation of the earlier rebellions resulting from unresolved Mijikenda grievances, which had been accumulating over the centuries.

The Digo

A deep friendship over the centuries between the Digo people and prominent Southern Swahili tribes such as the Vumba and the Funzi (or Fundi) led to complete domination of Swahili politics by this older Mijikenda sub-tribe. This, in turn, resulted in Digo culture (and by extension Mijikenda culture) receiving full recognition by the Swahilis, and vice versa. Apparently, from this intense interaction between the two friendly neighbouring peoples, the Swahili, who had converted to Islam much earlier, influenced the Digo to convert en-masse to the religion that was fast becoming the dominant faith in the entire sea-shore Coast. By 1850, the greater percentage of this Mijikenda sub-tribe had embraced the religion (Spear, 1978). It was not until more than a century later that a handful of Digo families (three to be exact) were to abandon Islam and convert to Christianity. This state of affairs was to remain as the status quo till this very day. In light of this state of affairs, it is inexplicable that to date, no Digo has ever been able to ascend to the top rungs of the leadership of coastal Kenya Islam. This is in spite of the fact that quite a number of Digos became leading Islamic scholars and were recognized as such by both Swahilis and Arabs. To be precise, no Digo has, for example, ever risen to the position of Chief Kadhi of Kenya. This has almost always been the preserve of Arabs; especially those with Omani roots. In this regard, it is worth noting that one Mazrui family has, for instance, produced four Chief Kadhis, one after another, within the short period immediately before independence and the present. With regard to this type of marginalization, even ethnic Swahilis have not fared better over the centuries; like the Mijikenda, they have also been marginalized.

Land Ownership Marginalization

After the "Mazrui" war, many loyal Arabs were rewarded with huge chunks of land all along the Coastal littoral; regarded as Arab territory anyway. It is to be noted that both the British and the Zanzibari sultanate went out of their way, blatantly skewing the scales in regard to the issue of land distribution, in favor of sea-shore inhabitants who had evidence of Arab origin. This policy not only alienated the Twelve Tribes (i.e.the twelve Swahili tribes of coastal Kenya) but, more perversely, it completely disenfranchised the Mijikenda people, particularly those who had been resident in the disputed area for centuries. The policy alienated the Digo all along the South Coast to the border with Tanganyika, the Giryama in Malindi, Mambrui and Magarini, the Chonyi in the area today known as Bahari, the Duruma in parts of Changamwe such as Miritini, Bokole, Mwagosi, Mwamlai, Chamunyu, and Chaani, as well as, the Rabai in Buni/Jomvu area, not forgetting the Kauma in Takaungu and Vipingo areas.

Henceforth, all these people were treated and referred to as 'squatters' illegally settled on other people's lands. On the other hand, Mazrui Arabs were screened and those deemed loyal during the rebellion were also awarded large tracts of land designated '*wakf*' possession both in the South and North coasts.

The bare-knuckles marginalization described above has remained a sore spot and strained relationships between and among diverse groups of coastal peoples for over a century now. This is the single-most important issue that was responsible for the flare-up of new hostilities in 1914 that pitted the Mijikenda against the British. The event, already referred to above, has come to be known as the 'Giryama War'. This war, ably led by the daring woman, Mekatilili wa Menza, led to further marginalization of all Mijikenda people, instead of resulting in any gains to their credit.

Marginalization in Education

The racial British colonial administration system known as 'colour bar' brought about a unique type of marginalization based on a person's skin color. This resulted in the stigmatization of people of non-mixed black complexion at the sea-shore coast; people who came to be derogatorily referred to as "*Nyika*", henceforth viewed as uncultured, uncivilized, dirty, uncouth, and worse still, sub-human. These individuals happened to be the Mijikenda. Once the system was fully implemented, these people were openly discriminated upon by even their allies over many centuries, the coastal Arabs and Bantu Swahilis (albeit arabized) most of whom, owing to non-discriminatory centuries' old interracial marriages, were brown, not white (i.e. both "Arabs" and "Swahilis"). Furthermore, it was a fact that most of the so-called Arabs and their Swahili co-religionists had taken in marriage Mijikenda women. Actually, before the British divide-and-rule policy, the relationship between the three peoples could be described as having been more or less, harmonious. This is clearly attested to by Abdulaziz (1979) who writes:

> "The Mijikenda and the Miji Kumi na Miwili (Twelve Swahili Tribes) relied greatly on one another both in times of peace and war. The MijiKenda not only provided a near market for articles imported through Mombasa, but it was through their territory that trade with the interior was carried on. In times of war they gave each other refuge and material support, for their enemies were often mutual. It was for reasons such as these, apart from the considerable intermarriage that took place between them, that the Nyika often referred to the Swahili as **adzomba**, meaning uncles and nephews! In fact there would hardly be an indigenous Swahili family in Mombasa which could not trace some MijiKenda blood in them *(Abdulaziz, 1979:23)*.

The above comments are supported by the works of Kindy (1972), Salim (1973), Spear (1978) and Krapf (in Spear, 1978).

Discrimination and Marginalization

The British colonial education system was pegged on the above described discriminatory and marginalizing practices. Schools were established for European, Indian and Arab children; but for Africans, governed by Local Native Councils, facilities for primary education were practically nonexistent. Later on, a school system for Africans was implemented under the auspices of District Education Boards (D.E.Bs). However, the D.E.B schools received very little support from the colonial administration and were poorly equipped or completely ignored as they were not meant to help the educationally marginalized Africans and particularly their children.

It is worth noting that, in contrast, there was a vibrant Arab Primary School in Mombasa which today is known as Serani. Further, a well-built and fully equipped secondary school was founded at Shimo la Tewa, just outside the island of Mombasa, to cater for Arab children. The status of the school was changed later and it was donated to take care of the educational needs of African children. However, this happened after the Second World War when Arabs panicked and chose to safely stay with their children on the island rather than risk sending them to the far off Shimo la Tewa mainland. The British understood the Arab concerns and helped them build another school for their children on the island on land donated by a rich Swahili landowner known as Khamis. That school was named after him and is known as Khamis High School to this day. No secondary school was established specifically for African children at the Coast during the entire duration of British colonialism; at least not by any express design or intention. It is therefore no wonder that most of the earliest indigenous professors from the coast were to be found only from among the 'Arabs.' Anyone looking for evidence of educational marginalization during that period and beyond need not search far and wide.

Suffered Worst

Swahilis and Digos suffered the worst in the scenario described above. Although they were Moslems, and therefore it would have been expected that their children were qualified to attend schools built for their fellow Arab Moslems, on the contrary, those children were not allowed to join such schools just because, in the first place, the schools were exclusively aimed at benefitting people designated as *white*. Arabs were those who could produce evidence of Arabian Peninsula descent. The British regarded them as favored subjects, and argued that they should not be lumped together with Swahilis. To entirely disqualify any Swahili pretentions, the Arabs kept insisting that Swahilis, together with their kin, the black African Mijikenda, were not only different but they, in fact, had no record of having contributed anything to human civilization, and therefore had no business expecting to reap the fruits of modern civilization. In this, they were supported by the British, who were readily available to fan the flames of segregation. Finding themselves betrayed and abandoned by their treasured guests (the Arabs), the Swahilis, on their part, sought a middle ground in which, even though they accepted that they were not Arabs after all, they were not Africans either, but "Afro-Asians". The aim of this surprising claim was, quite obviously, to counter the negative effects of raw discrimination and marginalization. Focused and dependent on this rather strange reasoning, the Swahilis used it as a weapon to ardently fight to be recognized as a unique, separate people. Nonetheless, their efforts came to naught as no school was built specifically for their children. However, they were later allowed to take their children to the Arab schools on condition that those who made any such claims had to prove their Arab origins (Kindly, 1972).

For the Digo, their case was straightforward according to the British and the Arabs. They had no claims to such privilege whatsoever and as such, it was legitimate to band them together with their fellow African brethren, the Nyika/Mijikenda. Consequently, it was no contradiction for them to be placed under the jurisdiction of the Local Native Councils. Fitted in that marginalizing hole, it was up to them to take their children to the far spread - out D.E.B. schools, their religious affiliation notwithstanding. Besides, some prominent Arabs were preaching water and drinking wine as the (English) saying goes. While their children were directly benefitting from the discriminatory British educational system and policies, they were at the same time telling the Digos that it was sinful and against Islamic teachings to take their children to European type schools where they would be exposed to infidel learning and thinking, in order to avoid actively receiving influences to convert to Christianity. This propaganda was so thorough that a good number of Moslem Digos accepted the reasoning as the truth. Needless to say, this enhanced the marginalization of the Digo people, in education which subsequently led to their being left behind by not only their fellow Moslems, the Arabs and Swahilis, but also by their fellow ethnic Mijikenda who had not converted to Islam.

Kenyatta and Moi: The "Conquistadors"

These two post-independent black African presidents took over the reign of national power as conquerors. With regard to their mode of leadership, the first and second presidency of independent Kenya was no different from British colonial rule. They imposed their relatives, their sycophants, cronies and fellow tribesmen and women whose appetite for land and other national resources they first had to satisfy before considering "the others".

Both Kenyatta and Moi discovered the straight-jacket of marginalizing people who were outside their immediate circles and consequently their taste and convenience. Acquisition with impunity, skewed distribution of resources and development programs as crafted by the British were never reformed but, instead further refined and even enhanced during their tenure in office. These presidents quite smoothly continued with the discriminatory and marginalizing practices introduced by the colonialists, thus consolidating and perfecting the plunder of the sea-shore coast. This application of an unreformed colonial system inevitably further alienated the coastal people, particularly the Mijikenda who were deprived of their traditional lands. These two rulers had no desire to right any historical wrongs that Arab and British colonialisms bequeathed to coastal Kenyans who could not lay any claim, even remotely, of being of Arab descent. In this respect, it is not surprising that some wish to break away from Kenya altogether, or else yearn for a return of the British rule, which they view more positively compared to that of black Africans from *Bara* (i.e. upcountry, non-coastal Kenya).

The third President of the Republic of Kenya, Emilio Mwai Kibaki has so far, not shown any shift in the way he intends to deal with the centuries of discrimination and marginalization against Coastal black Africans (i.e. Mijikenda and Swahili). Apparently, this president has decided to follow the trend of his predecessors in dealing with a people who have been pitilessly brutalized by centuries of administrative maltreatment. Ostensibly, he has chosen the beaten path of treating them in the traditional colonial manner, thus lacking the slightest feeling of concern or even remorse. For Kibaki, it is "business as usual".

Kaya Bombo and the Mombasa Republican Council

It is obvious that sea-shore coastal people, particularly those with no legitimate claim to Arab descent do not think that African rule has brought about anything worth celebrating. Not only are Coastal people hungry in an independent black African country, they are also an angry people. The pervasive view from within is that they suffer blatant and systematic trampling of their civil rights. To ignore these strong sentiments is tantamount to distorting their reality, which is that of Kenyans who do not see themselves as being anywhere near the Kenyan dream, as envisaged upon the attainment of political independence.

For one, they view Africans from outside the Coast as 'foreign' as the British were, or even more foreign; particularly those Kenyan communities that have produced a president. From the coastal people's point of view, they have borne witness of marginalization from fellow Africans since independence, virtually on a daily basis. Coastal people do not find themselves on an equal footing anywhere in the modern sector even in their home base at the Coast, a fact that adds to their extreme frustration and bitterness. The apex of the bitterness was physically manifested in the Kaya Bombo/MulunguNipa clashes that took place in 1997 and 2007/8 respectively. The occurrence of the clashes marked the culmination of decades of frustration since the Mekatilili war of 1914. The clashes also shed a different light on the famous calmness of the Coast people. These two episodes, if nothing else, provided proof that the desire to go to war among this dehumanized people is still alive. The ultimate price in any such future war is a complete secession of the Coast from mainland Kenya and the formation of an independent Pwani Republic, a la Southern Sudan. Obviously, something has to be done to right the wrongs, otherwise the threat of total war on the scale of the 1914 one, resulting in secession, will always be there.

Way Forward

Should Coast secede as envisaged by the Mombasa Republican Council (MRC)? Obviously not, as great danger lies ahead of any such plan. Coast people are not united; diverse groups are separated by disparate ethnicities, race, class, religious creed and a myriad of other socio-cultural differences, not to mention the cumulative animosities, thanks to the 'divide and rule' strategy of British colonial policing.

Given the history of the Coast from 1895 (when the British officially took over the administration of the Kenya Colony and Protectorate) all the way through the Kenyatta and Moi regimes to the present day, Coast people have been exposed to administrations that have viciously divided them, instead of uniting them. Coast people today do not respect or trust one another. Such groups would rather trust outsiders, any outsiders, even foreigners, rather than trust other coastal people perceived as being "different." At the extreme level, different coast groups hate each other. How then can these people ever dream of having their own country, separate from the rest of Kenya? What will happen in such a country? There will not be only one revolution, but rather one after another up to the end of times. It will be a state of perpetual upheavals of the type that will make the (1964) Zanzibar revolution look like a child's play. So much so that people will wish for a repeat of the Zimba episode, which will then be viewed as having been so mild and uniting factor.

Add all the above to the fact that Coast people, like all other Kenyans, have worked and sweated for the benefit of Kenya ever since that very idea of united country was conceived. How can they secede now after having invested so much in the country? Would they not be the losers? Rather than lose so cowardly and callously now when it is payback time, they should hang in there and stake claims to their rightful share in a nation they have actively built, sacrificing a lot in the process. This is no time to turn back to some cosy, comfort zones; rather it is the right time to make legitimate demands and follow them up to fruitful conclusions. In any case, the Constitution of Kenya (2010) offers ample space for one and all citizens' grievances to be adequately addressed. What coastal Kenyans must never do is to give up so late in the day. On the contrary, they must keep up the hope and strive even harder in their pursuits in order to realize their long smothered dreams from within the new dispensation. In order to be high achievers within the system, they must be ready, now more than ever, to release their pent up energies and claim their rightful stake in the nation.

References

Abdulaziz, M.H. (1979). *Muyaka: 19ᵗʰ Century Swahili Popular Poetry.*

Gray, J.M. (1957) *The British in Mombasa: 1824 – 1826.* London: Macmillan.

Kindy, H. (1972).*Life and Politics in Mombasa.* Nairobi: East African Publishing House.

Nicholla, C.S. (1971). *The Swahili Coast.* London: Allen &Unwin.

Prins, A.H.J. (1967). *The Swahili-speaking Peoples of Zanzibar and the East African Coast.* London: International African Institute.

Salim, A.I. (1973) *The Swahili-speaking Peoples of Kenyan Coast: 1895-1965*: East African Publishing House.

Spear, T.T. (1978). *The Kaya Complex: A History of the Mijikenda Peoples of the Kenya 1900.*Nairobi Kenya Literature Bureau.

Stigand, C.H. (1913). *The Land of Zinji:* London: Constable.

Strandes, J. (1961). *The Portuguese Period in East Africa.* Nairobi: East African Bureau.

Mainstreaming Gender in the Lake Victoria Region for Sustainable Regional Development

Easter Achieng

The Lake Victoria region is a multi-ethnic, multi-cultural, multi-lingual diverse hub whose potential has not been effectively and efficiently utilized despite various plans to do so by and with different actors nationally, regionally and internationally. To ensure regional development, it is important that an engendered multi-sectoral approach, which promotes access and equitable optimal utilization of the resources by the different nations around the Lake Victoria, is developed and actualized. This can only be possible if the different governments review the treaties and laws governing the Lake to ensure that rights based approaches are in line with Article 1 of the Universal Declaration of Human Rights (UDHR), which states: *"All human beings are born free and equal in dignity and rights. They are endowed with reason and conscience and should act towards one another in a spirit of brotherhood "*and Article 22 which states that *"Everyone, as a member of society, has the right to social security and is entitled to realization, through national effort and international co-operation and in accordance with the organization and resources of each State, of the economic, social and cultural rights indispensable for his dignity and the free development of his personality. "*

In addition, access to water is vital resource, as Koichiro Matsuura has asserted:

"Water is probably the only natural resource to touch all aspects of human civilization —from agricultural and industrial development to the cultural and religious values embedded in society. " – Koichiro Matsuura, Director-

General of UNESCO (1999-2009) and Chair of the World Heritage Committee (1999).

How can these declarations be marshaled to improve gender relations in the Lake Victoria basin? Gender is a terminology which needs to be unpacked so that it is effectively understood. Gender refers to the widely shared ideas and expectations (norms) held about women and men. It refers to the roles we learnt in our societies and responsibilities for women and men that are created and learnt in families, communities and cultures. Sex refers to the biological characteristics that make us male or female (anatomical, physiological and genetic). These biological differences are determined at birth and are universal. Sex also refers to sexual activity, including sexual intercourse. Sexism on the other hand, refers to attitudes and behaviours which promote stereotyping. Feminism is a collection of movements aimed at defining, establishing, and defending equal political, economic, and social rights and equal opportunities for women. Its concepts overlap with those of rights. Feminism is mainly focused on women's issues, but because feminism seeks gender equality, some feminists argue that men's liberation is therefore a necessary part of feminism, and that men are also harmed by sexism and gender roles. Feminism is thus an ideology for social change.

For Lake Victoria to be sustained as a resource, it is important to discuss gender as a live subject and the impact gender inequalities and inequities at different levels in the region have had on management and utilization of the lake as a resource. The discussion on mainstreaming gender in the effective sustainable utilization of the Lake Victoria as a resource will in turn give the different nations around the lake a common agenda and focus in working together to ensure that resource allocation and management has a gender based approach.

Fresh water is a renewable resource. Yet the world's supply of clean, fresh water is steadily decreasing. Water demand already exceeds supply in many parts of the world and as the world population continues to rise, so too does the water demand. Awareness of the global importance of preserving water for ecosystem services has only recently emerged during the 20th century, as more than half of the world's wetlands have been lost along with their valuable environmental services (*http://www.wateryear2003.org*). Biodiversity-rich freshwater ecosystems are currently declining faster than marine or land ecosystems. The framework for allocating water resources to water users (where such a framework exists) is known as water rights *(http://www.wateryear2003.org)*.

There have been many projects conducted on the Lake as well as for the Lake and her people but the integral question we ask is: What is their impact? To ensure that community members understand that the optimal utilization of the lake with its dwindling flora and fauna is their right and responsibility, radical measures need to be put in place for the community to realize their role in conservation of one of the major natural resources in the region.

The Lake Victoria region has not seen shared leadership in management of its resources or political leadership which is critical to any development agenda. The gender blind policies which are developed do not give space for women, female youth and girls to engage fully as their male counterparts do. To ensure that gender is mainstreamed at all levels, there is need for conscious and deliberate efforts to bring all spheres of the community to the realization that unless engendered policies and laws on the management of Lake Victoria are developed and enacted, the invisibility of women who still remain voiceless on sustainable development of the region, will continue.

To reach these goals is a huge endeavour, requiring substantial resources and coordinated actions, not just from governments but also from people who use water and those who invest in this precious resource, especially at the national level. The necessary actions in this regard include changing behaviour in water use, sanitation and hygiene; mobilizing and engaging regional communities in behavioral change and strategic plans for utilization of the lakes resources; setting regional and national targets and plans to generate investment; instituting and implementing policies and regulatory frameworks for water management that take into account both public health and ecosystem needs and forming partnerships between private companies, bilateral donors, development agencies, banks, civil society and local communities. It is imperative to keep up the momentum to reach the goals and make the best use of our water resources *(http:// www.wateryear2003.org)*.

The Lake Victoria region is also known for negative cultural beliefs and traditional practices such as wife inheritance, which has been a major contributing factor to the high incidences of HIV & AIDS in the region. This is partly due to the hetero-normative state of patriarchy which has contributed to subsequent deaths due to opportunistic diseases, and has had a huge negative impact in the region. This negative practice has seen women and girls disinherited thus increasing levels of poverty among the female gender in the region. The Bill of Rights in the Constitution of Kenya has addressed this form of discrimination by ensuring that all persons are equal and no culture which is repugnant supersedes the law. It is thus imperative that Kenyans ensure the implementation of the constitution *in toto*.

Some emerging negative practices e.g. *jaboya (a man who is assigned the task of fishing and bringing in the catch)* deny women access, accountability and still put agenda-setting in the domain of the male gender. In this case women are put in a situation where one has to have a male partner to enable her collect and sell her fish. This is due to patriarchal issues where women are believed to bring bad luck to the catch due to her "filth/dirt" even when she owns the boat. In addition, the culture of coercing women to have sexual intercourse in exchange for the fish has led to negative gains as there is increased devastation to human life in the region due to the continued practices of unprotected sex with multiple sexual partners. This also infringes on women's bodily integrity as it does not give them the opportunity to choose sexual partners thus infringing on the women's right of choice which is enshrined in the Universal Declaration of Human Rights (UDHR). This has in turn made cross-generational sex common place as a means of enabling women and girls to access the fish harvest. This could also be considered as a form of violence against women since they are denied equitable access to engage in socio-economic activities.

By mainstreaming gender at all levels, the visibility of females undertaking work and initiatives along with their male counterparts will increase. This can in turn be utilized to develop courses and training opportunities on water management, which countries in Europe such as Sweden, Norway and the Netherlands have optimized. Entrenching this aspect at all levels would then enable Kenya to eventually meet one of its goals of "Water for All". Unfortunately, this goal still seems unreachable yet it can be realized by ensuring the development and actualization of sustainable plans which ensure that the resources in the Lake Victoria are well managed at all levels.

The Kenya government has also developed programs such as fish farming in different regions and this has made the demand for fish from the Lake Victoria region to drop. Overfishing in the lake has also negatively impacted on the once thriving and vibrant industry. The introduction of exotic species such as Tilapia and Nile Perch into the Lake has contributed to unbalancing the natural ecosystem of the waters, contributing to dwindling fish stocks. This situation provides an opportunity for the region to look at other avenues of utilization of the waters within the Kenyan territory in accordance with the regional and international treaties. It is also an opportunity for Kenya to revisit treaties not favorable for optimal utilization of the water such as the Nile Treaty of 1929, and lobby for repeals for the country's benefit. This can only be possible if the citizens are aware of their role in management and proper utilization of the Lake Victoria waters. If citizens are also aware of their rights to the lake as a resource, then active citizen participation in regional development shall be realized.

"The International Year of Freshwater" (2003) provided the world with an opportunity to raise awareness, promote good practice, motivate people and mobilize resources in order to meet basic human needs and manage water in a sustainable way. World leaders at the United Nations Millennium Summit agreed to halve by 2015, the proportion of people without access to safe drinking water. This was held before 2003 and added a corresponding target to halve the proportion of people lacking access to basic sanitation by the same year. The meeting also agreed to develop national water management and efficiency plans by 2005. The question we need to ask ourselves is:How far has the Government of Kenya gone in implementing the action plans developed? It is also important to examine this in the Kenyan context and establishthe extent to which community members have related to this goal. In Kisumu for example, living next to the second largest freshwater lake in the world has not been beneficial, as many estates in the city did not have access to clean tapped water until the year 2011. This meant that significant portions of household incomes, which are marginal in many cases, went into purchasing water for daily household use.

On the aspect of water management, it is important to enable all gendersto understand how the utilization and preservation of Lake Victoria is key to ensuring that future generations will be able to enjoy the same resources and benefits. The Lake Victoria waters can therefore be utilized as a resource in the following ways:-

1. Agricultural – farming on the shores of the lake.

2. Industrial– reducing the effluence from the factories around the lake

which pollutes the lake and has greatly contributed to the near extinction of the natural biodiversity, and to the thriving of water hyacinth which is detrimental to the ecosystem of the Lake Victoria.

3. Household – utilizing the water in the city of Kisumu to enable all citizens have access to clean water.

4. Recreational – utilizing the water for water sports/hotels/tourism

5. Environmental – preserving the water to enable future generations enjoy the same.

Members of either gender can equally participate in the process of effective utilization of Lake Victoria resources. It is essential that the government invests more in the region to enable efficient utilization of this resource to generate revenue. The lake region is vast, but poverty in the rural areas where the lake crests the shores is high. The earlier mentioned economic activities could certainly help in alleviating poverty in the region with Lake Victoria serving as a key resource in that process. The new constitution of Kenya has embraced the protection of natural resources and it is up to the citizens of Kenya to be vigilant to ensure optimal utilization and conservation of the Lake.

It is imperative that the government of Kenya be put to task to ensure that the number of girls and boys in primary, secondary and tertiary education are equal from enrolment to completion. This will then ensure that participation of the female gender in the activities around the Lake Victoria will be from a knowledge-based and enlightened position. The mainstreaming of gender in management and utilization of natural resources is also seen in Goal 7 which seeks to ensure environmental sustainability through the following targets - *Target 7A: Integrate the principles of sustainable development into country policies and programs; reverse loss of environmental resources.* This aspect is core to the vision of this region where environmental policies are not effected thus resulting in situations such as having a slowly dying major water source as evidenced by the dwindling species which were once plenty in the lake. It is time for all persons to take charge, be sensitized and take the responsibility to develop sustainability strategies in the management of this resource.

There is linkage between the dwindling water sources, to the drying up of the once pristine rivers and streams due to the devastation of the forests in and around Mt. Kenya, the Aberdare Range, the Mau Complex, Mt.

Elgon and the Cherangani Hills which are the water towers of Kenya. The main influent rivers to the Lake Victoria are the *Sio, Nzoia, Yala, Nyando, Sondu Miriu, Mogusi* and the *Migori*. Combined, these rivers contribute far more water to the lake than does the largest single in-flowing river, the *Kagera*, which enters the lake from the west. The only river flowing out of the lake is the *White Nile* (Source: Wikipedia). Furthermore, it is stated in Daniel Kull's (1996), *Connections Between Recent Water LevelDrops in Lake Victoria, Dam Operations and Drought*, that about 55% of the lake's drop during 2004–05 is due to the Owen Falls dams (now known as Nalubaale and Kiira dams) releasing excessive amounts of water from the lake. The natural rock formation controlling Lake Victoria's outflow was replaced by the first Owen Falls dam in the 1950s. This lack of replenishment of freshwater into the lake is resulting in a rapidly dwindling resource which might cause serious conflict among the nations surrounding the Lake Victoria unless urgently addressed. It is thus very important to review regional historical agreements and treaties, to ensure that each country's rights and entitlements which are enshrined in Article 22 of the UDHR, are upheld.

The Target 7C of the MDGs - *Halve, by 2015, the proportion of the population without sustainable access to safe drinking water and basic sanitation-* is key to the sustainable development and management of Lake Victoria. The regional aspect of this is that water and sanitation programs should be central to the development agenda, and need to be integrated in all ministries and local authorities in and around the lake basin. This is the only way that a multi-sectoral approach can be sustainable. An engendered country budget will ensure that allocations would be made to sectors which reduce the burden on women due to lack of access to clean, safe water. An engendered water management policy at regional level would also ensure that information and resources would be equitably distributed to protect Lake Victoria as a precious resource.

Further reflection on access to water as a resource is found in the proposed amendment to the UDHR including Article 31 on the Right to Water, which states that, *"Everyone has a right to clean and accessible water, adequate for the health and wellbeing of the family, and no one shall be deprived of such access or quality of water due to individual economic circumstance"*, *(www.article31.org)*. This can only be achieved if gender is mainstreamed in the Lake region which will in turn ensure Sustainable Regional Development. The discourse on mainstreaming gender in the Lake

Victoria region for sustainable development is an opportunity for all citizens to start participating actively in the optimal use and management of Lake Victoria as is enshrined in the Constitution of Kenya, and not leave it to the government, civil society organizations or a few individuals alone: it is our right and responsibility. Kenyans and the East African Community at large need to ensure that the lake is not exploited and left devastated, unable to support itself due to the destruction of the eco-systems which support it.

The internalization of the process of preserving the lake is key to all for the management of this rapidly dwindling natural resource, which can be a source of conflict. A case in point is the Migingo and Ugingo saga where Kenya and Uganda were in conflict over the ownership of the water and the fish within it. Unless there is dialogue between the countries who share the waters of the lake for equitable and equal opportunities to exist for the communities around the lake and for the community members to feel protected to exploit their socio-economic activities to the fullest potential without fear of arrest by either government. Bank Ki Moon, the UN Secretary General states, *"Water, sanitation, stability, prosperity, and peace: these goals are closely, inextricably linked. Progress can be ours if we work together (UN Press Docs, July 27, 2011).*

An engendered multi-sectoral approach to development is the only sustainable way that will ensure that all sectors and citizens are included meaningfully in the discourse of Sustainable Development of the Lake Victoria as a resource and that women, men, youth (both male and female) and children (boys and girls) will move from awareness to internalization, conscientization and protection of Lake Victoria as a vital resource for generations to come. It is imperative for meaningful and greater involvement of women, female youth and girls to be involved in management of the Lake Victoria as a resource. This will ensure inclusion in planning and decision making is practically seen and contribute to an integrated and sustainable approach to management of resources.

References

Dolphine Okech, Kenya Female Advisory Organization (1997). *Practical Civic Education*.

Dolphine Okech, Kenya Female Advisory Organization (2001). *A Critical Look At Causes and Strategies for Reduction of Women's Human Rights Violation in Rural Areas*.

Dolphine Okech, Kenya Female Advisory Organization (2002). *My Struggles Hurdles and Achievements*.

Dolphine Okech, Women Action Forum for Networking (2008). Looking at the Nyanza Communities' Beliefs and Practices with Gender Equality and Human Rights Lenses (2007).

Kull, D. (1996). *Connections Between Recent Water Level Drops in Lake Victoria, Dam Operations and Drought*.

The Constitution of Kenya (2010)

UN PRESS DOCS (2007).

Universal Declaration of Human Rights (UDHR)

Wikipedia

www.article31.org

www.wateryear2003.org

The Politics of Identity

Ethnicity: The Jinx to Kenyan Politics and Economic Development

Felix Ngunzo Kioli

Introduction

Ethnic divisions as manifested before and after independence suffice to explain the ethnicization of politics and economic development in Kenya. Indeed, the roots to ethnicity and ethnic identification in politics and economic development can be traced to colonial Kenya. Kenya realized independence in 1963 from Britain and subsequently became a post-colonial African state when Jomo Kenyatta took over power as first as Prime Minister and later as President. Under the Kenyatta regime ethnic identity was used for inclusion and exclusion in the political arena and in development. Kenya was used as personal property of a clique and resources were inequitably allocated and distributed. This tendency continued under Daniel Arap Moi who was President between 1978 up to 2002. Moi's philosophy of following 'Nyayo za Mzee' heightened the process of exclusive development and political participation.

The repeal of section 2A of the Constitution of Kenya in 1991 which had banned multi-party democracy appears to have exacerbated ethnic consciousness and participation in politics and development. With the exit of Moi and the entry of Mwai Kibaki in the year 2002, things did do change much because regional imbalances in resource allocation and the entrenchment of ethnic consciousness in the conduct of public affairs were not confronted head on. Consequently, ethnicity has become the jinx of Kenya's politics and development. Indeed, the socio-cultural, economic and physical ramifications of ethnic politics in Kenya have been quite severe. This chapter seeks to address some of these issues.

Let us begin with some terminological clarification. The word 'ethnic' appeared in anthropological writings in the 1960s after the realization of the distortion of meaning and subjectivity in the usage of terms 'race' and 'tribe'. Jenkins (1997:17) observes that by the 1960s, the notion of "the tribe" was beginning to be replaced by perhaps the less derogatory concept, "ethnic group". The event which most clearly marked the paradigm shift within social anthropology from the study of 'tribal society' to social constructionist model of ethnic groups was the publication of Barth's work "Ethnic Groups and Boundaries" in 1969. The word tribe as used by anthropologists in 19th and early 20th centuries denoted primitivity, backwardness and non-Western practices. This was particularly the case in describing African and other cultures where European expansionist tendencies and colonization were prevalent. Similarly, the word race, associated with Count Joseph Arthur de Gobeneau (1816-82), proposed the existence of three races: White (Caucasian), Black (Negroid) and Yellow (Mongoloid). Giddens (2006:485) observes that de Gobineau was of the view that the white race possesses superior intelligence, morality and will power. This view strongly subscribes to the notion of evolution which is highly hierarchical and places human kind in a diametrical pattern – premised on color. According to Barth (1969b), the word "race" and "tribe" provided anthropologists (some of whom were sympathizers of colonialism) with grounds to classify human beings in terms of developed, civilized and vice versa. In a nutshell then, both terms "race" and "tribe" can be said to have been value laden lacking in academic neutrality and objectivity and hence the shift to the word "ethnic", which is less academically and socially contested, and adheres to the notion of cultural neutrality and relativism as propagated by the anthropologist Franz Boas (McGee and Warms, 2000:370).

Meaning and Nature of Ethnic Groups and Ethnicity

The word ethnic is derived from the ancient Greek word "ethnos" which originally according to Williams (1976) meant "heathen" or "pagan". It was used in this sense in English from the mid 14th century until the mid 19th century when it gradually began to refer to "racial" characteristics. In the United States, the word "ethnic" came to be used after the Second World War referring to distinct cultural groups such as Jews, Indians,

Italians, and Hispanics, and to social and cultural traits of immigrants to the United States (Ericksen, 1993).

In common usage, the word "ethnic group" refers to an assembly of people or collectivities of persons who share some characteristics premised on ancestry, language, culture, geographical locality and common objectives. Rupesinghe (1996:10-31) asserts that an ethnic group is not a mere aggregate of people but a self-conscious collection of people united or closely related by shared experiences and a common history. This argument brings to the fore the debate on whether membership to an ethnic group is only attributable to shared commonalities. Assefa (1996:32-51) argues that there are situations in Africa where an aspect of culture commonality, such as language or religion does not signify membership to the same ethnic group. Other scholars point out that membership to an ethnic group should not always be viewed in terms of shared characteristics. For instance, Eriksen (1993) observes that a person, regardless of primordial commonality, can become a member of an ethnic group if he or she feels and acts as a member and is accepted as such by the group. Moreover, this view brings into consideration other factors such as choice of a marriage partner which in many patriarchal cultures, especially in Africa, transforms an individual's identity. Indeed, according to Eriksen, membership to an ethnic group should be viewed as being both ascriptive and achieved.

The word "ethnicity" first appeared in the Oxford English dictionary in 1972, and is attributed to the American sociologist David Reisman in 1953. He used it to refer to a shared (cultural) and perceived (psychological) group identity (Glazer and Moynihan, 1975:1). Further, within American scholarship, the increasing use of "ethnicity" as a concept was part of a long term and gradual shift of analytical framework from "race" to "tribe" to "ethnicity" (Wolf, 1994). Anthropologist Fredrick Barth (1969b) played a key role in establishing the current anthropological understanding of ethnicity by associating the term with the conscious identity which individuals acquire for being members of a group. Clifford Geertz elegantly defined ethnicity as the "world of personal identity, collectively ratified and publicly expressed" and "socially ratified personal identity" (1973: 268, 309). Ethnicity can thus refer to a group identity, expressed behaviorally (by individuals or group) that emanates from membership to an ethnic group. British anthropologist Wallman encapsulates the concept of ethnicity by arguing:

Ethnicity is the process by which "their" difference is used to enhance the sense of "us" for purposes of organization or identification...Because it takes two, ethnicity can only happen at the boundary of "us", in contact or confrontation or by contrast with "them." And as the sense of "us" changes, so the boundary between "us" and "them" shifts. Not only does the boundary shift but the criteria which make it change (1979:3).

This view demonstrates ethnicity as being defined by cultural differences and the identity that emanates from it. Eriksen (1993) also emphasizes the idea of cultural distinctiveness between groups or individuals, and the concomitant identity that defines each group, in understanding ethnicity. Further, Giddens (2006:487) avers that ethnicity is the cultural practices and outlooks of a given community of people that set them apart from others. Members of ethnic groups see themselves as culturally distinct from other groups in a society, and are seen by those other groups to be so in return.

In the endeavor to understand the nature of ethnicity, it is important to note that ethnicity and ethnic consciousness is a product of socio-cultural orientation. This view is corroborated by Ogot (1996:19), Handelman (1997) and Giddens (2006:487). The view of ethnicity being a result of cultural orientation is predicated on the perspective that as a behavioral pattern, it can be learned, shared, transmitted and transformed as human beings interact with each other. This view is well espoused by Aboud (2001:181) who in his studies of children found out that ethnic awareness and identification is social and not biological. Ethnicity is acquired as one gets inducted to become a member of society. In this sense then, behaviorism which is a set of principles defining the learning process in understanding human behavior can be applicable to the study of ethnicity. The primary architects of behaviorism include Ivan Pavlov, a Russian Scientist (1849-1936) and B.F. Skinner, an American (1904-2009), and their theories ('classical conditioning' and 'operant conditioning' respectively) emphasize social learning as critical in understanding developmental behavior, which can include ethnicity. A synonym of social learning as applied by sociologists is the concept socialization, while anthropologists use the equivalent term, "enculturation". Giddens (2006:487) emphasizes that there is nothing innate about ethnicity; it is a purely social phenomenon that is produced and reproduced over time. Through socialization, children assimilate the lifestyles, norms and beliefs of their communities.

Jenkins (1997:12) further observes that ethnicity is variable and manipulable, not definitely fixed or unchanging. This view emphasizes the dynamic nature of ethnicity and the capacity of the human being to manipulate ethnicity either for personal aggrandizement or to be in tandem with other changes in the socio-cultural arena. For instance, Smith (1993) points out that conditions of modernity give rise to increased ethnicity and make such identity a powerful symbol of meaning and worth. Indeed, present day ethnic consciousness has a scope and intensity that did not exist earlier. In the current political configuration especially in Africa, the sense of identity offered by ethnicity is quite evocative and has the power necessary for political mobilization. Additionally, Jenkins (1997:13) points out that apart from the manipulable nature of ethnicity, ecological issues are particularly influential in determining ethnic identity, in as much as competition for economic riches plays an important role in the generation of ethnicity.

Ethnicity as a social identity is collective and individually externalized in social interaction, and internalized in personal self-identification. This view on the nature of ethnicity is also associated with Jenkins (1997:13) who articulates that not only is ethnicity quite manifest at the group level, but also the individual level. Theoretically, the symbolic interactionist perspective associated with George Herbert Mead (1863-1931) and his student Blumer (1900-1987) comes in handy. It observes that the self is a reflection of the group and it is difficult to divorce the self from the society. Farganis (1993:145-146)) points out that Mead and Blumer's theory of symbolic interactionism was concerned with the self as a consequence of complex social interactive process. In relation to ethnicity then, the active involvement of an individual in the life of a group affects the social development of the individual, including ethnic identity.

Genesis of Ethnicity in Kenyan Political and Development Arena

The trajectory of ethnicity in the political and development participation of the Kenyan people was well laid down during the colonial period. Indeed, before the colonialists penetrated into the territories of Africans, the notion of borders was not of concern. People of different cultural backgrounds interacted without too much regard for their ethnic base, while cultural limitations couched in stereotypes, prejudices and bigotry were relatively non-existent. Were (1967) and Ogot (1996:16) argue that there were no water tight ethnic categories between cultural groups in Kenya before colonialism, while Muriuki (1974) demonstrates how various cultural groups in Eastern, Central and Rift Valley provinces in Kenya had intimate relations with each other in total disregard to ethnicity by the 18th and 19th centuries. This scenario changed after the East African region was declared a protectorate in 1895.

As a strategy to annihilate, control and subjugate the Africans, the colonialists established borders largely configured in line with language and culture, and this satisfied their Eurocentric desire to create "tribes." Ogot (1996:17-18) observes that in furthering the policy of a gradual extension of British influence outwards from established colonial stations and forts, the new rulers established internal borders and district boundaries that were supposed to coincide with "tribal" and linguistic units. Their efforts were vitiated by the definition of ethnic groups as "tribes," a concept that was racist and historical in the sense that it regarded the various nationality groups as being static, exclusive and homogeneous. In this sense then, Ogot observes that the concept of "tribe" was therefore an intellectual abstraction; a mental invention of the colonialists which was intended to convey or portray the picture of a people without government, culture and history in order to justify colonialism. Physical borders were enacted to freeze movement and interaction and in order to avoid "contamination" from neighboring, but culturally and linguistically different peoples. Fines and corporal punishment were imposed to deter movement from one locality to another while Africans were to be governed in their own language units. As a consequence, "tribal" uniqueness was very well formulated, while strategies for inter-ethnic tension and conflicts were well enacted. The culmination of this was to divide and rule, in cahoots with colonial sympathizers.

The process of balkanization of Kenyan African groups into ethnic enclaves as strategized by the British colonialists succeeded and by 1920, indicators of ethnic consciousness among the Africans came to the fore (Ndege 1996:65). Ethnic oriented pressure groups started cropping up and indeed, the involvement in the struggle for independence by Kenyans was inevitably ethnicized. This assertion is exemplified by regional groups agitating for recognition and independence in the 1920s namely Kikuyu Central Association (KCA) in the Mt. Kenya region and the "Piny Owacho" in Luo land. Later, in 1944, KCA transformed itself and became Kenya

African Union (KAU). After the State of Emergency was declared in Kenya on October 20, 1952, Africans were advised to go back to their ethnic regions. This strategy ensured they were confined to their regions of origin and invented their own pressure groups to safeguard their interests and welfare.

Ndege (1996:65-73) observes that the emergence of such associations as the Nairobi District African Congress, the Mombassa African Democratic Union, the Kisii Highlands Abagusii Association, the Taita Democratic Union and the Nakuru African Progressive Party is a manifestation of how barely a decade to independence, the colonial state was still determined in localizing African politics.

In 1957, the colonial government legalized the creation of parties by locals but such parties were to be confined to their own districts as opposed to national operations throughout Kenya. When later national parties were allowed, the Kenya African National Union (KANU) was the first to be formed in 1960 in circumstances that made it the natural heir to the Kenya African Union (KAU). KANU emerged as a party to cater for the interests of larger ethnic groups (especially the Kikuyu and Luo), while Kenya African Democratic Union (KADU) was established for the concern of the so called "smaller communities". Behind these political groupings, ethnic consciousness was quite prominent. Later on, KADU was absorbed into KANU and became part of government. Despite the merger, ethnic suspicions and mistrust persisted.

Political and Economic Development participation since Independence

Kenya gained independence from Britain in 1963 and since then successive governments have demonstrated that ethnicity invariably remains a fervent tool for political mobilization and participation. Seeds of ethnic divisions planted during the colonial rule got anchored and perfected after independence.

The Kenyatta Era (1963-1978)

Jomo Kenyatta, abhorred competitive politics and that is why he strategized very fast to dismantle KADU immediately after independence, and later the Kenya Peoples Union (KPU) pioneered by Jaramogi Oginga Odinga in 1966. He set the stage by personalizing politics and development in Kenya placed his loyalists in strategic governmental institutions and subsequently, entrenched and perpetuated Kikuyu hegemony. Atieno Odhiambo asserts:

> After Kenya became a post-colonial African property, Kenyatta took over political power. Having captured the state, Kenyatta fell back to his lifelong and primary agenda, tending to the needs of his basic community, the Agikuyu. This he succeeded in doing very effectively in the fifteen years of his presidency. At the end of 1978, it could legitimately be stated that his was a story of spectacular success for his primary constituency, the Agikuyu. He had secured the state for them, the government and vast homeland in the Rift Valley and along the Coast. He had put commerce in their hands *(1996:76)*.

The economic elite from Central Kenya under Kenyatta's patronage controlled major financial lending bodies after independence with the aim of empowering "their" people financially and ultimately, controlling the political dispensation. Rothchild (1969:693) in his paper, *"Ethnic Inequalities in Kenya"* states that "the statistics on I.C.D.C. and National Bank loans up to April 1966 show that Kikuyu people received 64 percent of the industrial loans and 44 percent of the commercial loans."

Moreover, as a strategy to perpetuate Central Kenya into the political, economic and social sphere of the country, the Kikuyu and communities surrounding them saw the efficacy of ethnicity and ultimately created the Gĩkũyũ, Embu, Meru Association (GEMA) (Atieno Odhiambo, 1996:74-83). GEMA evolved into a powerful political entity in the 1970s and had a high influence in the socio-economic and political empowerment of its members. The fall-out between Oginga Odinga and Jomo Kenyatta in 1966 was grounded on the injustice and control that the Central province elite was subjecting the rest of Kenyans. This fall-out set the pace for the political alienation of the Luo community. KPU, the vehicle which Oginga Odinga clung to for political survival, was proscribed in 1969 and opposition politics criminalized. Atieno Odhiambo (1996:74-83) argues that with criminalization of competitive politics, the "ideology of order" moved to centre stage. Proscription of party politics gave room to the growth of government-supported ethnic associations headed by "ethnic kingpins" who acted as the leadership elites and avenue for control of ethnic groups. Ethnic-based associations permeated almost all public institutions. Atieno Odhiambo states that the democratic pillar became an orphan in Kenya, and ethnic interests superseded nationalism.

Kenyatta presided over Kenya as a one party system – a trend all over the African continent during the 1960s and 1970s (Tordoff,1997: 4, 134). Kenya's one party system was under KANU and clientelism shaped and colored Kenyan politics with Kenyatta himself as patron. Political alliance and patronage became increasingly important and politicians relied on ethnic linkages and networks for support. Many supposedly apolitical bodies were politicized, such as trade unions, universities, co-operative societies, women organizations, police and the army (Tordoff, 1997:154-155). In a similar version, provincial administration officials (provincial commissioners, district commissioners and chiefs), majority of who also had strong ethnic connections, executed and controlled party policies and ultimately determined political and economic dispensation. From 1963-1978 Kenya was synonymous with Kenyatta and his clique in controlling political and economic development affairs of the country.

The Moi Era (1978-2002)

Daniel Torotich Arap Moi presided over Kenya from August 1978 to 30th December 2002 and inundated the state with politics of patronage and ethnic clientelism, deception and hypocrisy, politics of anxiety and subservience. In the initial stages, his clarion call of following "Nyayo za Mzee" translated to simply following the footsteps of Kenyatta, and by implication meant subscribing to the ideologies and philosophy of his leadership. Like Kenyatta, Moi appeared to loathe competitive politics. Atieno-Odhiambo (1996:74-82) argues that throughout 1970s into 1990, discussing possibilities of democracy was anathema. Furthermore, every means at the disposal of Moi's ruling party KANU was used to derail the formation and registration of opposition parties including detention without trial, brutality of provincial administration and the police, control of the registrar of societies, courts of law and KANU youth-wingers. Through these machinations and other overt efforts, Kenya became a *de jure* one party system in 1982 after a failed military coup whose instigation was imbued by ethnic discontent in the running of the country.

As a strategy to entrench himself and his clique of leaders, and out of sheer paranoia, Moi started dismantling the Kenyatta Empire. Simatei (1996) points out that Moi embarked on "de-Kikuyunization" of the civil service including strategic state institutions (parastatals, security, diplomatic circles, and learning institutions) by means of the "Kalenjinization" of the same. Anecdotes abound how one would find people of the same ethnic group from the Rift Valley turning their local language into the official language of some parastatal such as Kenya Posts and Telecommunications Corporation, among others. Kalenjinization of key institutions was compounded with empowering ethnic chieftains (kingpins), handpicked by Moi himself to champion his interests at local (ethnic) level and to perpetuate subservience among other communities. Such tribal kingpins wielded a lot of power among their ethnics: Mulu Mutisya in Ukambani region; Shariff Nassir at the Coast; Kariuki Chotara and Joseph Kamotho in Central Province; Joseph Lotodo in North Rift Valley; Ezekiel Barngetuny in Uasin Gishu; and William ole Ntimama among the Maasai; Wycliff Mudavadi among the Abaluhya; among others. Paradoxically, after coming into power in 1978, Moi had disbanded all tribal caucuses formed during Kenyatta's time including GEMA, but in turn, endeavored to use ethnic chieftains to entrench himself. Through Moi and his henchmen, intra- and inter-ethnic dissent was confronted with extra judicial repercussions. To cite Wamwere (2008:187-202), this is how one would explain the demise of individual dissenters such as Bishop Alexander Muge, Jean Marie Seroney, Robert Ouko, and the incarceration of Kenneth Matiba, Charles Rubia, Raila Odinga and Koigi Wa Wamwere.

Indeed, the balkanization of African regions into "ethnic units" as happened during colonial times was efficiently rekindled in Moi's era. Ethnic dictatorship and in turn, ethnicizing Government and politics in Kenya were rampant during the entire 24 years of Moi's rule. Wamwere (2008:48) broaches the idea of ethnic dictators who handpicked leaders, manipulated elections and created fear, anxiety and despondency at the expense of democracy.

In the 1990s, there was an agitation to democratize the African continent; a political phenomenon which was more intense in former British colonies. Daniel Moi and his ruling elite eventually succumbed to both domestic and international pressure. This led to the repeal of Section 2(A) of the Constitution of Kenya and allowed creation of plural democracy in 1991. Fascinatingly, emerging opposition parties such as Ford Kenya, Ford Asili, Kenya National Congress, Democratic Party and other smaller ones failed to forge a unified platform to challenge Moi's ruling party, KANU. It is imperative to note that ethnic parochialism among leaders, and an ethnically driven population was a leading factor; keeping in mind that most of these leaders had grown and nurtured their leadership skills under Kenyatta and

Moi. Throup and Horby (1998) offer three main arguments to explain failure to unite by the emerging parties and their presidential aspirants. First, Kenyan voters had always rewarded politicians who could guarantee "*maendeleo*" (literally, 'development,' but usually understood as patronage of state resources). The second factor was that in the minds of voters and politicians alike, ethnic calculations had always outweighed any ideological consideration. Lastly, the euphoria of pluralism created unrealistic expectations of change in the era of multiparty competition.

The voting patterns for the presidential candidates in 1992 suffice to demonstrate ethnicization of political participation in Kenya. President Moi had managed to consolidate Kalenjin votes together with those of smaller ethnic groups to emerge the winner. Kenneth Matiba and Mwai Kibaki shared all Kikuyu votes, while Oginga Odinga's bulwark for his votes was from Luo Nyanza. Prior to the election of 1992, ethnic tensions had been very high with "ethnic" clashes in the Rift Valley and Western Kenya, which were politically instigated to drive away "non-indigenous" people.

The second multiparty election in December 1997 presented a myriad of political parties to compete against KANU. Indeed, the proliferation of these parties confirmed sentiments by Bratton and Van de Walle (1997: 239) that "democratization in Kenya has resulted in reaffirmation of ethnic identities with political parties emerging along ethno-regional criteria rather than ideological ones." Each aspiring politician was under the illusion that they could marshal their ethnic group behind them to trounce Moi and KANU. This cost the opposition candidates the presidency. Once more, Moi trounced them (Moi 40.64%; Mwai Kibaki 31.49%; Raila Odinga 11.06%, Michael Wamalwa 8.40% and Charity Ngilu 7.81%). Their combined votes would have led to a win, but factionalism driven by ethnic chauvinism and fixation was their undoing. Just as in 1992, prior to the 1997 elections, there had been "ethnic" clashes in the Coast province to eject non-Coastal people from the South Coast, while after the election, ethnic groups clashed again in the Rift Valley.

The period between 1998 and 2002 experienced an era of political realignment and strategizing with the main desire to succeed Daniel Arap Moi – who according to the constitution was not eligible to stand for presidential election. These realignments and political maneuvers were couched in ethnic calculation. National Alliance Party of Kenya (NAK) fronted by Mwai Kibaki's Democratic party (DP), Social Democratic Party

(SDP) by Charity Ngilu and FORD Kenya by Michael Wamalwa — all aspired to embrace the Kikuyu, Akamba and Abaluhya and to confront KANU (read Kalenjin) which had found a political alignment for convenience with National Development Party (NDP) fronted by Raila Odinga, a Luo kingpin. Moi and Raila were later to fall out when Moi anointed Uhuru Kenyatta as his heir. Together with other formidable forces from KANU (George Saitoti, Stephen Kalonzo Musyoka and Moody Awori), Raila joined forces with NAK prior to election of 2002 and formed National Rainbow Coalition (NARC). Ethnic calculation and patronage appeared to be the dominant factor when Raila Odinga pronounced "Kibaki Tosha" (Kibaki is Enough) in 2002 at a rally in Uhuru Park, Nairobi. Kibaki became the sole opposition candidate to square it out with Uhuru Kenyatta, heir apparent to Moi. Through ethnic balance, Kibaki came to power in December 30, 2002.

Mwai Kibaki's era (2002 to 2013)

Although the ethnic factor may have played a significant role toward the ascension of Kibaki to the presidency of the country, the diverse representation of key regional figures in his government in the beginning gave rise to hope that the ethnic factor in politics could dissipate. To the chagrin and disillusionment of many, Kibaki gradually started reviving the politics of patronage and what Maina Kiai and Paul Muite (2009) term as politics of ethnic "entitlement." To demonstrate that he was not for change, Kibaki reneged on a Memorandum of Understanding he had presumably signed with key figures that spearheaded his campaign, which prominently had been led by Raila Odinga. Secondly, in critical government positions and appointments, Kibaki retained some of the bureaucrats or remnants who had presided over Moi's system.

The Kenyan leadership of 2003 which had given hope and fortitude to its citizenry after many years of misrule, ethnicity and despondency, turned into a farce. By the year 2004, Kibaki had started facing a revolt from prominent figures in his government who had played a key role in his campaign for presidency. Consequently, a total fallout was quite imminent in the beginning of 2005. Apart from their grievances in affairs of running the country, the opposition by Kibaki and his inner circle to a comprehensive constitution review aggravated discord within the revolting group in the cabinet.

The emerging animosity culminated into two extreme antagonistic groups towards constitution making, and by extension, demonstrated the political trajectory in the country. As Kenya approached a national constitution referendum towards the end of 2005, the disintegration of NARC Government was quite imminent and inevitable. Ethnic passions and sentiments pervaded the campaigns to either adopt piecemeal constitutional change or a comprehensively review of the existing one. KANU, under Uhuru Kenyatta, teamed up with the renegade ministers, led by Raila Odinga. The fact that Uhuru Kenyatta and his followers belonged to a different camp from Mwai Kibaki is illustrative of the complexity of politics in Kenya. In addition to ethnicity other factors are at play. The referendum was won by the Orange team, thus reaffirming people's discontentment with the centre. Kibaki sacked the "renegade" members of his cabinet (those in the Orange team) – most of whom had been very critical to his presidency. Thereafter, as Kenya approached legislative and presidential elections in 2007, ethnicity once again took a prominent centre stage as politicians strategized for the elections. The Orange team portrayed themselves as nationalists, but it was very clear that ethnic mobilization and participation was paramount. Indeed, the Orange team appeared to sail comfortably within Nyanza (Luo), Western (Abaluhya) and Rift Valley (Kalenjin).The population of these regions was behind their leaders, namely Raila Odinga, Musalia Mudavadi and William Ruto, respectively. On the other hand, the Banana team had its bulwark of following in Central (Kikuyu) and Eastern (Embu and Meru) provinces.

Prior to the elections in 2007, Kenya projected itself as a very politically ethnicized society. The politicians and the mass media played a very crucial role in directing Kenya towards ethnic politics. Disturbingly, the religious fraternity with its diversity also demonstrated a penchant for discrimination and favoritism in political affiliation and party participation. Moreover, ethnic hate speech, reminiscent of the period preceding the general elections of 1992 and 1997 put the country at risk. Much of the campaign was beset with reckless and derogatory comments that undermined national unity. Statements such as, *"tutatoa madoadoa kati kati yetu"* translated to mean "we shall do away with those different from us" – attributed to a politician from the Rift Valley, were not different from the ones associated with a Maasai politician in 1991, who championed for "making the Kikuyu in Maasai land lie low like an antelope". Kenya was also treated to "politics of circumcision" and "Majimboism" or federalism which, to many, meant ejecting those who never belonged to certain regions or ethnic groups. These among many other speeches and outbursts that embody ethnic animosity associated with Kenyan politicians, illuminated the political arena.

The results of the legislative and presidential elections of December 2007 which pitted Mwai Kibaki against Raila Odinga clearly showed Kenya as highly ethnicized politically. Kibaki's potent electoral zones were Eastern and Central provinces. Indeed, in Central province (Kikuyu), Kibaki received the people's votes to the last person. The same scenario was indicative of Raila's votes, especially in Luo Nyanza and in other regions such as the Rift Valley (Kalenjin) and Western Province (Abaluhya), where emerging ethnic chieftains namely William Ruto and Musalia Mudavadi, respectively, played a key role in his campaign. The intrigues of ethnic politics were also exemplified in Ukambani region where Kalonzo Musyoka carried the day in presidential votes with his ODM-K political flagship.

Mwai Kibaki was pronounced the winner of the presidential elections in the year 2007 amid intense protestations from his competitors. The aftermath of these protests was the post-election violence in January and February 2008 which epitomized deep, inbuilt and passionate ethnic tensions between certain ethnic groups in Kenya. The international community intervened to restore "normalcy" in Kenya, which culminated in the formation of a Grand Coalition Government between President Kibaki and Raila Odinga as the Prime Minister. Intriguingly, ethnicity appeared to play a key role in the formation of this coalition government. With the inclusion of Kalonzo Musyoka in the government, each party appeared to champion for the political and economic interests of its ethnic group as well as rewarding their kinsmen and women. Marred by squabbles relating to appointments to the civil service as well as allocation of national resources the coalition government could not serve Kenyans well enough to deliver economic and political reforms.

Implications of Ethnicity in Kenya

Ethnicity is a jinx in Kenyan political and economic development. The ethnic mistrust aggravated during and after independence has had severe socio-cultural, economic and physical ramifications to the Kenyan society. First and foremost, it has become quite difficult and an uphill task to build a national culture or character. Atieno Odhiambo (1996) observes that,

Kenyans consciously first belong to an ethnic group before identifying with their country. This is manifested in their socio-political and religious organizations and affiliations as well as in their mother tongues. This divisiveness which militates against nationalism is further exhibited and exemplified in the mental entrenchment of ethnic stereotypes and prejudices amongst Kenya's ethnic groups. Ethnic stereotypes and prejudices are not conducive to amicable coexistence between groups. Politicians have systematically used the prevailing stereotypes and prejudices to breed hatred and suspicion between groups, culminating in ethnic rivalries, belligerence and conflicts. Indeed, the ethnic conflict experienced in Kenya since independence to the most recent post-election violence in 2007/2008, suffice to demonstrate that ethnicity is the jinx of Kenyan politics.

Kenya has witnessed politically and ethnically instigated conflicts before and after every presidential and general election held in 1992, 1997, 2002 and 2007, especially in Western Kenya, the Rift valley and Coast region. For instance, before the multi-party elections in 1992, politically instigated ethnic clashes flared up in the Rift Valley culminating in the killing of around 2000 people and displacement of thousands of others (Tordoff, 1997). The main victims were the Kikuyu community. Similar ethnic strife and tension replayed again before the 1997 elections, this time in the South Coast. Those targeted were ethnic groups from upcountry. Lives were lost and a lot of property destroyed. The aftermath of this conflict was also felt in the decline in the tourism industry in Kenya which was a major source of public revenue at the time.

The climax of ethnic conflict in Kenya was witnessed after the disputed presidential elections of 2007. The ethnic jinx played itself in a very wanton manner. The Kikuyu and Luo communities bore the brunt of this conflict. In the Rift valley and Western Kenya, the Kikuyu community and their economic empire were highly decimated. In retaliation, a section of the Kikuyu "warriors" blockaded a section of Nairobi–Nakuru highway and its environs in Naivasha and physically targeted Luo people for physical assault. Luo men were humiliated with forceful physical circumcision, torching of their houses and killings. Same scenarios of conflict between the two protagonists were experienced in certain estates in Nairobi (especially Kibera, Kawangware, Kariobangi, and Dandora). The post-election violence in 2008 led to the phenomenon of Internally Displaced Persons (IDPs) numbering almost one million people, around 1,500 people lost their lives, thousands of women and young girls were raped while property worth billions of shillings was destroyed.

Ethnicity plays out in the employment sector. Patronage in job employment was strongly entrenched during Kenyatta's presidency while Moi and Kibaki perfected it. It is evident that those in power craved to employ those from their ethnic groups in the institutions they presided. The Kenya of the three subsequent presidents since independence has seen some government institutions such as universities, colleges, parastatals, ministries, security agencies and even private companies being the domain of certain ethnic groups. This trend has infested and inundated the Kenyan socio-political and economic environment with the culture of impunity, corruption and subservience.

The Kenyatta and Moi regimes were highly identified with initiating selective and lop-sided development. During Kenyatta's regime, Central Kenya and its environs was the hub of good infrastructure, schools and hospitals. When Moi took over, there was a drastic shift of the development machinery to the Rift Valley and other well politically connected areas. Moi was popularly known for the slogan "*Siasa mbaya, Maisha mbaya*" translated to mean those outside KANU and not loyal to him would be alienated from sharing the national cake. Thus Moi's *modus operandi* was ethnic manipulation that set the stage for control of public resources without consideration to the whole society. Wamwere observes–

> President Kenyatta withheld development from Luo land because the Luo under Oginga Odinga opposed him. President Moi withheld development in Gikuyu land and Luo land because both Gikuyu and Luo had opposed him ever since he consolidated his ethnic power. Both Kenyatta and Moi governments withheld development from North Eastern province most likely in retaliation for 'shifta' war and rebellion (2008:213).

Despite the aforesaid negative implications of ethnicity, there exist some positive aspects as well. Aboud (2001:179-182) points out that ethnicity is a strong benchmark for identity and belonging. The self-consciousness of being Luo, Kikuyu, Meru, *inter alia*, offers to an individual a sense of security, comfort and identity. Moreover, cultural identification is pertinent to cultural preservation. In Kenya, the fact that individuals first belong to an ethnic group has enhanced continuity of cultural heritage. This cultural heritage is also demonstrated in the unique economic production of each ethnic group which enhances an elaborate symbiotic relationship between the various cultural groups in Kenya. This relationship is in the form of exchange and reciprocity between groups. Indeed, what one cultural group produces is exchanged with what is found in another group, but lacking locally. For instance, livestock bred by the pastoral peoples of North Eastern Kenya finds its market to Nairobi and Central province while vegetables and other manufactured goods from Central Province find their way to many other parts of the country. The same applies to fish from Luo Nyanza which is exported to many parts of the country while those in Nyanza in turn acquire cereals and vegetables from other regions and, vice versa. Additionally, certain talents associated with some cultural groups are a source of not only individual wealth but also the country. The athletic endowment of the Kalenjin community suffices to elaborate the strength of cultural diversity and ethnic identification.

Conclusion

The tendency for ethnicity to define politics and economic development has been quite pervasive before and after independence in Kenya. Ethnicity, expressed negatively, has become the Achilles heel upon which any political dispensation has been grounded. This kind of scenario has systematically entrenched a dangerous and harmful political trend. Indeed, Kenya has for a long time been subjected to guided democracy, that is, a democracy that borders on authoritarianism and the perpetuation of the interests of the minority. For Kenya to divorce itself from negative ethnicity there must be the desire to put in place a government which has the interests of the entire nation at heart, devoid of ethnic underpinnings and sentiments. This calls for what Pinkney (1993:12) calls "consociational democracy". This would ensure that all significant groups are incorporated in government without alienation of "others". The system recognizes society as consisting of distinctive groups, based on language, race or religious autonomy of one another and the state. Indeed, the object of consociational democracy is to seek consensus between the different groups through a political process that brings all leaders into a governmental process, through carefully tailored forms of proportional representation or by specifically reserving offices of state for members of the different groups. Moreover, there is need for legislation to guard Kenyans against politicians who whip ethnic emotions for political survival and aggrandizement. The law must be very clear, with severe penalties for those who violate such laws. Lastly, Kenya requires elaborate civic education targeting its citizens with information on inclusion and diversity, while emphasizing on building a national culture.

References

Aboud, F. (2001). The development of ethnic awareness and identification. In A.Giddens (ed.), *Sociology: Introductory Readings*.PP.179-182.Cambridge: Polity Press.

Assefa, H. (1996). Ethnic conflict in the Horn of Africa. In K. Rupesinghe and V. A. Tishkov (Eds.), *Ethnicity and Power in the contemporary world*, PP32-51.Tokyo; The United Nations University.

Atieno-Odhiambo, E. S. (1996). Reconditioning the terms of fact. Ethnicity, nationality and democracy as political vectors. In B. Ogot (ed.), *Ethnicity Nationalism and Democracy in Africa*, PP 74-84. Kisumu: Institute of Research and postgraduate studies, Maseno University.

Barth, F. (ed.) (1996b). *Ethnic Groups and boundaries: The social organization of culture difference*. Oslo: Universitet for Laget.

Bratton, M. and N, Van de Walle (1997). *Democratic Experiments in Africa: Regime Transitions in Comparative Perspective*. New York: Cambridge University Press.

Eriksen, T. H. (1993). *Ethnicity and Nationalism: Anthropological Perspectives*. London: Pluto Press.

Farganis, J. (1993). *Readings in Social Theory: The classic Tradition to Post-Modernism*. NewYork: McGraw-Hill, Inc.

Geertz, C. (1973). *The interpretation of Cultures*. New York: Basic Books.

Giddens, A. (2006). *Sociology*. 5th Edition. Cambridge: Polity Press.

Glazer, N. and Moynihan, D. (eds.) (1975). *Ethnicity: Theory and Experience*. Cambridge, Mass: Harvard University Press.

Handelman, D. (1977). The organization of ethnicity. *Ethnic Groups, 1, PP. 187-200*

Hobsbawn, E. and T. Ranger (eds.) (1983). *The Invention of Tradition*. Cambridge University Press.

Jenkins, R. (1997). *Rethinking Ethnicity: Arguments and Exploration*. London: Sage Publications.

Kiai, M. and P. Muite (2009, April, 17). Ethnic entitlement does not bode well for our country and communities. *Daily Nation, P. 4*

Mcgee, R. and R.L. Warms (2000). *Anthropological Theory: An Introductory History*, 2ⁿᵈ Edition. Mountain View: May field publishing Company.

Muriuki, G. (1974). *A History of the Kikuyu, 1500-1800*. Nairobi: Oxford University Press.

Ndege, G.O. (1996). Ethnicity, nationalism and the shaky foundation of political multi-partysm in Kenya. In B. Ogot (ed.), *Ethnicity, Nationalism and Democracy in Africa*. PP. 65-73. Kisumu. Institute of Research and Post Graduate studies, Maseno University.

Ogot, B. A. (1996). Ethnicity, nationalism and democracy - a kind of historiography. In B. Ogot (ed.), *Ethnicity, Nationalism and Democracy in Africa*. PP. 16-25. Kisumu: IRPS, Maseno University.

Pinkney, R. (1993). *Democracy in the Third World*. Buckingham: Open University Press.

Rothchild, D.(1969) Ethnic inequalities in Kenya. *Journal of Modern Studies, Vol. 7.No.4.*

Rupesinghe, K. (1996). Governance and conflict resolution in multi-ethnic societies. In K. Rupesinghe and V. Tishkov (eds.), *Ethnicity and Power in the Contemporary World* PP. 10-31. Tokyo: The United Nations University.

Simatei, P. T. (1996). Ethnicity and otherness in Kenya cultures. In B. Ogot (ed.), *Ethnicity, Nationalism and Democracy in Africa*. PP. 51-55. Kisumu: IRPS. Maseno University.

Smith, J. (1986). *The Ethnic Origin of Nations*. London: Oxford University Press.

Throup, D. and C. Hornsby (1998). *Multi-Party Politics in Kenya: The Kenyatta and Moi States and the Triumph of the System in the 1992 Election*. Oxford: James Currey.

Tordoff, W. (1997). *Government and Politics in Africa*. Bloomington: Indiana press.

Wallman, S. (1979). Introduction: The scope of ethnicity. In S. Wallman (ed.), *Ethnicity at Work*. London: Macmillan.

Wamwere, K. (2008) *Towards Genocide in Kenya: The Curse of Negative Ethnicity*, Nairobi: Mvule Africa.

Were, G. S. (1967). *A History of the Abaluhya of Western Kenya, C.1500-1930*. Nairobi: East African Publishing house.

Williams, R. (1976). *Keywords*. London: Flamingo.

Wolf, E. R. (1994). Perilous ideas: race, culture and people. *Current Anthropology, 35. pp.1-2.*

Deconstructing the Mindset of Poor Communities in the Coast of Kenya for Socio-Economic Development

Shauri Halimu & Lusweti Sellah

Introduction

The Coast Province is home to the nine coastal communities of Kenya commonly referred to as the Mijikenda. They comprise the Giriama, Rabai, Ribe, Kambe, Kauma, Duruma, Jibana, Chonyi and the Digo. Historically, these communities occupied well defined geographical regions called *'Kayas'* (shrines) before the Arab and European incursion of the early centuries dispersed and displaced them. The *'Kayas'* were held in high esteem by the Mijikenda community as places of worship (Schaaf 1998, Robertson 1986).According to Coastal Forest Conservation, there are more than fifty (50) *'Kayas'* which have been identified in Coast Province. Out of these, 41 are protected by law with 37 being under the National Museums of Kenya as national monuments, while the rest are safeguarded by the Kenya Forest Service (KFS) (Robertson and Luke 1993).

Given the Mijikenda classification, there are nine primary *'Kayas'* representing the sub-communities, while the other shrines were established much later. The primary *'Kayas'* include Kaya Fungo, Kambe, Ribe, Rabai and Jibana in Kaloleni, Kaya Kauma in Kilifi, Kaya Duruma, Gandini and Digo in Kwale. Apart from the nine Kayas, there are also shrines such as Kaya Chonyi in Kilifi district, Kaya Mudzi Mwiru in Kaloleni, and Kaya Kinondo in Kwale.

Located on the Indian Ocean coast, the region has excellent and vibrant access to other continents by sea. There is very productive agricultural land, and the potential for tourism is immense. The long history of contact with early Portuguese, Arab and Turkish explorers brought civilization to the area long before it reached other parts of the country. The province also shares borders and light craft air links with other countries such as Somalia, Zanzibar and Tanzania.

Despite these potentialities, there exists a pessimistic attitude and mindset among most of the coastal people. Academically, the province ranks very poorly among other provinces as evidenced by the results of the 2009 national examinations which ranked Coast Province second last, followed by only North Eastern province which has considerably less resources in comparison (KNEC 2009). There is a culture of apathy towards education and towards work, and especially manual work. This apathy is defeatist in itself since Kenya's key potentiality lies in agriculture and in its human resource competencies. Given that the Coastal people are not eager to participate in either of these very basic drivers of development, they will always be left far behind, economically.

Socio-cultural Hindrances to Development in the Coast Province

There are certain beliefs that have hindered forward thinking among communities of the Coastal region. These can be categorized into five aspects which aptly explain the current lack of development in the province, namely economic, social, cultural, political and spatial. Successful societies tend to possess more positive economic beliefs than their non-successful counterparts. Strong positive economic beliefs can act as drivers for the other pillars of society (economic determinism). Unfortunately, the communities of the coastal region have more negative economic beliefs than other communities in the country. This problem is both cultural and historical in nature. The pre-colonial and colonial period, for instance, gave the region's economic dominance to Arabs, Portuguese and Britons. This created a mindset where outsiders were perceived as the owners of means of production and the locals as workers. This negative perception has persisted even to date, forty seven years after independence.

There is a misconception in the region that all resources accrued from the different economic sectors, especially from tourism and transport, are transferred upcountry. This is commonly used as an excuse for not putting effort in work. The question of social inequality and inequitable distribution of resources in the region stirs controversy in many contexts. Whenever inequality is mentioned, it is quickly understood as income inequality yet in its wholeness inequality includes social exclusion and the inability of certain population groups to access key social services (Society of International Development, 2004). A region's initial level of income distribution is an important determinant of future growth prospects. An area with high levels of inequality, especially of assets, may achieve lower growth rates. When a part of the country feels disadvantaged, for example the coastal region, development efforts are watered down by the perception of being suppressed.

Apparently, there is apathy towards manual work in the region, which may be as a result of a conflation of many factors including culture, religion, climate and the economy. This culminates into a deep disadvantage that is translated into accepted social behavior. The idleness that comes with this behavior has led to alcoholism and drug abuse and consequent incapacitation and loss of life (Shauri, 2007). At the district level for example, life expectancy in Meru is double that in Mombasa at 68.6 and 33.1 years respectively (Kenya Demographic and Health Survey, 2003). This shows that by the time an individual reaches the most productive years, his or her life is over.

Though we acknowledge the positive role played by religion and culture in socio-economic development, the existence of multi-cultural and religious beliefs, attitudes and mindset has had a negative impact in the coastal region. In keeping with cultural and religious beliefs, for instance, there are social and economic activities that one cannot engage in as they are considered taboo. There is also the belief in witchcraft which is very retrogressive since it allows escapism and blame games that may not necessarily yield a solution to the health, economic or social problems being addressed.

The cultural belief that the place of a woman was never one that allowed her to make decisions has been held on to by many communities in the region and elsewhere in the country. While people are aware that educating a woman is educating the society, limited inroads have been made in this area. Given the marginalization, self or otherwise, women tend to suffer double tragedy in the lack of socio-economic wellbeing. First because they were born at the coast, with all its socio-cultural disadvantages, and second, the fact that they are women trying to make ends meet in a patriarchal system entrenched within their culture and religion. Thus, it is imperative that girls and women are encouraged to participate in education and development not only as beneficiaries but as policy makers and implementers.

Kenya is a democratic state with politics dominating its landscape and thus playing a significant role in the socio-economic development of the country. Since politics has become a game of numbers and bargaining, regions with this combination benefit more in the country. Those regions that play their politics well tend to develop more than others as allocation of resources tends to be skewed towards those areas that vote in a particular way and have the numbers. Thus, the divisions among the coastal indigenous communities rob them of both the numbers and unity of purpose that is needed in political machination and strategy in negotiating for equitable distribution of national resources.

The politics of resource distribution in Kenya, especially in the Rift Valley and Coast Province cannot be complete without addressing the question of land. Land ownership in most of the Coastal region was ill defined with only a few parcels demarcated and registered. This leaves the rest being held under communal and traditional tenure. State policies on land and structures are susceptible to deliberate misinterpretation and abuse (Society of International Development, 2004). This gave space for political interference as some leaders illegally allocated themselves and their cronies land belonging to coastal people. There have been many land injustices meted on the communities of the Coastal region. Over the years, the unfulfilled promises of compensation and resolution of past injustices have been used as the pawn in political campaigns. The phenomenon of squatters and land related violence, for instance "Kaya Bombo", "Mlungu Nipa" and the ongoing Msambweni-Ramisi Sugarland skirmishes, have become permanent features of the coast.

Finally, it is true that temperature and humidity at the Coast Province is significantly higher than it is in most parts of the country, with exception of North Eastern Province. Such conditions have the potential to slow people down by reducing the number of hours that they can humanly work in the day. Despite the existence of large tracks of land, a larger portion of this is unproductive as a result of frequent droughts which are normally followed by heavy floods that destroy the little that was cultivated, as well as the already weakened soil. Kwale District for example has only 1% of its land classified as arable/productive land (Society of International Development, 2004). There is also a serious shortage of fresh water in most areas of the Coast Province. These factors compromise the adoption of agriculture in the region hence enhancing food insecurity. This coupled with the effects of climate change has eroded the hope of development as food is a basic need and a cornerstone in Maslow's (1943) hierarchy of needs.

Formation of Defeatist Beliefs, Attitudes and Perceptions

People's beliefs are based on the culture of the communities or the families they come from. These beliefs inform an individual's attitude with regard to a wide range of issues. This process shapes the individual's perception or mindset which in turn defines the way they respond to events in their environment. Thus, depending on the level of skewedness of the socialization process towards building the individual's beliefs, attitudes and mindset, a person can develop a positive or negative orientation towards life. A negative orientation towards socio-economic development is the focus of this work as it is an obstacle to sustainable development.

When one does not fully subscribe to the culture of a given community, there must be some social force or sub-community (religious, educational, etc.) that is influencing their thinking, for them to digress from popular belief or practice. A belief is simply a principle accepted as true, a conviction which stems from culture. If culture is sluggish, laid-back or permissive then the people's beliefs are reflective of this weaknesses in culture since they convince themselves that there is no other way of life. Where a defeatist culture exists, it breeds beliefs, attitude and mindset of incapability. The people dwell so much on their misfortune, their lacking, and their suppression, that they do not give a second thought to their potential - collective or individual.

Apparently, when self-belief is crushed, the attitude towards any form of achievement is destroyed. Attitude is a complex mental state involving beliefs and feelings, values and dispositions to act in certain ways. The predisposition or the tendency to respond positively or negatively towards a certain idea, object, person, or situation depends predominantly on attitude. Thus, attitude influences an individual's choice of action or inaction. The four major components of attitudes include *affective* (emotions/feelings), *cognitive* (belief/opinion), *conative* (inclination for action) and *evaluative* (positive or negative response to stimuli). A person with defeatist beliefs/ attitudes or mindset is one who has lost confidence in his/her ability and hence cannot stand up to a self-confident self-assured competitor, even when all the odds are against the competitor.

The Process of Deconstructing the Defeatist Mindset for Development

In the process of changing beliefs, attitudes and mindset of people, knowledge of the need for change in orientation is critical. Unfortunately, many coastal communities do not know or are in denial that they need to change their defeatist beliefs, attitudes and mindset. However, for those who are searching for change of the status quo in the region, here are a series of steps that can generate a rebirth of the coastal populace.

In order to change the coastal person's defeatist beliefs, attitudes and mindset, it is critical that we endeavour to change their long held habits. Since mindsets are habitual tendencies that dictate the way an individual interprets and responds to social contexts, the implication here is that a positive mindset for the coastal people has the potential of changing the way they make decisions towards socio-economic development. Conversely, a defeatist mindset is a recipe for failure. An individual interested in making changes in their defeatist beliefs, attitudes and mindset should embrace positivities and shun negativities in life. The trick is to choose the positive all the time and observe the successes that come with the choice. Since we acquire negative thinking through socialization, then it is possible to unlearn it by re-socializing ourselves to the positives of life. It is important to acknowledge that somewhere in the past, during the domination by Arabs, Portuguese and early colonialists, and in post-independence era, the coastal people were socialized to view themselves as non-performers in various aspects of life. Accordingly, the key to have the correct mindset for socio-economic development is by erasing the negative orientation in favor of a more positive outlook to social life. Thus, to realize sustainable socio-economic development in the region, there is need for the cultivation of favourable beliefs, attitudes and mindset towards development. Suffice to note that the people's beliefs, attitudes and mindset have power over their socio-economic development and hence they should strive to tap this potential to reverse the downward trend in development in the region.

In this process of change for the coastal communities, individuals and groups must be conscious of what they say in any social situation. The rationale behind this is simply that we hear the words that we utter. Thus, if an individual is negative about themselves or others it goes to feed and nourish the cycle of negativity of orientation. The remedy for the coastal people of Kenya, as individuals or a collective, is to stimulate a wave of encouragement in form of dialogue and discourse that can meaningfully uplift performance and productivity in the region. This approach has the potential of stimulating success. The coastal people should face the defeatist beliefs, attitudes and mindset without fear. Once this process is started by the communities, they should soldier on without looking back. This is because looking back will expose them to the old patterns, which in most cases look good in that they constitute what they know and are used to. To change the defeatist mindset requires a complete break from the past negativity and a sustainable reliance on the newly acquired positive orientation.

Finally, to complete the process of change, the coastal communities, as individuals or a collective, should refrain from socializing with promoters of negativity. If allowed, this group can fuel and speed up the decay, leaving the individuals or the collective wallowing in self-pity and negativity. In the principle and theory of differential association, you become who you associate with. In fact, the "friends" or community members discourage attempts by the individual to break from their mindset. In group dynamics, this is explained aptly by the "we" (in group) as opposed to "them" (out group) with a view of protecting the identity and culture of the group. Simply put, the communities wallowing in defeatist cultural beliefs, attitudes and mindset will do all in their power to protect their negative image, identity and destiny. However, it is important to mention that the sorry state of the region was created by the communities themselves, for social life is how an individual or collectivity makes it - reality is socially constructed.

Methodology of Deconstructing Negative Mindset of the Communities

The paradox in this paper is whether to begin by dealing with the culture which feeds the belief, so that a new belief system can be reconstructed around a richer, more aggressive culture, or the mindset, which is a product or outcome of this process. The aim should be to boost positive self-belief, self-concept, attitude and mindset of the coastal indigenous communities. Accordingly, there is a state of cognitive dissonance on where actually to start the deconstruction process. A three faceted approach may be appropriate, whereby the process of deconstruction targets new recruits (children), the youth and middle age people and the advanced in age, with a progressive mindset.

The three tier approach is considered beneficial to the coastal communities especially when taking into account the resistance that can accrue due to cultural change. Children will be growing within the right environment, while the changing youth will be the drivers of this process, and those advanced in age act as custodians of the vision and wisdom needed to guide the process. Thus, change in the communities beliefs, attitudes and mindset should be introduced within the family, targeting children and in the community, targeting the youth and the elderly. This multi-faceted approach to social change has the potential of generating positive collective consciousness needed to spur performance for socio-economic development.

The idea here is to build a sense of collective consciousness among the local communities, to acquire a positive orientation towards development. In this regard, the new self and collectivity should be able to influence beliefs and consequently impact on the culture of the coastal people. The current state of affairs depicts the coastal society as one at crossroads. The expectation is that leaders – religious, political, educational or heads of families – make decisions that will turn around the culture or mindset and save the people. Leaders, on the other hand, should expect the local communities to take charge of their lives and destinies envisioning them using local resources and whatever can be accessed such as schools, mosques and churches, job opportunities, democratic space and business opportunities to rise up from the defeatist and impoverished state and stir the indigenous communities to greater heights of prosperity. This is the element of belief, attitude and mindset that needs to be strengthened. The missing link is to translate this conviction into a comprehensive system that can spur individual and collective social action.

The Pragmatism of the Deconstruction Process

The practicality of the deconstruction process of the coastal communities can be envisioned in four ways. First, most coastal cultures have religion as the strongest influence. This is because it provides hope in desperate situations and provides answers where science and technology have failed to explain. Religion provides the push for the desire of the most desperate people to continue living, hoping that life will be different with each coming day. In the words of Karl Marx (1818-1883), 'religion is the heart of the heartless and the opium of the masses'. This is construed to mean that people use supernatural powers (religion) to explain the unexplainable in society.

Culture and religion feed on beliefs, giving room for the formation of attitudes and mindsets. Since most of the coastal communities are followers of some religion, they have certain positive or negative beliefs, attitudes and mindset. It is the negativity, born out of the local communality's religious cultures that form the gist of deconstruction since it has the potential of hindering socio-economic progress. Accordingly, it is prudent and effective for beliefs, attitudes and mindsets generated by religion to be changed. The fact that most coastal people subscribe quite strongly to one religion or the other, is therefore a good thing, which can be tapped and used as the basis for change. Religious leaders are trusted by the masses and whatever they endorse passes within the community. Religious leaders should for this reason spearhead this process of social change to their adherents and be at the forefront of development projects as they hold the key to social change among their followers. The deconstruction of defeatist religious beliefs, attitude and mindset should therefore start with religious leaders.

Education is the second agent of change that society should embrace. Far from the belief that education equals schooling, the region should concentrate on continuous education of its people. This education has to cut across all age sets. The rationale behind this is that education takes on specific significance when it is considered that the older generation has to advise and finance the younger people's dreams and aspirations. If these advisers and financiers are not aware of the opportunities available, then their efforts will be in vain. On a different but complementary note, the coastal region has seen the growth of universities during the last few years. While this is a positive step in the country's milestones to attain positive cultural transformation of the coastal people for socio-economic development, the hope that more young people from the area can access higher education is still a mirage. This is evident in the low enrolment rates of communities in these university colleges which can be attributed to poverty and culture – negative beliefs, attitude and mindset towards schooling, sex tourism, and drug abuse among others. Thus, in the absence of efforts to change the defeatist mindset of the communities and mainstream education in the realm of their social life, these communities will continue wallowing in ignorance. This ignorance is the most critical hindrance to sustainable development in the Coast Province of Kenya.

In this regard, all the development stakeholders should then be involved in the creation of awareness on the value of education for the transformation of the mindset of the local people. This awareness should begin in the family and be propagated by all agents of socialization and re-socialization. The process should be spearheaded by professionals whose role would be to provide guidance on the relevance and appropriateness of courses offered by different institutions. It will be prudent also to encourage mainstreaming of mechanisms to deconstruct defeatist beliefs, attitudes and mindset of learners within the framework of the various courses being offered in these educational facilities. These institutions should also participate by collaborating with nursery, primary and secondary schools to boost performance from an early age. More emphasis should be placed on early childhood education to build a firm foundation. The rationale behind this is that, what people learn in their formative years is profound and long lasting. Therefore, if deconstruction of beliefs begins in earnest during this phase, its impact on the whole person cannot be gainsaid. In addition, the wider community should also be engaged in continuous education. There are also very many Non-governmental Organizations (NGOs) and Community Based Organizations (CBOs) that should be encouraged and enlisted in the campaign to target the youth and women with innovative, deconstructing educational approaches. These efforts should be coordinated to ensure that they reach the most affected areas/communities. If the right beliefs, attitudes and mindset are instilled in these young people, the region will soon be enjoying the fruits of its investment.

Complacency that is seen as traditionally *'Coastarian'* is a myth that needs to be dispelled. There are areas of specialization for which the Coast has been renowned for centuries: architecture as evidenced by the steady and sturdy structures, products of masonry skills passed down by the early Portuguese and Arab settlers and explorers; skillful traders and merchants, growing of fruits, nuts and spices, rich mineral deposits, diversity in flora and fauna, pottery, iron forging, curio industry, fishing and deep sea diving, musical talent of both males and females, acrobatics, world class hospitality, narrator and oratory skills, culinary talents and of course the potential in local and foreign tourism cannot be overemphasized.

Two other aspects that stand out in the history of the Coast of Kenya include the fact that the very first schools in Kenya were established at the Coast by Christian missionaries and Arabs. Conversely, other areas of the republic expanded their educational facilities faster (even though missionaries reached them later) while the Coastal people still prided in 'the first schools'.

Secondly, as far back as the sixteenth century when the Portuguese still occupied the island of Mombasa, the transport system in the coast was unique and advanced. Of course there was the seafaring, but there was also inland transport in form of hand pushed trams with railway lines that ran throughout the town. If then the Coastal region was to advance at a normal rate since the sixteenth century, then the present state of the province is a far cry from the potential it had then.

The areas mentioned above are therefore areas that need to be focused on, as each of them defines who the people of the Coast are, and can therefore be seen as areas of potential growth. In this case the investment that will be put into these activities in terms of sensitization and training will be minimal; all that will be needed is capital, further training and monitoring. New trades and technologies are good for any community but first, existing potential should be harnessed to the fullest. The coastal people need to re-own their heritage and the variety in economic activities that once existed. This will provide opportunities for more people to do their part in changing the culture of complacency and inaction.

References

Central Bureau of Statistics (CBS) [Kenya], Ministry of Health (MOH) [Kenya], and ORC Macro. (2004). *Kenya Demographic Health Survey 2003*. Calverton, Maryland: CBS, MOH, and OCR Macro.

Central Bureau of Statistics. (2004). *Economic Survey 2004*. Nairobi: Government Printer.

Maslow, A.H.. (1943). *A Theory of Human Motivation*, Psychological Review 50(4):370-96.

Robertson, S. A. (1986). *Preliminary Floristic Survey of the Kaya Forests of Coastal Kenya*. Unpublished report to the Director, National Museums of Kenya and WWF International. Nairobi, Kenya .

Robertson, S. A. and Luke, W. R. (1993. *Kenya Coastal Forests: The Report of NMK/WWF Coast Forest Survey*. WWF Project 3256, Coast Forest Status Conservation and Management. Nairobi: WWF.

Saad S.Y. (1998). *Who Owns the Kenya Coast? The Climaxing of Land Conflicts on the Indian Ocean seaboard.http://www.payson.tulane.edu/conflict/Cs%20St/ SAADFIN5.html,* Retrieved 29/07/2010.

Schaaf, T. (1998). *Report on the Workshop on Natural Sacred Sites: Cultural Integrity and Biological Diversity* (Unpublished) Workshop held at UNESCO Paris from 22nd to 25th September 1998. Paris: UNESCO.

Shauri, H. S. (2007). *Substance and Drug Abuse: The Effectiveness of Heroin Rehabilitation Centres at the Coast of Kenya.* PhD Thesis (Partially published)

Society of International Development. (2004). *Pulling Apart: Facts and Figures on Equality in Kenya. http://www.scribd.com/doc/2223295/Pulling-Apart-Facts-and-Figures-on-Inequality-in-Kenya.* Retrieved 22/07/2010.

United Nations Development Programme (2004). *Human Development Report 2004.* New York: Oxford University Press.

The Change of Gĩkũyũ Value-Systems in Central Kenya: From Pre to Post Independent Kenya

Frederick Kang'ethe Iraki

Introduction

Central Kenya is currently in a grave socio-economic condition. A visit to the region reveals scores of young men hovering around trading centers in search of hand-outs from relatives or simply dead-drunk and lying by the roadside. The media, especially K24, a popular national TV station, have also documented the lives of young men and women who lead a lowly life of alcoholism, drug-abuse, and total disregard of age-old values among the Gĩkũyũ. As a result, Central Kenya has lately been identified with high crime rates, extreme poverty, low educational achievement, alcoholism and dissolute life. This paper provides a glimpse of Gĩkũyũ value systems from a traditional stand point and discusses the erosion of the same by colonialism and westernization. It argues that although culture is dynamic there is need to inculcate and promote positive ethos and mores for the socio-economic and political development of a people. Finally, a set of ideas are proposed as a way forward for the Central Kenya people, especially in view of the new Constitutional order. The value-systems of the Gĩkũyũ have transformed from a closely-knit system of value and norms to what many call today "lack of culture" among the Gĩkũyũ. How has this happened?

The Gĩkũyũ nation is stereotyped as consisting of members who are thieves, money-lovers, wheeler-dealers, misers, Shylocks, opulent and very hard working. Whereas it is important to redress some of the biases, it is a fact that some values such as hard work and procurement of wealth are ingrained in the culture of the Gĩkũyũ. There is therefore need to re-examine the Gĩkũyũ people both from inside and from outside with a view to charting the future of the Gĩkũyũ community. First, it is a fact that the value system of the Gĩkũyũ has deteriorated dramatically in the last ten years or so. The decline is manifested by high rates of alcoholism and drug-abuse, idleness among the youth, low educational achievement, increased unemployment, poor parenting, low self-worth, increased insecurity and loss of cultural identity.[1] Secondly, the community is viewed with mistrust by other communities in matters of politics and economics. Economically, the Gĩkũyũ are considered swindlers, wheeler-dealers and highly corrupt people and very few people from other communities would like to do business with them. In the social domain, the Gĩkũyũ man is hardly enthusiastic to embrace intermarriage with other Kenyan communities.

In contrast, the Gĩkũyũ woman is more flexible in this respect. She is nonetheless dreaded for taking away the children with her after a failed marriage with a non-Gĩkũyũ[2]. This article will outline the Gĩkũyũ value system prior to colonization with a view to presenting the reader with an idea of what has given way in modern times. Secondly, it will briefly review the impact of colonialism and western education system and modernism on the culture of the Gĩkũyũ people. A brief parenthesis will encapsulate the effects of Kenya's presidential administration on the Gĩkũyũ. Finally, a few proposals will be raised on how the Gĩkũyũ people, especially the youth, can lift themselves by their bootstraps to regain dignity, decency and prosperity.

Value Systems prior to Colonization

In general terms, a *value* could be material, immaterial or abstract constructs that are considered necessary and therefore very important by a person or community. This also includes patterns of behavior, attitudes and aspirations. In addition, a set of values that provide the fundamental world view of a people constitute a *system* since they act in sync and in synergy. In other words, they are interdependent, interrelated and mutually-reinforcing. The *value system* therefore becomes the basic reference or beacon that underpins the social, economic and political life of a community, in this case the Gĩkũyũ people. Before delving into the Gĩkũyũ value system, let us first provide a sketch of Gĩkũyũ society, i.e. the political and socio-economic bulwark. It would be foolhardy to attempt to describe these structures in any form of detail as that would surpass the confines of this chapter. As a result, only a succinct review will be provided.

Gĩkũyũ Political System

Leakey (2007) explains that the Gĩkũyũ territory was administered by two entities, namely the *Kĩama kĩa athuuri* (council of elders) and *Njama* (war regiment). Each village or ridge (itũũra) contributed to the establishment of these two ruling entities. Leadership was based on ability and intelligence and no one was elected on the basis of family influence, neither was it possible for anyone to accede to power on the sole basis of being someone's son. Whereas the *Kĩama* adjudicated over judicial matters, the *Njama* was largely involved in protecting the community against invaders such as the Maasai (Ũkabi) and also raiding the same Maasai for their livestock. Of essence, the *Njama* was made up of young and strong men. There was a regiment in power and another one in the wings waiting to take over. The older regiment retired to pave way for the younger blood to replace them in view of the rigor required to protect the Gĩkũyũ territory (bũrũri). The retired regiment was now eligible for leadership in the *Kĩama* council.

The *Kĩama* had several stages. When a man married his first wife, he could pay a fee and be admitted to the grade of junior elder (Kamatimũ). After acquiring a second wife, he could pay a fee and pass to Second grade elder; and when he had a child old enough to be circumcised, i.e. a 14 year-old, he could pay a fee and be initiated into the Third grade elder.[3] This was a very respectable stage and the elder was now required "to maintain law and order, administer justice, and oversee religious ceremonies" (Leakey 2007: 4). Elderhood continued as one advanced in age and wisdom and upon death, the elders transcended the material world and entered the spiritual realm. They were now the ancestral spirits that played a key role in the religious life of the community. Other than death, leadership among the Gĩkũyũ was also regulated by age-groups. One generation of leaders was required to pass over the baton of leadership to a younger generation during the *Itwĩka* ceremony. This happened every 30 or so years. The two generations were Iringi and Mwangi.[4] In sum, the two councils, *Njama* and *Kĩama* maintained the political and judicial stability of the Gĩkũyũ people.

The Gĩkũyũ Economy

The Gĩkũyũ economy was chiefly based on land; land had both economic and spiritual importance. Gĩkũyũ bartered products such as maize, millet and sweet potatoes in exchange for beads, copper wire and cloth from the Arabs and Swahilis, and goats, sheep and cows from the Maasai (Leakey 2007: 53). They also bartered their farm produce and livestock to obtain land from the Athi people. The latter were hunter-gatherers who controlled an immense territory in Central Kenya and therefore provided the already sedentarized Gĩkũyũ with an opportunity to buy new lands. Even before the advent of European settlers in 1883[5], the Gĩkũyũ community was under pressure to expand their territory due to population pressure and also personal ambition. Land or *gĩthaka* was the ultimate acquisition as it provided a man with respect, self-worth and a great sense of achievement. Further, the soil (tĩĩri) created an incredibly strong bond between a man and his ancestral, spiritual 'umbilical cord.' To this end, a man did his level best to acquire his own piece of land, and invariably moved his family away from the *mbarĩ* (extended family). Kenyatta (ibid) argues that there was no land among the Gĩkũyũ that could be said to belong to no one, as claimed by colonialists. Land was bought from other people and put to communal use; but it belonged to someone.[6] Leakey (2007:113) notes that "...it was the ambition of every Kikuyu to found a sub-clan of his own." To this end, he had to procure goats (mbũri), the only recognized unit of value, to purchase land[7].

Social Organization – The House, Clan and Age-set: *Nyũmba (Mbarĩ), Mũhĩrĩga na Riika*

Culture is, of necessity, dynamic and the Gĩkũyũ culture is no exception. It is therefore misleading to describe the Gĩkũyũ norms and values as if they were in a glass casing or an artifact for display. The intention here, however, is to highlight the core values held dear by the Gĩkũyũ prior to colonization. This is important as Ogot (1976:6) notes "After all, the most important agent of change during this time was colonialism".

Kenyatta (1938/65) notes that, "The Gĩkũyũ tribal organization is based on three most important factors, without which there can be no harmony in the tribal activities". These factors, he argues, include the *mbarĩ* (family or house) *mũhĩrĩga* (clan) and *riika* (age-set). The *mbarĩ* consisted of a man, his wife or wives, children, grandchildren and great grandchildren. A man was respected for having several wives and very many children since the entire team was a formidable workforce indispensable for breaking new grounds in the forest and expanding cultivation land. An extended family could therefore own very large pieces of land, a huge collection of goats, sheep, cows and oxen. The proverbs *kamũingĩ koyaga ndĩrĩ* (collective work helps to lift a huge mortar) and *kĩara kĩmwe gĩtiũragaga ndaa* (One finger cannot kill a louse) may explain the need for joint work to achieve greater success. Further, a big family was salutary for family security as evidenced by the proverb *Mũndũ ũtarĩ hinya ndaugaga kwao* (a weak person does not give directions to his family). However, as families increased in number there was increased pressure on land and some families moved out to search for more land though maintaining their blood ties with the remaining families. Such related families constituted the mũhĩrĩga or clan.

The Gĩkũyũ peoplewere initially matriarchal before becoming patriarchal as it is today. Kenyatta (op.cit) notes that there are nine clans, but Cagnolo (1933:19) seems to be more precise with the *nine top* figure (kenda mũiyũru). These clans include *Aithĩrandũ, Aithekahuno, Aithiegeni, Aichakamũyũ, Ambũi, Anjirũ, Aceera, Agachikũ, Akĩũrũ/Ethaga* and the *Agathigia* or *Airimũ* (Cagnolo: 19). The clan alliance is crucial in matters of ceremonies or rituals and its members enjoy a great sense of community and communion.

The *riika* or age-set was made up of people who were circumcised at the same period. The ensuing bond between initiates was extremely solid and lasted a lifetime. It was during the initiation period that the youth were introduced to adulthood. In other words, the *mbarĩ, mũhĩrĩga* and the *riika* provided the ethical bulwark of the Gĩkũyũ; they determined the ethos of an individual and regulated the life of the entire community wherever it was in Kenya. Kenyatta (1938/65:95) observes that "...the character of the individual is formed within the family circle and then within the local group, and then within the whole tribal organization through a course of initiation ceremonies..."

Practical traditional education

Gĩkũyũ children learned a great deal from observing what their parents and siblings were doing but also they were supposed to learn practically by doing (Kenyatta 1938/65: 96). He further notes that girls spent their time with their mothers learning how to cook, draw water, and most importantly, how to behave in society. In fact, aspects of personal hygiene, diligence, sitting properly (not exposing oneself) and modes of address were very important in ensuring that the girls would find suitable suitors when the time came. Girls were socialized by their mothers and aunties on their prospective roles as wives, home-makers, mothers and advisors for their children. They were also exposed to a wide range of do's and don'ts to make their marriages work. These included faithfulness, integrity, good cooking, diligence, cleanliness, etc. A girl who got pregnant before marriage attracted a very low bride price (if she got a suitor other than an old man) and brought shame to her family. Great value was placed on chastity.

On the other hand, boys spent their time with the father learning how to be responsible, and more important, independent. Leakey (2007:3) notes that boys were socialized by their fathers on their future role "to defend the tribe against the Maasai but also to raid the Maasai for goats, sheep and cattle." In this way, they thus maintained the economy of the community. Tending sheep and goats or helping till the land were important aspects of preparing the boys for their role in society. Stock was critical for a wide range of rituals such as birth rites, initiation rites, marriage, death, burial, etc.

Children also benefitted immensely from the counsel of their grandparents, uncles and aunts. Apart from the learning-on-job approach, Gĩkũyũ children were also exposed to a wide repertoire of riddles, puzzles, ogre stories, lullabies, songs, legends, games, dances, proverbs and sayings that served directly or indirectly as moral beacons (Chesaina 1997:54). These also helped enhance the intellect and memory of the children as well as protect them from physical harm. This practical and intellectual exercise was termed *kĩrĩra kĩa mũcĩĩ or ũtaari wa mũcĩĩ)* (family education). Indeed, children who fell short of the expected social behavior brought shame and embarrassment to their parents since the latter were supposed to provide quality education at home (Kenyatta op cit: 101).

It is important to note that the Gĩkũyũ subscribed to a system of continuous education whereby learning began at childhood and continued all the way into eldership. Indeed, the life of a Gĩkũyũ had grades or echelons starting from childhood, adulthood, warriorhood, first-level elder, second-level elder and senior-level elder. Upon death, a Gĩkũyũ joined the spirit world (ngoma) as an ancestor and continued to commune, guide and sanction the living. For each of the grades or levels, the individual was initiated into more and more ancient secrets of the people such as magic, poisons, plant life, relationships, etc. The first serious initiation was circumcision.

Circumcision/incision

Cagnolo (1933/2006) observes that at adolescence – 14 years for boys and about 12 years for girls – a Gĩkũyũ underwent the all-important *rite de passage*, circumcision for boys and incision for girls. The rite was one of the three pillars of the Gĩkũyũ society alongside the family and the clan and was the beginning of a new life for the initiates. Indeed, the young men (*anake*) received instructions and guidance to enable them to join the warrior class and also prepare to begin their own hearths through marriage. They were advised to work very hard in order to acquire wealth that would enable them acquire land, sheep, goats and cows – the traditional currency of the Gĩkũyũ.

Conversely, the girls (*airĩtu*) entered an age where they were now being prepared to marry and start new homes. The gap between the uncircumcised boy (*kĩhĩĩ*) or girl (*kĩrĩgũ*) and the initiated young man (*mwanake*) or girl (*mũirĩtu*) in terms of social expectations was considerable. In fact, the *kĩhĩĩ* was expected to be childish, dependent on the mother, silly, uncouth (e.g. breaking wind at short notice), unfocussed, etc. But a *mwanake* was the exact opposite. After enduring the pain of the knife andundergoing the traditional education reserved for him, a *mwanake* was independent, brave, well-mannered and very responsible. Cagnolo (op.cit:104) observes that the *mwanake,* who now adorned different regalia and long plaited hair (as a warrior), was exemplary in behavior due to his respect of Gĩkũyũ customs and law. The Gĩkũyũ were very proud of a *mwanake* and even stopped short of idolizing them. Agĩkũyũ proverb concludes that, *"Mwanake nĩ kĩenyũ kĩa Ngai"* – a young man is a piece of God.

The boy initiates were exposed to basic Gĩkũyũ expectations of a man. The proverbs *'ng'ombe itionagwo nĩ kĩgũũta'* (cows are not for the lazy fellow), 'beer is for the hard-working man,' *"gũtirĩ kĩega kiumaga hega* 'nothing good comes easily' (Chesaina op cit: 128-134), 'good things come from hard work', etc., drive home the high premium that the Gĩkũyũ people placed on hard work and diligence. Furthermore, Chesaina (op.cit: 184) notes importantly that the Gĩkũyũ/Meru people had no belief in good luck or sheer benevolence from the Heavens. The proverb *"mũnyaka wĩ mbere ya gĩthaka"* (luck comes after the acquisition of land) underscore man's determination to be a master of his destiny. Clasen (1988:58) observes aptly that "Men of action are favored by the Goddess of Good Luck".

Cagnolo (op. cit: 51) also notes that young men were supposed to be diligent so that they could provide well for the women they would marry. They were also meant to be generous and kind to in-laws who had given him their daughters in marriage (Chesaina, op.cit:139).

The education provided during this stage also involved sexual matters and respect for women. Young men were taught self-restraint through the *Ngwīko* ritual where lovers were allowed to be intimate without sexual penetration before marriage (Kenyatta op.cit). Similarly, they were taught how to handle a woman during her various stages: menstruation, pregnancy, sickness, etc. In addition, the young man was supposed to be respectful and well-behaved as he enjoyed the full membership privileges of being initiated. Conversely, the *kīhīī* had absolutely no rights in the traditional arena. A young man falling short of these high expectations was at once reprimanded: *you have now passed the period of childhood and you cannot behave like this; you are circumcised and you are a man to know right and wrong* (Kenyatta, op.cit: 104). In a nutshell the young man was taught to be responsible, diligent, honest, well behaved, respectful, generous, considerate, level-headed and brave as per the Gīkūyū customs and law. He was also required to marry and have children in order to perpetuate the Gīkūyū community.

As for the girls, there was great respect for a young girl who had undergone the incision rite. She was not expected to prattle like her younger sisters; rather, she was reserved and respectful as required by custom. She also redoubled her diligence in farming and keeping the home properly in order to attract the best suitor. Her mother and aunt spent time with her educating her on how to make a successful home. Iraki (2003) notes however that with the disappearance of the rite for girls, the dichotomy *kīrīgū/mūirītu* has also disappeared[8]. In fact, the term *kīrīgū* is deemed uncouth or uncivil; now the term *mūirītu* describes the two states of a girl.

Undergoing the rite of circumcision enabled a person to belong to an age-set or *riika* in which he remained all his/her life. The saying *Nyūmba na riika itiumagwo* – one cannot leave his family or age-set – underpins the high value placed on the family and the age-set. This new brotherhood or sorority provided the initiate with further knowledge and secrets about life. Mbiti (1969) notes that the initiates "... learn to live with one another, endure hardships, obey, and keep secrets of man-womanhood relationships".

Gĩkũyũ family

The family was an integral part of the Gĩkũyũ society. As we discussed earlier, it was within the homestead (*mũcĩĩ*) that the child first got the values of the community. These values also included religion, an important aspect of the Gĩkũyũ life. Leakey (2007:2) observes that "The Kikuyu family was the centre of all religion, and family worship was more important to the Kikuyu than pubic worship..." In a word, the family was the bedrock of the Gĩkũyũ social organization.

A man was required to marry one or several wives and have many children. Kenyatta argues that the average was two women to a man, and a man should have at least four children. Further, he was the head of the family and made sure that his family never lacked anything. This meant that he had to make his sheep and goats multiply to increase his wealth and also break new farm lands or buy more land for his extended family. A woman was supposed to obey her husband and make him happy but also procreate as much as she could. In this logic, a barren woman (*thaata*) suffered stigma and her life could be very miserable. The role of the wife was subordinate and she worked extremely hard in the field to provide food for her children and husband. She was also considered the property of the man (Chesaina, op.cit:10).

It was therefore imperative that a young man should found his own family shortly after acquiring the requisite number of sheep and goats for marriage. He had been instructed during childhood and later after circumcision on the virtues of a good husband and a model family. Through legends, songs, proverbs and sayings, he had a clear mind about what was expected of him. The role models provided in the society via this orature guided the young man and exhorted him to become very ambitious in life. Marriage constituted the next stage after a stint in warrior-hood.

I have mentioned above that in order to marry, goats, sheep, cows and oxen were used as currency. They were not only expressions of wealth; they also have a deep spiritual meaning among the Gĩkũyũ. For instance, goats and sheep were sacrificial animals used in worship of God and ancestors. They were also used in purification rites, witchcraft, etc. (Kenyatta op. cit:65). Thanks to his diligence, the young man could marry with the help of his father. An average of 30-40 goats was enough for a bride. The symbolic rite of marriage united two families and two clans thereby extending the confines of kinship. The young family was now guided by all that both the man and woman had learnt from the family, clan, *riika* and society at large. Within this system terms such as senior bachelors, spinsters, prostitutes, street children had no place since all men and women were supposed to marry and children belonged to the entire society. Indeed, Chesaina (op.cit:146) notes that *"Mūciari wa mwana ti ūmwe"* – a child has many parents.

The children within the family were taught via observation and action as described above. The family through various teaching processes such as legends, ogre stories, folk tales and songs imbued the children with values such as patience, diligence, honesty and fairness, logical and critical thinking, equanimity, courage, avoidance of excesses and appropriate behavior. In addition, they were taught to ridicule greed, stupidity, meanness or even loneliness. In a typical Aesopian ethic there was no mercy for dullness of mind. Stupid children got mauled by ogres and there was hardly any 'happy-ending' for fools.

Community work for socialization and bonding was also emphasized as Chesaina (op.cit. 135) notes in the proverb *'Njara īmwe ndīkandii wīra'* – one hand cannot do work properly or Barra (1991), *'Kīara kīmwe gītiūragaga ndaa'* – one finger cannot kill a louse. But at the same time some proverbs check excess socialization and promote individual enterprise such as *'Mūrimū wa mūndū ūngī ndūngīgiria ūmame'* – another man's disease cannot stop you from sleeping (Chesaina op.cit: proverb 355). Proverbs are in the main ambiguous and oftentimes contradictory – a double-edged sword – and they require context to signal the intended meaning. Finally, the children were taught how to worship God and commune with the ancestors; they were also reminded of the ephemeral nature of life and the need to "make hay while the sun shines". Proverbs such as *'warūgaga nī atobokaga'* – the one who used to jump now wades in and *'wainaga nī eroragīra'* – the one who used to sing and dance now just watches (Barra 1991) - emphasized the need to recognize and accept change in age as inevitable; hence the need to prepare and provide adequately for old age.

The impact of Colonization and Westernization on Gīkūyū value-systems

Colonialism impacted the entire Kenyan country, from the nineteenth century to the second part of the twentieth century. The Gīkūyū society was subdued and modified tremendously by the British rulers. During this time, the colonial government changed the landscape of Gīkūyū value systems, especially in the areas of education and land tenure. The prime lands of the Gĩkũyũ were reserved for the settlers and the indigenous people were moved to "native reserves". Further, due to the need for labor, the Gĩkũyũ were compelled to work on the settler farms for meager wages. This was a way to enable them pay the compulsory taxes that had been introduced so subjugate Africans. These moves were encapsulated in various government instruments such as the Crown Lands Act of 1902, the hut and poll taxes, the Kipande Act of 1915, etc. The net result was a coerced change from a traditional economy based on barter, land, sheep and goats to the money capitalist economy. The proletariat class had been created ushering in the capitalist–worker dialect that would bedevil Kenya even after independence.

In the arena of education, the colonial Administration provided formal and informal education via the missionaries who had set root since 1902. Thanks to missionary zeal, many Gĩkũyũ people converted to Christianity in view of its apparent affinity with Gĩkũyũ religious paradigm and the concomitant benefits that came with accepting the new faith. Christianity provided education that came with a new culture, which appealed to many Gĩkũyũ. Nonetheless, the relationship between the Church and the Gĩkũyũ was not always smooth, especially in the area of female circumcision and polygamy. This led to conflict and the subsequent rise of independent churches and schools in the 1930s (Thomas, 2003). On the other hand, Kenyatta was already crying foul in 1938 about the impact of Western-type of education on the future of the Gĩkũyũ nation. He notes "...children who have been taught under European influence have almost forgotten or disregarded the Gĩkũyũ customary law of behavior." (Kenyatta, op.cit: 106).

The displacement, acculturation and economic disempowerment of the Gĩkũyũ led to the Mau Mau movement in the 1940s. The main contention was that the Gĩkũyũ should get back their land. The colonial administration responded by defending the settler rights and bolstering its stranglehold on the Gĩkũyũ people. From 1952 to 1960, the Gĩkũyũ were subjected to cruel containment measures that left the society in tatters (Anderson 2006; Elkins 2006). Many were tortured, detained or simply killed. The resettlement schemes by the colonial administration were mainly ineffective in redressing the land issue (Swynnerton plan). As a result, by independence in 1963, the land issue and the disintegration of the Gĩkũyũ society remained to be addressed. This was to be Jomo Kenyatta's task – the same man who had objectively and at times emotively explained that the Gĩkũyũ society was premised on family, clan and age-set, and in all these, land was of cardinal importance.

The Gĩkũyũ after independence

Some scholars claim the Gĩkũyũ benefitted a great deal when their "time to eat" came with the Kenyatta presidency. Alwy & Schech (2004:269) note that:

> During President Kenyatta's regime (1963-1978) certain parts of the Kikuyu community gained considerably, while President Moi (1978-2002) granted similar advantages to his tribe – the Kalenjin.

As a result, the argument continues, the Gĩkũyũ community obtained free land from the departing settlers. Further, Kenyatta is said to have settled "his people" in the Rift valley, Coast province, etc. The ethnic favors made the Gĩkũyũ not only recover quickly from many years of deprivation but also to become one of the wealthiest communities in Kenya[9].

However, if this perspective has some seed of truth in it, it oversimplifies the reason for the rapid economic transformation of the Gĩkũyũ community. In fact, a great deal of the transformation can be attributed to some positive aspects of the Gĩkũyũ culture such as personal ambition, diligence and desire to acquire personal property. To be true, the blanket description of the Gĩkũyũ as a wealthy community can be extremely misleading. Indeed, rather than explain things in terms of ethnicity, Wa Thiong'o (2008) preferred the dichotomy of "haves and have-nots" to describe the Kenyan society. The SID (2004: 8) report also had interesting observations. It noted that "... the country's top 10% households control 42% of total income while the bottom 10% control less than 1% and that the difference in life expectancy between the central and Nyanza is a staggering 19 years!" Therefore, this is hardly an ethnic issue.

The blanket description also ignores internal divisions among the Gĩkũyũ themselves. First the distinction home guard (*ngaati*) or collaborators vs. freedom fighters (Mau Mau). In the modern Gĩkũyũ contestations[10], it is claimed that Kenyatta's land policy favored the erstwhile collaborators and punished the freedom fighters (Gatheru 2005). The emergence of the Mũngĩkĩ movement was fueled largely by this distinction. The Mũngĩkĩ) (or even its mutations such as the Thaai) claim they are the neglected children of the Mau Mau fighters, the people that Kenyatta ignored and punished.[11]

Secondly, the Gīkūyū unless threatened, politically or otherwise, from without, view themselves as distinct entities from Murang'a, Kiambu, Nyeri, Embu, Kirinyaga, Meru, etc. The linguistic similarity is often used to include or exclude depending on political expediency. For instance, during the Moi presidency, the groups were separate for individual survival but under Kibaki the distinctions are rather blurred. It is now easier to talk about the "Central Kenya people" or the "Mount Kenya region people". It would be unfair not to mention corruption, nepotism and cronyism as important aspects of Kenyatta's administration. But if some Gīkūyū people did indeed benefit, it would be misleading to claim that "most" of them did so, in the absence of convincing statistics. These aspects were continued by President Moi and to a lesser extent President Kibaki. Ngirachu (2010) wrote, for instance, that the appointment of Kenyan ambassadors in 2010 by Kibaki was about ethnicity and "rewarding cronies".

The Gīkūyū dilemma in a nutshell

At the risk of oversimplifying the current dilemma of the Gīkūyū, it can be stated that the Gīkūyū community is confronted by a dicey political, economic and social malaise. Firstly, in the area of culture, it is abundantly clear that the Gīkūyū have evolved tremendously to embrace a hybrid identity that is Western and Gīkūyū. But it is also clear that the Gīkūyū have been moving away from their ancestral roots very fast to the extent that a great number of urbanized Gīkūyū people hardly understand the Gīkūyū language.[12] Moreover, the Gīkūyū place an incredibly high premium on the education of children. But modern education as Kenyatta had noted in 1938 is Westernized and based on Western value systems. As a result, the products of the educational system do not necessarily espouse Gīkūyū values. These products are also ill fitting in a modern world that requires intelligent, creative and diligent individuals to survive and prosper. One of the symptoms of social malaise due to collapse of traditional Gīkūyū values is the wanton drunkenness and idleness of most of the men in Central Kenya. The situation is so critical that a law has been promulgated to curb alcohol abuse in the entire country.[13] The self-destruction of the youth can also be attributed to economic disempowerment.

Economic Disempowerment

Until recently, successive Kenyan governments had only paid lip service to the youth whose value only increases during the General Elections. Central province depends heavily on cash-crop farming (tea, coffee, *mīraa*, etc), dairy farming and subsistence agriculture. Sustained rain failure or declining world prices can seriously harm the purchasing power of the farmers. But even more alarming could be planned economic sabotage by the country's leadership to frustrate the farmers whose political support seems to be elsewhere. This conspiracy is especially directed at the Moi administration for sabotaging the central province economy by meddling with the Coffee Board of Kenya. Such claims, however, may need more investigation. Suffice it to say, the youth of Central Kenya have not had much to do in the way of gainful employment. The only avenue left to them was to join the exodus to the cities or join the militia to extort money from local people. Alcoholism, crime and idleness describe the situation in Central Kenya. However, the activation of the Youth Fund, Women Fund and Constituency Development Fund (CDF) has presented unique opportunities to change the situation in Central Kenya. Further, the new Constitution is another opportunity for Central Kenya to pave its way to economic prosperity and social development. But politically, the region would need to re-invent itself.

Political Suspicion

Winning and consolidating political power in the years preceding Kenya's independence required great ability to create a coalition of big ethnic groups. Kenyatta and Oginga Odinga cobbled up a coalition of two big ethnic groups, the Gĩkũyũ and the Luo, to create a winning machine: Kenya African National Union (KANU). However, Moi, adverse to political pluralism, transformed KANU into a monolithic political institution. Therefore, he did not need ethnic coalitions[14.] The return of political pluralism in 1992 necessitated the return of the old game of creating ethnic groupings. Karega-Munene (2003) noted that the politics of Kenya had returned to the ethnic polarization of the 1960s.

Kenya is yet to become a fully integrated nation-state, therefore ethnic interests are likely to persist in the political arena. No government has managed to reassure the 40 plus ethnic groups that their interests are safe without one of their own being the President. In this context, the Gĩkũyũ are viewed with much suspicion by other communities mainly due to their numerical strength. For instance, some politicians claimed that the 2007 General Elections were a vote against the Gĩkũyũ people.

Amidst the political suspicion, the Gĩkũyũ community has a great challenge to promote healthy coalitions with other ethnic communities, especially in view of the 2012 General Elections and the requirements of the new Constitution. It might be more reassuring to create all-inclusive political and governance structures in lieu of perpetual ethnic coalitions and re-arrangements. The Gĩkũyũ, by dint of sheer great numbers, could push for such a system to alleviate feelings of ethnic marginalization. Not even the new Constitution can help here.

Way Forward

In light of the situation of Central Kenya, there is need to address a few issues as a matter of urgency. First, the crackdown on alcoholism, drug and substance abuse was long overdue. But it needs to be accompanied by a re-education on Gĩkũyũ values, especially expectations of responsibility, diligence, individual prosperity, community service and honor. The second important component is the conscientization of the youth on the opportunities now available to them to improve their lot. These include ICT hubs, investment in SMEs, market gardening, rabbit and pig farming, knowledge economy just to mention a few.

Secondly, and in line with Gĩkũyũ culture, the youth should be exposed to role models in the areas of education, business, religion, politics and sports. Gĩkũyũ folklore is replete with *njamba* stories that can be re-told and re-energized via modern role models. Men and women who represent the "get-rich quick" mentality should be lampooned and derided, not worshipped as is the case today. Children should be exposed by the family and the school to time-tested values of diligence, patience and determination to excel. These are very clear in the Gĩkũyũ value system.

Thirdly, there is need for the youth and women (since they are the ones who vote most) to review their attitude towards political leadership. Creative and productive leadership will be required to revamp the economy of Central Kenya. Empty political talk and short-termism should be replaced by leadership with a solid economic agenda. To this end, the youth and women should consider offering themselves if they can deliver. Overdependence on the so-called "rich families" can only constrain the development of the region.

Fourthly, the family and the school systems in Central Kenya should strive to inculcate values of nationhood in the children. These could be institutionalized via home stays in other communities, externships, joint social events, collaboration between counties on projects, new narratives and books that promote national harmony and so forth.

Fifthly, the current educational system will need to be re-examined for its relevance in modern or evolving Kenya. Of particular interest is how to strike a creative balance between theory and practice. Gĩkũyũ traditional education was mainly practical and geared towards success in life. What is the current education about? In addition, Central Kenya will need an audit of its educational institutions in a bid to understand the reasons for poor performance in national examinations. Have the children lost interest in an education they deem "useless" or are there other social or economic factors at play? Should we create more centers for practical education?

Sixth, Central Kenyan counties can create a model for other counties to emulate; a county with good governance, employment opportunities, a disciplined work force, good schools, good infrastructure, electricity and security. In turn, the other counties will now have reference point to improve their own areas.

Finally, and probably more importantly, the children should be inculcated in life-long values that are indispensable in the pursuit of happiness. These include independence, culture of saving, entrepreneurship, innovation, diligence, honesty and self-pride (see Clasen 2008 and Johnson 1998). These values should be promoted by both the family and the school system. The current trend where the products of education are inordinately dependent on the family could be attributed to inappropriate or inadequate preparation for real life. It could also be imputed to a disempowering economic climate. As a result, our youth remain in the family nest way beyond the age of 18 years, with some reaching the age of 30 years. A combination of relevant and adequate education at home and at school accompanied by an enabling economic environment could reduce the current derisory dependency on parents. In fact, traditionally, Gĩkũyũ youth were independent from parents after the rite of passage to adulthood and on-the-job apprenticeship; this was around the age of 16-17 years.

Conclusions

In this chapter, we have presented a synopsis of the Gĩkũyũ value systems as gleaned from the existing literature and oral interviews with older Gĩkũyũ people. In addition, we have summed up the issues bedeviling the Central Kenya people and proposed some avenues of reflection as to why this is the case. The Gĩkũyũ society/community is in crisis: low achievement, idleness, unemployment, insecurity, immorality, alcoholism, inordinate love for money, and decline of cultural values are the main features of this decadence today. This situation contrasts sharply with the traditional Gĩkũyũ value system. Admittedly, culture is dynamic but it is important not to throw away the baby with the bathwater in the name of modernism. There is urgent need to address the crisis and resolve it via culture, the current Constitutional order, and the recent infrastructural developments. We have also made some suggestions that could correct the current malaise in the Central Kenya region and place it on a fast-track of social, economic and political development. The way forward will no doubt bring back hope and optimism among the people of Central Kenya.

Notes

[1] The claim does not mean that all the youth are afflicted by these ills. In fact, there are also very many young Kenyans who are diligent and a source of great pride and inspiration.

[2] Traditionally, Gĩkũyũ women took away the children from a failed marriage as she felt they were safer among her relatives than with those of her husband.

[3] Kenyatta (op.cit) describes the passage from the junior elder (Kamatimũ) to Kĩama kĩa Matathi (elders who carry ruling leaves) and finally to Kĩama kĩa maturanguru (seniormost elders).

[4] Iringi was the son of Mwangi; Mwangi then bore Iringi and so on and so forth. The idea is power should be passed from one generational set to another in a ping-pong fashion.

[5] Joseph Thompson in 1883. He had been sent by the British to stake out Kenya.

[6] This was the case with salt licks, watering points and grazing grounds.

[7] Leakey observes that unless a man could afford to purchase 50 acres of land, he continued to work hard to find the number of goats required.

[8] Influence of Christianity. See Lynn Thomas (2003) for a detailed discussion on the furor around female incision in the 1930s.

[9] Report by the Society for International Development (SID)-(2004).

[10] See especially Ngugi Wa Thiong'o's works: *The River Between*, and *Ngahika Ndeenda* (I will marry when I want).

[11] The movement or militia is accused of subversive acts, murders and harassment of ordinary people. However, some people find them extremely useful, peaceful and orderly.

[12] Most of the urban youth, especially the teenagers cannot hold a conversation in the Gĩkũyũ language.

[13] The now nicknamed "Mututho law" after the Member of Parliament, Mututho, came into effect in 2010 limiting alcohol consumption from 5.00 p.m. to 11.00 p.m. on weekdays and from 2.00 p.m to 11.00 p.m. on weekends.

[14] But he managed to consolidate the diverse communities (Nandi, Kipsigis, Tugen, Marakwet, Elgeyo, etc) into a single Kalenjin identity.

References

Alwy, A., Schech, S. (2004). "Ethnic Inequalities in Education in Kenya" in *International Education Journal,* Vol 5. No.2. 2004: 266-274.

Anderson, D. (2006). *Histories of the Hanged: Britain's Dirty War in Kenya.* New York: W.W. Norton & Company.

Barra, G. (1939/1991). *1000 Kikuyu Proverbs.* Nairobi: Kenya Literature Bureau.

Cagnolo (1933/2006). *The Agĩkũyũ: Their Customs, Traditions & Folklore*, new edition by Wambugu H., Ngarariga J.M,. & Kariuki, P.M. Nyeri: Wisdom Graphics Place.

Chesaina, C. (1997). *Oral Literature of the Embu and Mbeere.* Nairobi/Kampala: East African Educational Publishers.

Clasen, G.S. (1926/1988). *The Richest Man in Babylon.* Signet: USA.

Elkins, C. (2006). *Britain's Goulag: The Brutal End of an Empire in Kenya.* New York: Henry Holt & Company.

Johnson, S. (1998). *Who Moved my Cheese?* New York: G.P. Putnam's sons.

Karega-Munene (2003). "Polarization of Politics in Kenya along ethnic lines", *Wajibu* Vol 18: 1-2: Nairobi.

Kenyatta, J. (1938/1965), *Facing Mt. Kenya.* New York: Vintage Books Edition.

King, K. (1976). "Education and social change: The impact of technical education in colonial Kenya" in Ogot, B.A (ed), *History and Social Change in East Africa:* 145-165.

Leakey, L.S.B. (2007). *The Southern Kikuyu before 1903,* Vol.1: Nairobi: Richard Leakey.

Mbiti, J.S. (1986/1992). *African Religions and Philosophy,* 2nd edition. Nairobi: Heinemann.

Mugo, G. (2005). *Kenya: From Colonization to Independence, 1888-1890,* USA: McFarland & Company Inc.

Mwanzi, H. (1976). "Social change among the Kipsigis" in Ogot, B.A (ed), *History and Social Change in East Africa,* 31-44.

Ngirachu, J. (2010). "It's all about rewarding cronies" in *Daily Nation* of 18 October 2010.

Ngugi Wa Thiong'o (2008). *"The Myth of Tribe in African Politics",* Transition 101, 16-23.

Ogot, B.A. (1976). *"History, Anthropology and Social Change",* History and Social Change in East Africa: 1-13. *East Africa.* Nairobi: East African Literature Bureau.

Thomas, L.M. (2003). *Politics of the Womb: Women, Reproduction and the State in Kenya.* California: California University Press.

Reports

"Pulling Apart: Facts and Figures on inequality in Kenya" by Society for International Development (SID), 2004.

The Kadhi's Court and the Constitution of Kenya

Mohamed Mraja

Introduction

The search for a new constitutional dispensation in Kenya was long, expensive and polarized. After the process of writing a new constitution stalled following the defeat of the government side (Wako Draft) in the 2005 referendum, the Constitution of Kenya Review Bill 2008 was passed in parliament. This Act of Parliament created the Committee of Experts (CoE) and effectively revived the process of constitutional review. Under this Act, the CoE was given the mandate to identify contentious issues and to invite representations from the public, interest groups and experts to prepare a Harmonized Draft Constitution. The non-contentious issues were duly identified as agreed and closed, and the contentious ones as outstanding.

According to the statute that created the CoE, a contentious issue was where there was no consensus or agreement in all the draft constitutions including the Bomas Draft, Wako Draft, etc., as well as the Independence Constitution of Kenya. All were to serve as reference points in coming up with a Harmonized Draft Constitution. According to the chairman of the CoE, there were three contentious issues identified by his committee and in line with the provisions of the law; namely, the Executive and Legislature, devolution, and transitional clauses.[1] The debate that emerged following the release to the public of the Harmonized Draft Constitution and thereafter the Proposed Constitution of Kenya was, however, not been limited to the aforementioned three areas of contention. Rather, the Kadhi's Courts occupied a centre stage in public discourse and submissions to the CoE particularly pitting Christian against Muslim groups. While such a debate may be healthy in a fledgling democracy such as Kenya's, people often lose sight of fundamental issues that are key in overcoming the challenges of coming up with a new constitution, which meets the aspirations and interests of all ordinary citizens; the "Wanjikus" of Kenya.

This Chapter examines some of the core issues which surrounded the debate on Kadhi's courts, including the call for their retention in the constitution and the demand by a section of the Church to remove them from the proposed constitution. The views presented are drawn from a cross-section of Kenyans regardless of their religious affiliation. The primary source of data used is newspaper reports, where this was a key area of discussion.

Entrenching *Kadhi*'s Courts in Kenya's Constitution

In the 1960s, negotiations between the future first president of Kenya and the Muslim government of Zanzibar paved the way for entrenchment of the *Kadhi*'s courts in the Constitution. Thus a treaty signed between representatives of the Sultan of Zanzibar and Kenya's Prime Minister Jomo Kenyatta on 5th October 1963, committed Kenya, *inter alia*, to grant its Muslims citizens in the protectorate (formerly the Sultan's 10-mile coastal Strip) the following:

1. The free exercise of any creed or religion will at all times be safeguarded and, in particular, the Sultan's present subjects who are of the Muslim faith and their descendants will at all times be ensured of complete freedom of worship and the preservation of their own religious buildings and institutions.

2. The jurisdiction of the Chief *Kadhi* (Muslim Judge) and all the other *Kadhi*s will at all times be preserved and will extend to the determination of the questions of Muslim law relating to personal status (for example, marriage, divorce and inheritance) in proceedings in which all parties profess the Muslim religion.

Following this Agreement, the 10-mile Strip (the Protectorate) was to be part of independent Kenya under those terms. Indeed the map of Kenya would be quite different if it were not for the foresight of the Founding Fathers of this nation, who exhibited the spirit of accommodation of minority interests for the sake of national unity. Kenya's Independence Constitution therefore provided for the establishment of *Kadhi*'s courts as part of judiciary arms of the government. Thus, section 66 of the Constitution of Kenya gave those courts constitutional recognition. The constitution spelt out the qualification of being a *Kadhi* (Muslim judge) as being a person who "possesses such knowledge of the Muslim law applicable to any sect or sects of Muslims as qualifies him, in the opinion of the Judicial Service Commission, to hold a *Kadhi*'s court." The mandate of the courts was stated as "the determination of questions of Muslim law relating to personal status, marriage, divorce or inheritance in proceedings in which all parties profess the Muslim religion." The sphere of operation of the *Kadhi*'s courts was also defined as applicable to areas within the former protectorate or within such parts of the former protectorate as may be prescribed by an Act of Parliament.

To give practical effect to the *Kadhi*'s courts in the country, parliament passed four Acts namely: (a) The *Kadhi*'s Courts Act, Chapter 11 of the Laws of Kenya, (b) The Mohammedan Marriage and Divorce Registration Act, Chapter 155 of the Laws of Kenya, (c) The Mohammedan Marriage, Divorce and Succession Act, Chapter 156 of the Laws of Kenya, and (d) Amendment of Laws of Succession Act, Chapter 160 of the Laws of Kenya.

The following may be deduced from the Constitution and subsequent Acts of Parliament:

a) *Kadhi*'s Courts were only to apply to members belonging to the Muslim faith. The courts have no jurisdiction over Christians or members of other non-Muslim faiths.

b) The courts have no jurisdiction on criminal or matters pertaining to commercial disputes. Thus to impute, as some Christians do, that these courts apply the *Sharia* (total legal system of Islam) is sheer ignorance.

c) The Chief *Kadhi* is recognized as an official of the *Kadhi*'s courts. The constitution and various Acts of Parliament have not defined the duties of this person or the procedure leading to his appointment. The Chief *Kadhi* is not a member of the Judicial Service Commission, which as stated in the constitution, is the appointing authority of the *Kadhi*s.

d) The *Kadhi*'s courts are subordinate courts and do not have appellate powers. Thus, where a decision passed by a *Kadhi* is not satisfactory to one of the parties, the aggrieved party will have to refer the matter to the High Court. The Chief *Kadhi* or two other *Kadhi*s are allowed by law to sit in the High Court as assessor(s). In this capacity, their views are not binding in the final judgment of the High Court. In the Court of Appeal the Chief *Kadhi* is not admitted even as an assessor.

e) The various amendments made to the constitution of Kenya so far did not call for the *Kadhi*'s courts to be removed altogether, even as parliament has been dominated by parliamentarians and heads of state who are Christians.

The Bomas and the Wako Drafts: A Critical Assessment

The Constitution of Kenya Review Act of 2000 established the Constitution of Kenya Review Commission (CKRC) chaired by Yash Pal Ghai, which was mandated to collect and collate views from Kenyans on what they wanted to be included in a new constitutional dispensation. The CKRC received submissions from Kenyans from all sections including political parties and religious organizations (Christians, Muslims and others) between December 2001 and 2002. The views collated resulted in a draft that was discussed by the National Constitutional Assembly held at Bomas of Kenya and culminated in the publication of a final draft on 15th March 2004. Although the general mood in the country was that the draft constitution was to be people- or "Wanjiku"- driven, the Bomas constitutional conference was, however, highly politicized and polarized, with the NARC government and other parties fronting partisan interests above national ones. With regard to *Kadhi*'s courts, the Bomas draft retained these as constitutional offices. Section 198 of the Draft thus provides:

1. There are established *Kadhi*'s Courts, the office of Chief *Kadhi*, office of senior *Kadhi*, and office of *Kadhi*.

2. There shall be a number, being not less than thirty, of *Kadhi*s as may be prescribed by the Act of Parliament.

The jurisdiction of the *Kadhi*'s courts was retained, with an addendum to determine civil and commercial disputes between parties who are Muslims. The Bomas draft, however, gave parties to such disputes the right to take the matter to other courts or tribunals with similar jurisdictions. The *Kadhi*'s courts were also given appellate jurisdiction and provided with an enhanced structure based on the following hierarchy: District *Kadhi*'s Courts,

Provincial *Kadhi*'s Courts and *Kadhi*'s Court of Appeal. According to the Bomas Draft, any dispute arising from the *Kadhi*'s Court of Appeal was to be referred to the Supreme Court.

The Bomas Draft also established the required qualifications of the Chief *Kadhi* or *Kadhi* to be a minimum degree in Islamic law from a recognized university. The person to be appointed as Chief *Kadhi* was also obligated to have had at least 10 years of experience in legal practice, and a *Kadhi* a minimum of five years. The Judicial Service Commission, to which the Chief Kadhi was to be incorporated as a member, was mandated to be in-charge of the task of recruiting *Kadhi*s. The Chief *Kadhi*, the Chief Justice and the Law Society of Kenya were given the mandate by the Bomas Draft to consult and formulate the rules and procedures to be applied in the determination of cases brought before the *Kadhi*'s courts. It should be noted that Christian groups did not agitate for the creation of Christian courts in the country when presenting their memoranda to the CKRC. The Bomas Draft was never presented for a referendum by the government. It was dismissed by the Executive and its political allies as too expensive and impractical to implement, especially those aspects dealing with reduction of powers of the executive and the devolved units of government. Led by the Parliamentary Select Committee on constitutional review, pro-government law-makers met in Naivasha and Kilifi to amend the Bomas Draft. The modified Draft was then handed over to the Attorney-General's office for "fine tuning" before it was presented to the public for a referendum. The draft dubbed "Wako Draft" established religious courts; namely, Christian courts, *Kadhi*'s courts and Hindu courts, which were to be subordinate courts. In instituting these courts, Section 195 of the Wako Draft thus stated, *inter alia*, that:

> Christian courts, *Kadhi*'s courts, Hindu courts, and other religious courts shall respectively – (a) consist of Chief presiding officers, Chief *Kadhi* and such number of other presiding officers or *Kadhi*s, all of whom profess the respective religious faiths; and (b) be organized and administered as may be prescribed by respective Act of Parliament.

The jurisdiction of these religious courts was however restricted, just as in the current constitution, to matters of religious law relating to personal law, marriage, divorce, inheritance and succession, and matters consequential to them in proceedings in which all parties profess same religious beliefs. Parliament was also empowered to enact legislation to establish other religious courts as circumstance and need may arise.

Through such constitutional provisions, the Wako Draft ostensibly aimed at treating religious groups equally by granting them the right to govern their respective personal laws via formal structures within the judiciary. However, the fact that members of various religions in Kenya other than the Muslims had not requested for such courts, begged the question whether the government was merely strategizing to garner the crucial support of members of all faiths in the impending referendum. The issue of denominational differences and the nature of personnel to be employed in such courts were raised by various Christian groups as an impediment to the functioning of the Christian courts. Muslims, on the other hand, were incensed by the provisions of the Wako Draft that greatly weakened the *Kadhi*'s courts. The Muslims argued that unlike the Bomas Draft, the Wako Draft expunged the appellate jurisdiction of the *Kadhi*'s court. In addition, the Wako Draft made it easier for parliament to remove the religious courts from the Constitution by a mere simple majority of votes. The Wako Draft was rejected at the referendum.

Kadhi's Courts in the Harmonised Draft Constitution and the Proposed Constitution of Kenya

As aforementioned, the CoE did not consider the *Kadhi*'s courts as contentious in the statutory sense that they had been enshrined in Independence Constitution and that all the other Drafts that were to form the basis of reference in guiding the work of the Commission provided for these courts. According to Nzamba Kitonga, the chairman of the CoE, the decision not to regard the courts as contentious was not that of the CoE. Rather, it was arrived at out of the many submissions presented to the Commission. He asserted that:

> "A small section of evangelicals (Christian) who are dissatisfied with our failure to categorise the *Kadhi*'s courts as a contentious issue made their submissions that, in their view, *Kadhi's* courts is a contentious issue. But that is not our view because we had invited memoranda from Kenyans and received over 12,000 written ones; very few said the issue is contentious."[2]

Thus, the Harmonised Draft included the *Kadhi*'s courts among other subordinate courts such as the magistrates' Courts, and the Court Martial.

Section 209 of the Harmonised Draft Constitution of Kenya, *inter alia*, provided:

(a) There shall be a Chief *Kadhi* and such number, not being fewer than three, of other *Kadhi*s as may be prescribed by, or under an Act of Parliament.

(b) To qualify to be appointed as *Kadhi*, a person must profess the Muslim religion, and possesses such knowledge of the Muslim law applicable to any sects of Muslims as qualifies that person, in the opinion of the Judicial Service Commission, to hold a *Kadhi*'s court.

(c) The Chief *Kadhi* and other *Kadhi*s shall each be empowered to hold a *Kadhi*'s court having jurisdiction within the former Protectorate or within such part of the former Protectorate as may be so prescribed.[3]

(d) The jurisdiction of a *Kadhi*'s court shall extend to the determination of questions of Muslim law relating to personal status, marriage, divorce or inheritance in proceedings in which all parties profess the Muslim religion.

It should be noted that while the Muslims had demanded that the *Kadhi*'s courts have a High Court and a Court of Appeal, these issues were not included in the Harmonized Draft or in the Proposed Constitution. Nor wasthe Chief *Kadhi* included as a member of the Judicial Service Commission. Despite such misgivings, which arguably went against the demands made by Muslims and which the CoE ignored, the Harmonized Draft was well received by a section of Muslim leaders for retaining the *Kadhi*'s courts in the constitution; among them the Chief *Kadhi*, Sheikh Hamad Kassim, and the Supreme Council of Kenya Muslims (SUPKEM) Director-General, Abdulatif Shaaban.[4]

Sections of the Christian population, especially the Evangelical and the Protestant churches, strongly opposed the Harmonized Draft and the Proposed Constitution because of the *Kadhi*'s courts, among others reasons. In fact, Bishop Margaret Wanjiru led a group of evangelical churches that vowed to have the *Kadhi*'s courts "removed" from the Draft. The National Christian Council of Kenya (NCCK) led by its General-Secretary, Rev. Peter Karanja added its voice in expressing reservations in entrenching the *Kadhi*'s courts in the new constitution.[5] Karanja emphatically expressed that "If the Draft presented at the referendum has loopholes for legislation of abortion, exempts Muslims from the Bill of Rights or includes the *Kadhi*'s courts, we shall mobilise Kenyans to reject it," and that "Our demand for removal of the courts from the Constitution is not negotiable."[6]

It should be noted that this is not the first time some Christian leaders have taken such strong opposition to the inclusion of the *Kadhi*'s courts in the Constitution. In August 9, 2005, for instance, Bishop Kihara Mwangi, also MP for Kigumo, when asked by President Kibaki to close a meeting of MPs discussing constitution-making with a prayer, invoked divine intervention to save Kenya, adding that the "new constitution should not condemn the country into a *Sharia* state."[7] In 2004 a group of Church leaders including the Rev. Jesse Kamau (then PCEA Moderator), Bishop Silas Yego of the African Inland Church and Bishop Margaret Wanjiru of the Jesus is Alive Ministries filed a case against the Attorney General and the defunct Constitution of Kenya Review Commission (CKRC) for, among others, the extension of the jurisdiction of the *Kadhi*'s courts beyond the 10-mile coastal strip and sections of the current constitution that provide for their introduction. Six years later and long after the 2005 referendum that had determined the fate of the said challenges (contained in the Bomas Draft), three High Court judges ruled that the *Kadhi*'s courts were unconstitutional and funding them amounted to favouring one religion. Such, they argued, contradicted the principle of separation of State and Religion.[8] This ruling did not, however, have the force to expunge the *Kadhi*'s courts from the Constitution nor affect the provisions of the Proposed Constitution. The decision by the judges was declared by the Attorney General as "itself unconstitutional". He opined that "The court lacked jurisdiction, (and) the judgement is wrong in law." Muslims argued that the Constitution did not regard family matters such as those under the purview of the *Kadhi*'s courts discriminatory. Abdulghafur Al-Busaidy, Chairman of SUPKEM, found fault in the decision by the judges on the courts arguing that, "They conveniently ignored sub-section 4 of the same section (Sec. 62 of the Constitution) which says that matters of divorce, adoption, marriage and inheritance are excluded from the definition of discrimination."[9]

It has been argued that the judges also overstepped their mandate, since the court had no jurisdiction to grant the orders sought.[10] They also veered off to constitutional matters, a reserve of the Interim Independent Constitutional Dispute Resolution Court. According to Ben Sihanya, the former Dean of the School of Law at the University of Nairobi, the *Kadhi*'s courts are constitutional and recognize the need to protect minorities and historical agreements, and that the judges arrived at the decision without considering historical circumstances.[11] Martha Karua, the then Minister for Justice, National Cohesion and Constitutional Affairs declared the ruling as "legally and socially unsound."

Another bid by yet another group of Church leaders under the auspices of Mombasa Pastors Fellowship was to move to the High Court in 2009, requesting it to declare the *Kadhi*'s courts in the Proposed Constitution illegal. They wanted the review process stopped because they alleged that their rights would be infringed upon by among other things, the inclusion of *Kadhi*'s Courts in the new law. In mid-2010, the presiding judge ruled that the High Court had no mandate to determine the case, arguing that the courts had no jurisdiction to deal with any matter touching on the Constitutional Review Process and to do so would be unconstitutional. He pointed out that the High Court lacked the power to decide whether sections of the Constitution were legal or illegal. As though making reference to the earlier ruling by the three judges, the judge of the High Court in Mombasa pointed out that any attempt by the Court to question and interpret the constitutionality of the Constitution itself "would be the height of judicial arrogance and usurpation of the supremacy and legislative functions of Parliament."[12] The implication of this ruling is that, it showed that the Judiciary had no powers to declare any section of the Constitution to be unconstitutional.[13]

The leadership of the Catholic Church also added their voice against the Proposed Constitution, expressing their "gravest reservations" on the articles touching on *Kadhi*'s courts and abortion, among others. Although the Catholic clergy were in agreement that the Proposed Constitution was better, they remained adamantly opposed to the referendum, pointing out that "the Constitution is not a bag of potatoes, which you can remove five bad ones and retain the 95 that seem to be good. It is like an egg. If it begins to go bad, it goes bad wholly."[14]

The stand by a section of Church leaders to oppose the Proposed Constitution and specifically the *Kadhi*'s courts was described by public figures and other Christian leaders as unfair[15], a fronting of the interests of the Church in the West and their inconsistence in guiding their congregations. The Church was accused of serving the interests of evangelicals in the United States, particularly on their stand on the *Kadhi*'s courts and abortion.

One may opine that there is no scriptural basis for the Church's stance against the courts. Regarding the issue of abortion, some within the religious ranks have argued that issues such as abortion are moral subjects that the Church should have effectively dealt with at the congregational level.[16] Kiraitu Murungi, the Energy Minister, accused the Church of goal-shifting and posited that "during the 2005 referendum, Catholic bishops told their faithful to vote with their conscience while the provisions on abortion (and *Kadhi*'s Courts) were not any different from todays. Why can't they ask them to vote with the same conscience now?"[17] It is imperative to note that not all Church leaders were opposed to the Proposed Constitution. The most visible Church clergy in support of a new constitutional dispensation included former Anglican Archbishop David Gitari and Reverend Timothy Njoya.

Reasons for and against the *Kadhi*'s Courts

While the arguments against entrenching these courts in the Constitution by some Christians were varied, they may be summarized as follows:

1. It is against the constitution which provides that the state and religion shall be separate and that there shall be no state religion. The fact that the independence constitution guaranteed that all religions shall be treated equally was interpreted by some Christians to mean that the existence of *Kadhi*'s courts implies favouritism of the Muslims by the state or primacy of Islam above other religions.

2. Though nowhere stated in the constitution, some Christians and other Kenyans argued that Kenya is a secular state and no religion should be embedded in the constitution.

3. That the Bill of Rights already provides for the freedom of conscience, religion, thought, belief, and opinion. Why should Muslims have such "religious" courts which are already catered for in the Bill of Rights?

4. That *Kadhi*'s courts are a burden to the exchequer and tax payer, yet they do not cater for all the people. As one reader put it: "Remove the *Kadhi*'s courts, the exchequer cannot use public resources to satisfy a section of religions."[18]

In response to these sentiments, the Muslims and a number of non-Muslims writers and commentators advanced the following views to defend *Kadhi*'s courts:

- *Kadhi*'s courts are part of Kenya's judicial system, subordinate to the High Court and the Court of Appeal. Though presided over by the Chief *Kadhi* and *Kadhis*, these courts, like the rest of country's courts, are all under the ambit of the Chief Justice. The *Kadhi*'s courts are thus not a religion.[19]

- The constitution is a document that addresses the needs of all citizens, including those of the minorities and special interest groups who ask for such interests to be provided for and protected by the constitution. Muslims in this country have always felt the need for the courts and have asked for them. It would be unfair for the government to deny the Muslims such courts on the ground that other communities or religious groups have not asked for them.

- The notion that the country needs to separate state matters from religious ones in a secular frame has been seen as wanting. The independence constitution and the Proposed Constitution had a national anthem which recognizes God as the Originator of all creation. Sunday, a Christian day of worship, not Friday, is recognized by the State as a holiday. The State also pays for the salaries for chaplaincy in the army and the public universities as well as teachers of religious education in government schools. Kenya's common law is also said to have been heavily influenced by Judeo-Christian traditions. Thus, the state-religion divide is an idealistic concept and practice has shown that many nations try to accommodate the religious needs, rights and freedoms of their citizens. In fact, the demand by a section of Church leaders for the inclusion in the Proposed Constitution that life begins at conception and their opposition to abortion borders on imposing Christian values to Kenyans, some of whom are not Christians.

- Muslims do not get the services offered by the *Kadhi*'s courts free of charge. Muslims also pay taxes like any other Kenyans. According to Lethome Ibrahim, "the court is part of the judiciary, a public office serving a special interest group of the Kenyan tax payers who happen to be Muslims, without infringing on the rights of others in any way."[20] Similar sentiments have also been echoed by Peter Mwaura, who writes:

> "*Kadhi*'s courts are part of the Judiciary and tax payers, including Muslims, are already paying for them, and will continue to do so regardless of whether they are entrenched or not."[21]

According to Andrew Kipkemboi, the Standard Foreign News Editor, it is not plausible to argue, as some Christians do, that because the *Kadhi*'s courts are funded by the exchequer, therefore the taxpayer is funding Islam. He notes that the Magistrate Courts are spread all over the country and apply the African Christian Marriage & Divorce Act in resolving disputes relating to marriage and divorce involving Christians. These courts also apply the Succession Act on matters relating to inheritance. The traditionalists too can go before the courts, and with the help of experts on local tradition, their disputes on issues on marriage, divorce and inheritance may be resolved. Thus, if the resolutions of the disputes affecting the personal status of Christians and traditionalists are funded by the Exchequer, why should Muslims be an exception?[22] Are such provisions in the Constitution catering for Christian interests through the use of public funds amounting to favouring one religion against the others?

- The process of re-writing the constitution does not involve taking away already existing rights enjoyed by a group of people. As Ahmednasir Abdullahi, the former chairman of the Law Society of Kenya puts it: "Constitutional making is a progressive process that makes what we already have just better. It is not about the curtailment of rights that are already in existence."[23] Muslims in Kenya have had constitutional rights to have their matters and disputes on law of personal status decided by these courts since the time of independence in 1963 and in some parts of Kenya long before the coming of the British colonialists.

Some writers considered the hard-line position taken by Christians as immoral and a sign of intolerance. Wanyonyi Wambilyanga, the Chief Sub-Editor of the *Standard* (*Weekend Editions*), writes:

"Intolerance has never been a virtue. Church leaders do not want to hear anything about *Kadhi*'s courts in the new constitution. Not even if the word comes from the experts. Is their call genuine? Will it be of national good to rally faithful to shoot down a new constitution on the premise of one idea viewed as giving prominence to one religion?...The Church should be at the forefront in fighting for a new constitution. For the Church to threaten to marshal faithful against the new constitution on the basis of *Kadhi*'s courts is immoral. If the new document will ensure development of the whole country and seal avenues the politically correct use to make illicit money, we should support it. It is wrong for the clergy to incite faithful to reject it because *Kadhi*'s courts have been acknowledged."[24]

Paul Aol also considered the statement by the Evangelical churches against the *Kadhi*'s courts as unwarranted. He accused the group of acting in ignorance and asserted that there are adequate provisions in the Constitution and international law – treaties and conventions that the Government has signed and ratified – to protect Christians and non-Muslims faiths from being subjected to *Kadhi*'s courts or '*Sharia* law'. In view of this, the (Christian) clergy should use their energy to strengthen existing relations between Christians and Muslims instead of provocations in a manner akin to political activism.[25]

The support for the inclusion of the *Kadhi*'s courts in the constitution should not be construed as a concern of Muslims only. A number of NGOs voiced their support for the entrenchment of *Kadhi*'s courts. For instance, the Centre for Multiparty Democracy – Kenya (CMD Kenya), on a statement on the work of the Parliamentary Select Committee on the constitution at Naivasha, wrote:

"We fully support retention of the *Kadhi*'s Courts and call upon the church leaders to avoid extremism and be magnanimous. *Kadhi*'s Courts are a judicial and not a religious matter."[26]

Entrenching the *Kadhi*'s Courts in the Constitution

Kenya, as a unitary state, cannot allow a judicial system, such as that of the *Kadhi*, to operate separately outside the watchful eye of the state. Such a state of affairs may lead to "Taliban-styled" courts or extremist interpretation of the Muslim law. Entrenching *Kadhi*'s courts in the constitution thus gives the government some leverage to control and regulate operations of such courts (which has been the case since the era of British rule), while at the same time safeguarding the genuine concerns of a section of its citizens. Indeed one such safeguard is the supremacy clause in the Proposed Constitution of Kenya, which states that "Any law, including customary law (and Islamic Law), that is inconsistent with this Constitution is void to the extent of the inconsistency, and any act or omission in contravention of the Constitution is invalid."[27] While it is possible for Kadhi's courts to operate outside the provision of the constitution, indeed much of the aspects of the Sharia are daily observed by Muslims without the trappings of the state machinery. It needs to be observed that other aspects of Muslim law require the safeguards of the state to fully operationalize them. For instance, there is nothing that a local Sheikh can do to compel a husband who refuses to appear before him to answer charges raised by his estranged wife in relation to provision of maintenance or over a dispute on the custody of children following divorce. The state, however, has the power to do so under the law of contempt of court thus ensuring justice to the aggrieved party is guaranteed. In the Kenyan context moreover, entrenching Kadhi's courts in the new constitution is necessary, given that Muslims are a minority.[28] Unlike their Christian counterparts, Muslims do not constitute a politically, educationally, or economically dominant group. Without any constitutional safeguard, such courts could also be easily expunged by an overzealous Christian-dominated Parliament.[29]

The Way Forward

Barely a week before Kenyans decided the fate of the Proposed Constitution in the 4th of August 2010 referendum, it was clear that a "Yes" vote at the referendum would have had the implication of retaining and entrenching Kadhi's courts in the new constitutional dispensation. A "No" vote would have been of no consequence to the fate of the courts as they would still have been provided for by the previous constitution. Thus, for Christians opposed to the Proposed Constitution, the above scenario presented a "lose-lose" situation. That view was shared by Archbishop Eliud Wabukala, the Head of the Anglican Church of Kenya, who reasoned that even if Christians ganged up to defeat the Proposed Constitution at the referendum because of the clause on Kadhi's Courts, they would still have lost the war since the Kadhi's courts were already in the Constitution. In addition, Christians would be blamed for failure to pass new laws that would do away with an imperial presidency among other positive aspects.[30]

Using the jurisprudential principle of choosing a "lesser evil rather than the greater evil", the prelate David Gitari urged Kenyans to accept the Proposed Constitution as being far preferable to the current supreme law, warning against turning the referendum into a battle between Christians and Muslims. He was unequivocal when he argued that "As a Kenyan and a Christian saying 'Yes' to the constitution is evil. But saying "No" will be a greater evil. If I was to choose I will go for the lesser evil."[31] While a section of Christian leaders rejected the possibility of amending the Proposed Constitution after it passed into law, the document itself provides for a mechanism through which an aggrieved party can seek redress. Section 257 (1) of the proposed law gives the Church the option of changing a section of the Constitution by raising one million signatures from among registered voters. The onus is thus upon the Church leaders, not to stand in the way of a new constitution because of the *Kadhi*'s courts, but to endorse it and rally their support to garner the requisite numbers to effect the changes they desire.

If the entrenchment of the *Kadhi*'s courts were to be the main bone of contention against the adoption of a new constitution, and that Christians felt disadvantaged and discriminated, instead of demanding the removal of the courts – a move which would certainly be rejected by Muslims, Christian leaders may have to demand for a provision in the proposed law or an amendment of the constitution once it was passed, granting any religious group the right to establish courts of their own to govern matters of personal status. Only when Christians make such a demand and it is rejected, would the provision on *Kadhi*'s courts be seen as discriminatory.

Conclusion

An analysis of the workings of the CoE shows that despite the many submissions made by Muslims demanding for some reforms on the *Kadhi*'s courts, the Committee simply retained the status of the courts as they were in the previous constitution of Kenya. Perhaps the CoE in so doing wanted to respond to the sensibility of the Christians by only accepting from the Muslims the least irreducible minimum, namely retaining the courts as they were before. In addition, the support for a new constitution in general and *Kadhi*'s courts in particular came from Muslims and non-Muslims alike.

Leaders of the Catholic, Anglican and Pentecostal Churches under the aegis of the NCCK voiced some reservations to the proposed new constitution. The retention of *Kadhi*'s courts in the proposed constitution has been shown to be supported by both historical and judicial precedents and practice in this country. To avoid subversive elements within the church and potential kindling of extremist tendencies among Muslims, majority Christians and Muslims of goodwill rallied together and midwifed a new constitutional dispensation that safeguards the rights of all. Instead of standing in the way of a new constitution, Christians who felt aggrieved by the retention of *Kadhi*'s courts in the Harmonized Draft may challenge the matter in the country's Constitutional Court, where they will have a chance to get a fair hearing. The Proposed Constitution of Kenya was overwhelmingly passed by the populace during the 2010 referendum and has since been promulgated into the supreme law of the country. Despite misgivings expressed by some sections of the Christian clergy, majority of Christians in the country supported the document.

Notes

[1] *Nation*, August 22, 2009, p. 5.

[2] *Nation*, August 22, 2009, p. 5; also *The Standard*, November 18, p. 11.

[3] The part under this clause touching on protectorate was subsequently removed following reservations by Muslims to read, inter alia, in the Proposed Constitution of Kenya as revised by the CoE and following the recommendations of the Parliamentary Select Committee on Constitutional Review as: "The Chief *Kadhi* and other *Kadhi*s shall each be empowered to hold a *Kadhi*'s court having jurisdiction within Kenya. "

[4] *The Standard*, November 18, 2009, p. 11.

[5] *The Standard*, December 13, 2009, p. 19.

[6] *Daily Nation*, April 8, 2010, p. 5.

[7] Peter Mwaura, "Kenyan Christians behaving like a dog in the manger", *Saturday Nation*, August 15, 2009, p. 11.

[8] *Daily Nation*, May 26, 2010, p. 9, 10-11; *The Standard*, May 26, p. 8.

[9] *The Standard*, May 26, 2010, p. 6.

[10]*Daily Nation*, May 26, 2010, p. 4.

[11]*Daily Nation*, May 25, 2010, p. 2.

[12]*The Standard*, June 7, 2010, p. 7.

[13]*Daily Nation*, June 1, 2010, p. 4.

[14] This statement was attributed to the Head of the Catholic Church in Kenya, Cardinal John Njue. *The Standard*, May 12, 2010, p. 7.

[15]Mutula Kilonzo, the Justice Minister, posits that "Christians opposed to this wonderful draft are unfair…The current constitution is silent on abortion but the new draft is clear that abortion is illegal…it holds responsible doctors who illegitimately terminate pregnancies…" *The Standard*, April 6, 2010, p. 7.

[16]*Sunday Nation*, April 18, 2010, p. 12.

[17]*The Standard*, April 6, 2010, p. 7.

[18]*Sunday Nation*, February 7, 2010, p. 2, a response by a reader, named Mzeemoja on the paper's week's debate entitled "Should experts change PSC proposals in draft?"

[19]Peter Mwaura, "Kenyan Christians behaving like a dog in the manger", in *Saturday Nation*, August 15, 2009, p. 11.

[20]*The Standard*, November 16, 2009, p. 15.

[21]*Nation*, August 15, 2009, p. 11.

[22]*The Standard*, May 26, 2010, p. 15.

[23]*Sunday Nation*, February 7, 2010, p. 18.

[24]Wanyonyi Wambilyanga, "There is more to law reform than the Church locking out Kadhi's courts", *The Standard*, November 1, 2009, p. 16.

[25]Paul Aol, "Clergy's views on Kadhi courts selfish", in *The Standard*, November 7, 2009, p. 17.

[26]*Daily Nation*, February 19, 2010, p. 36.

[27]The emphasis is mine.

[28]According to the 2009 National Census, the total population of Muslims are 4. 3 million while that of Christians including Catholics and Protestants number about 32 million. The country's population stands at 38.6 million. See *Nation*, September 1, 2010, pp. 1, 8.

[29]Mwaura, *Nation*, August 15, 2009, p. 11.

[30]*The Standard*, April 4, 2010, p. 19.

[31]*The Standard*, April 19, 2010, p. 7.

Channelling Youth Energies, Expanding Opportunities

Empowerment of Youth and Communities in the Coast Province through Strategic Investments in Education

Hamadi Iddi Boga

Background

For many years, Prof. Ali Mazrui, a renowned scholar lamented about the lack of a University at the Coast of Kenya. He described the Coast Province as being "the first to go to school and the last to graduate". But in the recent past the Government of Kenya has established the Mombasa Polytechnic University College, Pwani University College, and the Taita Taveta Campus in the Coast Region. Other universities have also rushed to create campuses in Mombasa Town. These Institutions hold much hope and promise for stimulation of excellence in education in the region and nationally, and also towards preparation of the region for some of the flagship programs of the country's Vision 2030. Despite this apparent progress, youth in the Coast Region continue to face a number of challenges in the provision of quality education. The challenges include limited access to education, negative attitudes towards education, low quality of education and poor infrastructure leading to poor performance in national examinations, and high student-teacher ratio among others. In this chapter, I will attempt to discuss some of these challenges in some detail.

Limited Access to Education at the Coast

Although the earliest schools were started at the coast, with some of the oldest schools such as Waa High school located in Kwale, the Coast Province currently faces a severe shortage of schools both at the Primary (ca. 1650) and Secondary (ca. 310) levels thereby limiting access (Ministry of Education, 2009). In 2009 there are 630,000 students attending public primary schools and 99,000 attending private primary schools in the Coast Province. At the secondary school level, there were about 70,000 pupils in public schools and 12,000 in private schools. It has been observed that a steady but gradual increase in enrolment of about 34.5% has taken place in primary schools since 2002. However, enrolment is weighed down by high dropout rates by both boys and girls, and overall, the number of girls steadily declines in upper primary. The Coast Province has done poorly in percentage mismatch between girl and boy enrolment with a disparity of 3.2 percentage points in favor of boys (Achoki *et al* 2007).

Enrolment rates are still low as a large number of children of school-going age in the province are not yet in school. In addition, majority of the pupils in primary schools do not proceed to secondary schools; only about 55% of those who complete Standard 8 transit to secondary school, making this one of the lowest transition rates in the country. Apart from lack of available places in primary and secondary schools, there are not enough training places at the polytechnics, middle level colleges and universities. Major towns such as Malindi, Kilifi, Lamu, Diani and Hola, lack any meaningful tertiary colleges and have to rely on Mombasa Polytechnic, Mombasa Technical Training colleges, Mikindani Islamic Teachers Training College and Shanzu Teachers Training College, all located in Mombasa Town. The only county in the Coast Province which has invested slightly more in tertiary level educational institutions is Taita Taveta, which has the Coast Institute of Technology, Bura Teachers Training College, and a number of youth polytechnics. In addition to the lack of educational infrastructure, poverty is a key factor which keeps out most of those who qualify for university admission but do not gain access to government funding including, for example, 2000 students who obtained between C+ and B (64 points) in 2008. Only 416 out of 15000 candidates (2.8%) received government support; the rest who attained C and below remained without any further education due to poverty and lack of information or a general misconception that completing Form Four is the end of learning. A high level of ignorance and lack of information on training opportunities on the part of parents and students also keeps most youth at home as they are unable to locate training places and funding opportunities after their tertiary education. These issues deny more of the youth and future citizens a chance for further training or higher education.

There is also a gender dimension to the issue of access to education. Completion rates for girls in primary schools stand at about 60%. Most of the girls drop out due to poverty, teenage pregnancy and early marriages. At the time of writing with chapter, Mombasa County had only one boarding school for girls, with many parents taking their children to Taita Taveta or Kwale County to access boarding facilities.

Quality of Education and Performance in National Examinations

Even when students have access to education, they still have to wrestle with the problem of poor and dilapidated infrastructure especially in public institutions. As a result of the free primary education program, some schools have become overcrowded, with learners sharing limited space. Most secondary schools are under pressure to expand spaces to 3 or 4 streams. This worsens a situation in which a high teacher-student ratio exists. In 2008, staffing levels were low in Coast Province with a shortage of 716 teachers in secondary schools and 3,858 teachers in primary schools. This situation might not have improved much since then.

The Coast Province has consistently performed poorly in national examinations, with counties such as Tana River, Lamu and Kwale perpetually underperforming. Between 2003 and 2008, Tana River County had only five candidates qualifying for university. Poor performance in Mathematics, English, Chemistry, Physics and Biology were mainly responsible for the overall dismal results. In the case of primary schools, rural schools generally perform poorly with results on subjects other than Kiswahili ranging mostly below 50%. This sorry state which has persisted over the years hardly portends well for the future of the coastal counties, which are struggling with hordes of uneducated, dissatisfied, and unemployed youth who could easily be manipulated into anti-social activities.

One observation is that most schools in the province are mixed schools. The environment in mixed schools is hardly conducive for learning and exposes learners to much distraction and burdens teachers with the enormous task of trying to manage boy-girl relationships. This could also be a contributor to the general low performance in the province. Research has shown that mixed schools tend to perform worse compared to boys' and girls' schools.

Attitude

Generally negative attitudes towards education by parents and students can also be blamed for the low education levels and poor performance. The common cliché that *"Mombasa kuingia ni raha, kutoka ni karaha"* alludes to the plenitude of leisure and pleasure in Mombasa, entrapping and enchanting visitors with a life of bliss. Youth while away their time dreaming about working at the beach or port without any training or skills. With increased competition, these dreams are no longer easily realized, yet these dreams are heavily etched in the minds of the youth in the area, and have become part of their very existence. Communities spend heavily on social activities such as weddings and funerals even while their children are at home for lack of school fees. A general sense that one can take a short-cut to success without working hard at school has driven young men and women into the arms of tourists old enough to be their great grandparents. The very beauty of the coast that attracts people from far and wide has become a trap for its resident youth, who are unable to cope with its delusions.

Teachers and education officials who find a laid back community have also developed a negative attitude towards teaching and therefore neglect their obligations. This fuels a cycle of apathy which leads to the never ending blame game between teachers, parents, and students about who is responsible for the low education standards.

Lack of Role Models

Immediately after independence in 1963, tourism was booming and the port was doing brisk business with ships landing with hordes of seamen. Seamen, beach boys and port workers became the role models for many youth at the coast. Many of the educated people from the coastal community ended up working in the civil service far away from home and therefore were not quite as visible or accessible to their local communities. People such as Mzee Samuel Maneno and Mzee Timothy Ramtu who had risen in the Civil Service could only influence the youth whom they taught at Kwale High School, Kenyatta High School in Taita or Alliance High School in Central Province. Even today, the competition between the educated elite and beach boys for influence over the youth is still being won by the latter hands down.

Indiscipline and Drug Abuse

It is an open secret that schools at the coast have become notorious for indiscipline. Students refuse to take mock examinations, resort to strikes and burning of schools and many believe their salvation lies in *gomba* (cheating in examinations). With such a mindset, these youth are already defeated, hence undermining education further in the region. Rampant drug abuse in the region contributes further to the challenges faced in schools at the coast.

The Political Dimension

Oginga Odinga and Tom Mboya are remembered for the airlift of Kenyan students to Russia and USA respectively which entrenched the culture of education among their people in Nyanza Province. No politician from the Coast Province appears to be remembered for any such an undertaking. Indeed these politicians have been known to look down upon education and to talk ill of the educated. A location such as Diani in Kwale County with a booming business centre and known all over the world has had only one day secondary school for over 40 years since independence, serving more than seven primary schools. Few political leaders have promoted education aggressively by word or deed. They have not focused on education as a key means of empowerment which would free coastal communities from poverty, disease, hunger and despair. Instead, the possibility has been treated casually, as one of the issues to be handled alongside others.

Religion

Due to the historical link between Western education and Christianity, some Muslims at the coast have refused to embrace Western education which they associate with Christianity. Groups such as the so called "Answar" around Ukunda still keep their children, especially girls, away from accessing education for fear of committing sin. In the past, many actually burnt their academic certificates, abandoned their jobs and withdrew from society in search of salvation for fear that embracing education would make them appear the same as the Naswara (Christians).

Empowering the Youth in the Coast Province

The Bible says "*My people perish from a lack of knowledge*" (Hosea 4:6, King James Version). The majority of youth at the Coast are desperate.

They have embraced drugs widely, are joining Al-Shabaab in Somalia or other proscribed groups such as the Kaya Bombo and Mulungunipa, in a desperate search for meaning and relevance in their lives. This sense of helplessness and despair can only be addressed if youth in the Coast Province could be empowered through provision of quality education and skills and the ensuing opportunities for employment. This can be achieved if political leaders and all stakeholders worked to address the issues proposed below:

1. More educational infrastructure should be put up. This includes early childhood education facilities, primary schools and secondary schools, youth polytechnics, tertiary colleges and universities. The private sector should also be given incentives to continue investing in education. Everyone who wishes to get education and training should be enabled to access these affordably and easily.

2. The various bursaries available will be better managed by targeting those in need and should be enhanced by raising more funds from well-wishers and other stakeholders.

3. Mixed secondary schools should be phased out. Teachers have enough challenges managing the teaching programs without having to manage youth boiling with hormones; besides, girls and boys learn differently (Bosire et al 2007).

4. Education officials should enhance monitoring of teaching and learning in schools, dealing with non-performing head teachers and transferring those who overstay in some schools.

5. Head teachers and school boards have to set clear visions for schools with quality of teaching and learning at the heart of their investments. Prudent management of resources, including time, should be the concern of every head teacher and board chairperson.

6. Appointment of boards and school management committees should be depoliticized and be based on merit to inject professionalism into the running of schools.

7. Political leaders should support head teachers who perform well and call to account those who do not. They should pay attention to what is happening in their schools, organizing sensitization meetings with parents, students and professionals from the area.

8. Political, religious groups and the media, especially FM radio stations should speak up for, and promote education. They should be at the forefront of fighting against the negative attitude and other retrogressive cultural practices that keep the region from developing further.

9. Muslim leaders should issue a "fatwa" decreeing that going to school is not "haram", and consistently speak for education in all available fora.

10. The newly established university colleges at the coast should work to sensitize communities, leaders, schools and students on education in general, career guidance and future trends. They can contribute to making education fashionable.

11. Youth should have easy access to information on education and training opportunities. This can be done through the media, religious venues, provincial administration and elected leaders.

Successful professionals from the coast need to be more visible in their villages, serving on school boards, providing information, offering advice and guidance and acting as role models for the youth.

Conclusion

The Constitution of Kenya states that the youth have a right to affordable and quality education, and also a right to information. The recommendations contained herein will ensure an improved education environment in the coast, hence fulfilling the constitutional promise for access to quality and affordable education. The communities at the Kenyan Coast owe it to their children and their survival in tomorrow's Kenya, to give them a good start by ensuring that they have access to quality education and training.

References

Achoka, J. S. K, Stephen O. Odebero, Julius K. Maiyo and Ndiku J. Mualuko (2007). Access to basic education in Kenya: inherent concerns. Educational Research and Review Vol. 2 (10), pp. 275-284.

Bosire J., H. Mondoh and A. Barmao (2008). Effect of streaming by gender on student achievement in mathematics in secondary schools in Kenya. South African Journal of Education 28:595-607.

Njeru, E. and J. Orodho (2003) *Access and Participation in Secondary School Education: Emerging Issues and Policy Implications.* IPAR Discussion Paper No. 037/2003.

http://chet.org.za/manual/media/files/chet_hernana_docs/Kenya/National/ MEST%202004_Development%20of%20education%20in%20Kenya.pdf (Development of Education in Kenya, MOE). Accessed 24th June 2011.

(2006) Globalization: A Major Challenge to Muslims in Kenya.

Mazrui A. (2005) Annual Mazrui Newsletter No. 29.

Search for Identity: Youth, Culture and Religion in the Mount Kenya Region

Margaret G. Gecaga

Introduction

Culture and religion provide an individual and group with identity. People define themselves in terms of ancestry, religion, language, history, values, customs and institutions. They identify with cultural groups, ethnic groups, religious communities, and at the broadest level, civilizations. Using the example of the *Mūngīkī*, this chapter shows the significance of religion and culture in crystallizing the identity of the youth for political and economic protest in the Mt. Kenya region. It is pointed out that any social transformation policy must take into consideration the two dimensions (religion and culture). The chapter concludes by providing practical steps essential for the participation of the youth in development.

Identity and Youth

According to Kathryn Woodward[1] identity gives us a location in the world and presents the link between us and the society in which we live. It is the interface between subjective positions and social cultural situations. Identity gives us the idea of who we are and how we relate to others. It marks the ways in which we are the same as others who share that position, and ways we are different from those who do not. In this regard identity is most clearly defined by difference. Identities are produced, consumed and regulated within culture by the language and symbolic systems through which they are represented.

The concept of youth is one whose use is heavily dependent on context. A majority of people understand this term in relation to age. For example, the National Policy Steering Committee[2] describes a Kenyan youth as one aged between 15 and 30 years. In this case "youth" means young people or adolescents. As adolescents, the youth are considered too immature to have anything significant to contribute to national politics, hence the common cliché "the youth are leaders of tomorrow". On this basis, they are marginalized in significant decision-making forums even those that concern their own category.

In this chapter, I use the term "youth" to denote not only young people in the transitional stage between childhood and adulthood – meaning they have undergone the *Agĩkũyũ* (Kikuyu) rite of circumcision – but also those who are capable of taking up societal responsibilities although they have not attained the stage of social elder-hood. Youth is a social category largely determined by cultural rites and the ability of the individual to perform capably in service to the wider society. Thus age, the circumcision rite of passage and performance of the individual in society are important identity makers of a youth.

Culture

Culture is a complex phenomenon. Many disciplines such as anthropology, sociology, history and philosophy have tried to define it in ways and paradigms particular to those disciplines. Culture is the whole way of life, material and non-material, of human society[3]. It includes norms and values of a society, their religion and politics, economics, law, and performing arts, amongst others.

According to Ali A. Mazrui[4], culture has seven functions. First it helps provide lenses of perception and recognition. How people view the world is greatly conditioned by one or more cultural paradigms to which they have been exposed. The *Agĩkũyũ* worldview is that there is one God (*Ngai*), the creator of all things. This has influenced their perception about the cosmos. Second, culture provides motives for human behavior. The behavior of a person is partly cultural in origin. Culture provides the norms and values which guide the behaviors of individuals. These are passed on through the process of socialization. Third, culture provides criteria for evaluation. The good and the bad are determined by culture. Fourth, culture provides a basis of identity. Culture includes a community reservoir of what defines them as people, in other words what gives them an "identity". Fifth, culture is a mode of communication. The most elaborate system of communication is language itself. Language is realigned and reconstructed to accord with the identities and contours of civilization[5]. Culture as communication can take other forms including music and performing arts among others. Sixth, culture is a basis of stratification. Class, rank, age and status are profoundly conditioned by cultural variables. In the *Agĩkũyũ* community the custom of initiation into adulthood (*Irua*)[6] or circumcision was the deciding factor in giving a boy or a girl the status of manhood or womanhood. During this rite, the initiates were introduced to the customs, religion and morality of the *Agĩkũyũ*. Unfortunately, to date the rite has been largely reduced to a surgical operation with little cultural significance. Boys as young as eight days go through this rite, certainly without any form of socialization.

The seventh function of culture lies in the system of production and consumption. The traditional *Agĩkũyũ* community's main occupations were agriculture and the rearing of livestock. Each family unit constituted an economic unit. This was controlled and strengthened by the system of division of labor according to gender[7]. Each member of the family knew what task they were supposed to perform in the economic productivity and distribution of the family resources, so as to ensure the material prosperity of the group. At present, the situation has changed due to socio-economic and political factors, such as the introduction of formal employment.

In conclusion, each African community has its own culture although there are broad similarities in norm, values, practices, beliefs and customs. However, cultural chauvinism brought to the African continent by European colonizers and their Christian missionary associates changed the situation. The newcomers denigrated African culture through the introduction of western education and Christianity. Many of the African elite received the European system of education. Although African cultures have remarkably resisted this onslaught and are reviving a broad ranging process of culture liberation and renaissance[8], a considerable gap exists between rhetorical expressions of pride in African cultures and the practical application of cultural resources in addressing the challenges confronting Africa today especially on the issue of governance.

Religion

Religion is a system of beliefs, values, symbols and practices which give meaning to individuals, groups, society as a whole and to the cosmos – all these with reference to some ultimate reality[9]. According to Mugambi, religion is one of the six pillars or components of culture. The others include politics, economics, ethics, aesthetics and kinship[10]. Politics has to do with patterns of decision making and distribution of social influence. Economics incorporates mechanisms for owning and distribution of resources. Ethics determines the values that govern social conduct. Aesthetics is founded on the notion of beauty (shapes and colors). Kinship determines social relationships.

Ninian Smart[11] has pointed out that religion has several dimensions. These are, the mythical dimensions that entail the significant historical events of a community to which they explain their origins, values, beliefs and practices that reinforce meaning. All rituals have symbolic meanings that emphasize communal identity and self-understanding. The system of values (both right and wrong), are articulated by the ethical dimension. All ethics in African society is centered on maintaining social harmony.

Experiential dimension is based on the individual's experience with the ultimate reality (God, or the "other"). The doctrinal dimension spells out the system or structured beliefs that are significant for religious traditions. Religion therefore is one of the most important elements of culture which determines the way of life of the people. Culture embodies norms and values, while religion is one of the value determinants. If religion is an integral part of culture, there is need to explain the role and function religion fulfills in the cultural matrix. This chapter focuses on the political domain.

The Functions of Religion in the Cultural Matrix

R.K. Merton[12] distinguishes between manifest and latent functions of religion. A manifest function is open and evident to actors themselves, the reason they acknowledge for maintaining the institution. The latent function is a hidden function which is neither intended nor recognized by the actors. In this case, individual religious leaders and clerical groups utilize sacred symbols to mobilize the masses for nationalist struggles, internal revolts and election campaigns.

This is possible because religion is the center of the order of symbols, values and beliefs which govern society. Religion provides powerful emotional symbols of group identity which bind people together even in the midst of great opposition. For example, all over Africa, the political elite make use of religious communities for mobilizing voters. In Senegal, the influence wielded by *marabouts* or Islamic holy men belonging to the main Sufi brotherhoods has been recognized as a source of political influence for decades[13]. Similarly, during the liberation war in Zimbabwe, the advice of mediums said to be possessed by spirits of ancestors played a vital role in securing the support of the population. In these two cases, religion serves as a vehicle of political mobilization through the enormous power of its symbols.

In the manifest functions, religion could either be ambivalent and limiting or constructive. The African experience shows that religion can be dangerous to human liberties of believers and non believers alike. It can threaten democratic principles, freedom and peace of public life and easily shatter the fragile moral bonds holding human societies together. Further, Tarimo and Manelo[14] have observed that despite their exhortation on peace, in practice religion has served to ferment endless conflicts. Most often, religious differences stimulate an attitude of dehumanizing the enemies in order to justify violence. This is true of fundamentalist groups among both Christians and Muslims.

Religion also has a positive role. It furnishes people with a sense of identity and a direction in life. Mol[15] posits that one of the main functions of religion is to provide personal identity. He argues that humans have a fundamental need for an identity. Mol defines religion as a 'sacralization' of identity and he presents three types of identity: personal, group and social identity. Personal identity relates to the meaning each person finds in life. Mysticism emphasizes personal identity. Group identity involves attachment to one or more particular groups. Sectarianism emphasizes group identity. Social identity refers to the place a person has in society at large. The established religion of a church which is integrated into the social structure of a society emphasizes social identity.

Resacralizing the Public Domain: The Case of *Mũngĩkĩ*

On the interplay between religion and politics in the public space, Stephen Ellis and Gerrie Ter Haar have observed that:

> ...religious ideas provide people with the means of becoming social and political actors[16].

Religion has been a central factor in the politics of state formation in many parts of Africa. Studies of the early colonial period in Kenya demonstrate the active role of religious based ideologies and organizations in mobilizing people to rebel against foreign rule. For example, the cults of *Mumbo, Dini ya Msambwa and Karīng'a* movements were main actors in the fight against colonial rule as they mobilized citizens to win political power from colonial administration. In this context, the citizens ritualized their struggle through religion.

There are a number of factors that trigger the emergence of religious movements, chief among them being the political and economic pressures afflicting society at specific points. The *Karīng'a* movement which was largely concentrated in the Mt. Kenya region emerged out of the political, educational and cultural struggles of the 1920s and 1930s[17]. The Agīkūyū reacted to an oppressive situation that the colonial government and missionaries had created[18]. Like other Africans they had experienced problems of land alienation, forced labor, squatter, unemployment and gross violation of human rights. The missionaries condemned the Agīkūyū tradition and culture by attacking female circumcision, a central feature of the Agīkūyū culture and identity.

The Agīkūyū religion and culture played the primary role in the development of the *Karīng'a* movement. Nine[19] Agīkūyū cultural and religious practices were utilized in the development of the movement including the concept of democracy, the sacredness of land, the social spirit of cooperation and communalism, songs (mūthīrīgū), the Agīkūyū concept of God (*Ngai*), oathing, initiation rites, folktales and prophetic tradition inherent in this community's culture. The administration of oaths was both a religious and political act, thus their effectiveness lay in both their traditional and symbolic force. They were for the purpose of creating social and moral solidarity. Oathing involved personal loyalty to the resistance movement backed by powerful mystical sanction[20]. The Mau Mau used these mystically sanctioned oaths to enforce strict adherence to the movement.

In the post independence period movements that claim to be religious have emerged in the public realm of many African countries with important political implications. These include the Lord's Resistance Army of John Kony in Uganda, the *Naprama* movement in Mozambique and the *Mūngīkī* movement in Kenya[21] with a large following in the Mt. Kenya region.

Mūngīkī emerged in the early 1990s as a religious movement at a moment of transition in the country from single party to a multiparty state. Even with the return to multiparty politics in 1992, authoritarianism persisted along with the entrenched socio-economic deprivation of the majority of Kenyans. Accordingly, it is within this context of poor economic performance, ineffectual provision of basic services, the collapse of social infrastructure, unbridled accumulation of power by the elite and ethnic violence, that *Mūngīkī* emerged.

The loss of identity implicit in the aforementioned situation led the youth to form *Mūngīkī*. A large number of this socially marginalized youth embraced conflict in a desperate search for empowerment. They combined a religio-cultural identity with a political agenda. *Mūngīkī* had the Agīkūyū tradition, religion and culture as its basis. It advocated a politics of cultural emancipation and clearly showed that spiritual liberation requires political liberation. The *Mūngīkī* youth emerged as a relatively coherent social group with cultural forms, such as sniffing tobacco, reggae music and keeping dreadlocks. They tended to be strongly anti-establishment and rebellious towards authority and were critical of the older political leadership.

In 2002, *Mūngīkī* set the agenda of political campaigns within Central Province by persisting on the theme of political position[22] of the youth in political systems. They demanded that politicians take into consideration the fate of the Kikuyu in the Rift Valley especially those affected by the ethnic cleansings of the 1990's.

Several scholars have sought out specific trajectories to explain the origin the *Mūngīkī* movement. The first is Grace Wamue's[23] analysis of *Mūngīkī* as a religio-cultural movement which calls for a return to African traditions and spiritualism as a means of resolving social problems. In this trajectory, religion is used as a tool for political mobilization.

Peter Kagwanja[24] in his analysis of *Mūngīkī* has criticized the overemphasis on its religious character to the exclusion of its political one. *Mūngīkī* has also been characterized as the local manifestation of anti-globalization forces. Terisa Turner and Leigh Brown Hill writing from a universalist, materialist standpoint suggest that *Mūngīkī* is part of an international movement "for globalization from below to rebuild civil commons"[25]. In their view, *Mūngīkī* as the claimants to Mau Mau heritage, are part of a grassroots movement of those at the margins of society. However, Anderson[26] argues that the movement is so deeply implicated in the politics of violence and vigilantism, and should not be termed as a religio-cultural movement or as a political voice of the Kenyan under class.

Subsequently, Anderson and Kagwanja provide the third view of *Mūngĩkĩ* as a criminal gang and vigilante.

This last interpretation conforms to the dominant public image of the movement in the print and the electronic media. In May 2007 the National Rainbow Coalition Government (NARC) led by President Mwai Kibaki embarked on a major crackdown of *Mūngĩkĩ* movement following a spate of attacks on public service vehicles (*matatus*) by its members[27]. Targeted killings of *matatu* owners, drivers and touts occurred in Nairobi and the Mt. Kenya region, sparked off by the decision of the *Mūngĩkĩ* to increase a daily fee they had been collecting from the *matatu* operators. In response, the *matatu* owners appealed to the government for protection against the group. The government responded by arresting members of the movement and in retaliation, members of the movement killed two chiefs in the Mt. Kenya region.

In the post election violence of 2008 that pitted the supporters of Orange Democratic Movement (ODM) against those of Party of National Unity (PNU) and in which approximately 1500 people died and 600,000 were displaced, ODM leaders alleged that PNU was mobilizing *Mūngĩkĩ* to undertake revenge attacks in Nairobi and in the Rift Valley. These allegations were strengthened by reports that gangs made up of Kikuyu youths identifying themselves as *Mūngĩkĩ* had attacked supporters of ODM in Nairobi and Naivasha[28]. The involvement of *Mūngĩkĩ* in the post-election violence remains largely a matter of speculation. The association of *Mūngĩkĩ* with violence has influenced public perception of Kikuyu youth who are consequently accused of engaging in criminal activities.

The title *Mūngĩkĩ* is invoked by various groups to achieve particular ends. It is invoked by the police to justify crackdowns and executions of suspected criminals. Once a suspect is labeled *Mūngĩkĩ,* there is less likelihood of public scrutiny on the circumstances of their killing[29]. For instance in November 2007, the Kenya National Commission on Human Rights[30] released a report suggesting that the police had executed about 500 suspected *Mūngĩkĩ* members between June and October of the same year. The Kenyan public that dreads *Mūngĩkĩ* criticized the Human Rights group for producing this alarming report.

Under such circumstances the Mt. Kenya region youth are disillusioned, have lost hope for the future, and view the society as hostile towards them. They are unwilling to participate in the agricultural sector because of low returns and consequently there is an influx of the youth into urban areas such as Nyeri, Thika, Maua, Embu, Meru, Ruiru and Kiambu towns among others, in search of livelihood. As a result, urban neighborhoods are being transformed into youth enclaves that foster criminality and pose security threats.

Conclusion

There is a clear indication that religion and culture continue to exert a very pervading influence on the lives of people and on the character of social, political and economic institutions. Culture and religion provide identity of individuals and groups giving them purpose and meaning. Religion gives support and sustains certain values which form part of a culture which in turn defines identity. From the example of *Mūngīkī*, people strengthen their identity by discovering their religious traditions. At the same time, religious beliefs help to develop mobilizing ideologies of opposition and self expression. Thus, any theory of political, social and economic change (social transformation) must recognize the significance of religio-cultural factors.

There is need to recognize the role of religion and culture in the formulation of social policy. In its constructive role, religion can challenge forms of social injustices thus acting as a force for social transformation.

Religion is also a key player in social reconciliation and peace building as justice and peace values form part of the basic teachings of most religions. In peace building, religion serves as a bridge between social groups in supporting social interaction and mutual care. These activities enhance friendship and solidarity. In addition, religious institutions such as churches and mosques perform a number of social and educational functions to compliment the efforts of the state. In Kenya, in the last decades religious groups have taken the responsibility of providing the citizenry with civic education in order to prepare them to participate in the realization of a democratic system of governance. Thus, religion has to be considered while formulating policies relating to the youth.

Knowledge of African culture is prerequisite for any social transformation. One of the greatest challenges in many African countries, Kenya included, is that the elites do not receive formal instruction in indigenous cultures. They tend to look down on these cultures as "primitive" in line with the perspective of their western orientation. This has been a major impediment to the cultural contextualization of governance in the continent. Therefore, African culture, values and worldviews need to be reconciled with other perspectives (western) while formulating new social and political frameworks relating particularly to the youth.

There is an urgent need to address the socio-economic and political factors that lead to the alienation of the youth. One of the major challenges is poverty which leads the youth to engage in anti-social behavior such as the criminal activities associated with members of the *Mũngĩkĩ* movement. The youth also migrate to towns where they are attracted by illusory allure of urban affluence and abundance. The informal settlements in the Mt. Kenya region today stand as monumental symbols of the depravity and immorality resulting from all this.

In order to reduce poverty the following measures are essential. There is need to consider the natural and human resources available in the Mt. Kenya region. The region has abundant arable land and natural resources (rivers and forests) which can be harnessed for increased productivity. Providing land and credit facility to the youth will enable them participate in the economic development of the region. The recently initiated Youth Enterprise Fund will go a long way in changing the economic status of the youth in rural areas. The credit facility if properly utilized will enable the youth to start income generating, small-scale enterprises. The youth should also be provided with non-formal education and skills training to reduce unemployment by equipping them with knowledge and life skills to be utilized in the entrepreneurial sector. Such skills include carpentry, leather work, tailoring, radio and mobile phone repair, handicrafts, making and mending fish nets (for the newly introduced fish farming in the region). These skills will entrench the idea and practice of self-employment. Moreover, the youth will enjoy a vast forum to display their creativity. Training on responsible leadership should also be an integral part of the non-formal education. This will prepare the youth for leadership. For practical purposes, responsibility should be delegated to them.

Kenya is a sporting nation. There is a high potential for sportsmen and women in the Mt. Kenya region. However, there is no specific policy to govern sports. The government in collaboration with stakeholders in the region should develop a comprehensive policy on sports. Such a policy should provide a framework for identifying and nurturing sportsmen and women in all disciplines. The policy should stipulate the method of recognizing and honoring the young men and women who bring fame to the country at the international level. This will act as incentive to the youth who in turn look to sports and games as lucrative career activities.

We must also encourage the youth in the Mt. Kenya region to form cultural groups to promote visual and performing arts. These groups could provide information and education through performances on health, including information on HIV/AIDS and dangers of drugs and substance abuse; economic, political, social and developmental issues. The artists can take a token as a wage for performing and others by selling art work. The performing groups can be assisted by the different counties in the region to hold workshops, festivals and exhibitions intended to tap artistic talents among the youth.

There is need to develop a reintegration program for the marginalized youth – particularly those who are members of the *Mūngīkī* movement. Such a program should provide skills training for self-employment as stipulated in this text. *Mūngīkī's* associational life can be harnessed for positive results. Their network can, for example, be utilized for the establishment of business cooperatives to empower the youth.

Notes

[1] Kathryn W. (ed) (1997) *Identity and Difference* Sage Publications, London.

[2] National Youth Policy Steering Committee (NYPCS) (2003) Draft of the National Youth Policy, *East African Standard* 21st Nov 24-5.

[3] Shorter A. (1998) *African Culture: An Overview* Paulines Publications, Nairobi.

[4] Mazrui A. *Cultural Forces in World Politics* James Curry, London (Pg7 -13).

[5] Huntington S.P. (2003) *The Clash of Civilization and the Remaking of World Order* Simon and Schuster, New York.

[6] Kenyatta J. (1938) *Facing Mt .Kenya*. Martin Secker and Warburg Ltd, London p.133.

[7] Ibid pg. 53.

[8] Deng F.M. (2008) *Identity, Diversity and Constitutionalism in Africa*, United States Institute of Peace Press, Washington DC.

Dietrich Gabriele(1978) *Culture, Religion and Development.* Sidma Press, Madrass p.14

[10] Mugambi J. (1999) *"Religion and the Social Transformation of Africa"* in Magesa L. and Nathamburi Z. (eds). *Democracy and Reconciliation: A Challenge for African Christianity.* Acton Press, Nairobi. (p.73-96). Also Mugambi (1989) *African Heritage and Contemporary Christianity.* Longman, Nairobi.

[11] Smart N. (1969) *Religious Experience of Mankind,.* Charles Scribners Sons, New York.

[12] Merton R.K (1975) *Social Theory and Social Structure.* Free press, Glencoe.

[13] O'Brien D.B.(1975) *Saints and Politicians: Essays in the Organization of Senegalese Peasants Society ,* Cambridge University Press, Cambridge.

[14] Tarimo A. and Manelo P.(2007) *Africa Peacemaking and Governance,* Acton Publishers, Nairobi P. 92.

[15] MoL H. (1980) *Identity and Sacred. A sketch for a New Social-Scientific Theory of Religion,* Basil Blackwell, Oxford p. 8.

[16] Stephen E. and Ter Haar G (2004) W*orlds of Power: Religious Thought and Practical Practice in Africa,* Oxford University Press, New York.

[17] Roseberg C and Nottingham R. (1966) *The Myth of Mau Mau: Nationalism in Kenya,* East African Publishing House, Nairobi, Tignor R. L(1976) *The Colonial Transformation of Kenya* Princeton University Press, New Jersey and Kanogo T.(1987) *Histories of the Hanged: The Dirty War in Kenya and the End of the Empire,* W.W. Norton, New York.

[18] Kamuyu wa Kangethe (1981) The role of the Agĩkũyũ Religion and Culture in the Development of the Karinga Religio-Political Movement 1900-1950, with particular reference to the Agĩkũyũ Concept of God and the Rite of Initiation, Unpublished Phd Thesis, Kenyatta University.

[19] Ibid.

[20] Gecaga M. (2007) "Religious Movements and Democratization in Kenya: Between the Sacred and the Profane". Murunga G. and Nasongo S. (eds) Kenya: The Struggle for Democracy Council for the Development of Social Science Research in Africa (CODESRIA) Zed books, London p. 59.

[21] Ibid p.59.

158 TOWARDS INCLUSIVE DEVELOPMENT IN KENYA

[22] Maupeu H. (2005) Religion and the Elections in the Maupeu. The Moi Succession in the 2002 Elections in Kenya. Trans Africa Press, Nairobi.

[23]Wamue G. (2001) "Revisiting our Indigenous Shrines Through Mūngīkī" *African Affairs Volume* 100 p.453-457. Anderson D. (2002) "Vigilantes Violence and Politics of Public Order in Kenya", *African Affairs Vol. 101 p.531-555 no. 405* Kagwanja P. (2003) "Facing Mt. Kenya or Facing Mecca? The Mūngīkī Ethnic Violence and Politics of Moi Succession 1987-2002", African Affairs Vol 102 p.25-49

[24] Kagwanja P. (2003) "Facing Mt. Kenya or Facing Mecca? The Mūngīkī Ethnic Violence and Politics of Moi Succession 1987-2002", *African Affairs Vol. 102.*

[25] Turner T.E. and Brown Hill L.S.(2001) "African Jubilee. Mau Mau Resurgence and the Fight for Fertility in Kenya, 1986-2002", *Canadian Journal of Development Studies , Vol. 22* (1037-88).

[26] Anderson D. (2002) *Vigilantes Violence and Politics of Public Order in Kenya,* African affairs Vol. 101 N o. 405.

[27] Ruteere M. (2008) *Dilemmas of Crime, Human Rights and the Politics of Mūngīkī Violence in Kenya.* Occasional Paper 01/08. Kenya Human Rights Institute, Nairobi.

[28] Ibid.

[29] Ibid.

[30] Ibid.

Integrating Tourism with Rural Development Strategies in Western Kenya

George Otieno Obonyo & Erick Victor Onyango Fwaya

Introduction

Tourism is widely recognized for its tangible, as well as less tangible outcomes. According to Hall and Brown (2002), tourism is one of the central means through which rural areas can adjust themselves economically, socially and politically to the new global environment. This contention has triggered increasing focus on tourism by primary producers and rural communities as an alternative means of achieving sustainable economic growth and development. Rural areas in this context refers to geographical areas in which primary production takes place and where populations are found in varying densities (Viljoen & Tlabela, 2007).

Rural development is considered indispensable for the overall progress of any developing country because very high percentages of people in these countries reside in rural areas (Barrera & Muñoz, 2003). Kenya, like other developing countries, faces the challenge of improving the lives of her rural folks and despite the existence of certain projects and programs meant for rural development, little success has been recorded. Poverty, food insecurity, unemployment and poor infrastructure are still key challenges faced by rural communities. Basic services such as primary education, health care, safe drinking water and roads remain deficient making it difficult to achieve the Millennium Development Goals (MDGs). Tourism is regarded as the best option for improving the living standards of the people particularly those living in rural areas (Barrera & Muñoz, 2003) because of the steadily increasing numbers of tourists visiting the countryside.

However, consideration of tourism as an instrument of development in rural areas has been ignored for several years by governments of most developing countries. Tourism has been concentrated in prestigious areas of these countries (Cabrini, 2002). Only until very recently have some governments in developing countries, including Kenya, started appreciating the role tourism can play in the development of rural areas. This paper focuses on developing rural areas through various forms of tourism that can be integrated into broader rural development strategies in western Kenya.

Tourism and Rural Development

The countryside is increasingly being viewed as a commodity that can be marketed by the tourism industry and consumed by the tourist (Kneafsey, 2001). Many countries have incorporated tourism into their economies in order to achieve even development in both urban and rural regions (Hall & Page, 2002; Briedenhann & Wickens, 2004). The most important factors to consider in this balancing act are rural environment, rural population and natural products. All these factors are known to contribute to the particularities of recreation, gastronomy, culture and ecology that rural tourism generally offers (Tane & Thierheimer, 2009).

Rural development strategy and programs in most developing countries reinforce the need for consistent growth, while conserving natural resources for present and future generations (Ashley, 2000; Cabrini, 2002). Tane and Thierheimer (2009) identified four main objectives for rural development strategies and programs: to increase agricultural productivity; to expand farm and non-farm income earnings and food security; to reduce disease and ignorance; and to achieve sustainable natural resource management. Tourism is regarded as a viable tool in achieving all these objectives provided that both the targeted final consumers of tourism and the local community are considered (Kim, Chen, & Lang, 2006). Tourism is emphasized in this case not only as a foreign exchange earner but also as a source of employment (Reeder & Brown, 2005), and a means by which rural communities can achieve their livelihoods if well planned and incorporated.

Sharpley and Sharpley (2006) define rural tourism as a state of mind, and technically, according to activities, destinations and other measurable, tangible characteristics. The Organisation for Economic Co-operation and Development (OCDE, 1994) states that this form of tourism varies from one country to another using various channels of rural tourism. These include interest in farms, nature, adventure, health, education, arts, and heritage (Bramwell and Lane in Jolliffe & MacDonald, 2003) and experiencing living history such as rural customs, folklore, local traditions, beliefs, and common heritage (Pedford in Jolliffe & MacDonald, 2003). Haghsetan, Mahmoudi and Maleki (2011) believe that in order to develop rural areas through tourism, it is important to first develop rural tourism because this is a strategy for improving economic and social life of poor villagers. This is attributed to the fact that rural tourism possesses strong social and economic potential, does not only involve local actors in sustainable resource use, but also generates new income sources and improves life conditions (Barrera & Muñoz, 2003; Aranda, Combariza & Parrado, 2009).

Viljoen and Tlabela (2007) explain that rural tourism is a way of involving ventures that feature local ownership and management of tourism facilities within a given touristic destination. This can be achieved by developing tourism in rural areas in order to increase participation of the poor in the development of tourism, thus bringing wider benefits to the areas (Holland, Burian & Dexy, 2003). Holland, Burian and Dexy (2003) further argue that, since the success of tourism development depends on commercial, economic and logistical issues (such as the quality of the product, accessibility and infrastructure of the destination, availability of skills and interest of investors), rural areas may well be at a disadvantage. This is attributed to what Kay (2008) refers to as "Urban Bias" (UB). Therefore, successful development of rural areas through tourism requires the involved parties to overcome this notion and develop tourism products that fulfill both the needs of the tourists and the local people (Rogerson & Visser, 2004).

Method
This article is based on research conducted principally through focus group discussions, in order to obtain in-depth information describing integration of tourism with rural development. Dean (1994) contends that a focus group is an informal, small-group discussion designed to obtain in-depth qualitative information, and is an excellent method to study processes. Participants were derived from hospitality and tourism organizations in the region, Community Based Organizations (CBOs), Non-Governmental Organizations (NGOs), and local business persons associated with tourism and concerned with rural development in Western Kenya. More specifically, the focus

groups explored rural development concerns, the various forms of tourism that can be integrated with rural development strategies and the mode for integrating tourism with rural development.

Participants were asked to discuss, in detail, their ideas of rural development through tourism, the various forms of tourism suitable for stimulating rural development and entrepreneurship in Western Kenya, tourism development strategies and how to integrate them with rural development, and the resultant benefit from the integration process as a whole. Great care was taken in selecting focus group participants, formulating the questions, and training moderators and assistant moderators for the discussions. Thirty participants were obtained for focus group discussions (FGD) from each of the ten counties in the region. Each of the NGOs and CBOs selected had been involved in rural development in the region for at least five years. Three focus group discussions were conducted, one with NGOs representatives, another with CBOs representatives, and the other with local business persons associated with tourism.

The discussions with local business persons associated with tourism consisted of three hotel managers, three tourism development and marketing officers, two tour operators in the region and one entrepreneur and businessperson. CBO representatives in the discussions included three youth and three women from development organizations and three farmer representatives in the region. The NGO group included three members concerned with poverty reduction, one member in the education sector, three members engaged in food security and two members with health service delivery in the region. The average number of participants for each focus group discussion was nine and the duration of the discussion ranged from one hour and 15 minutes to approximately two hours. Different sets of questions and focus group protocols were developed for the focus group participants. During the training sessions for moderators and assistant moderators, participants composed lists of guiding questions and probes for the three categories of discussants. The principal investigators and an extension specialist then reviewed and revised the questions and probes which were then pre-tested and further revised. Focus group moderators and assistant moderators included the principal investigators, and regional hospitality and tourism specialists. Additionally, the principal investigators with the help of extension specialists developed a set of focus group procedures that helped guarantee reliability and consistency across the focus groups. All the focus group discussions were tape-recorded. The assistant moderators took notes during every focus group discussion session. Debriefings were conducted and field notes were compiled as soon as possible after each focus group discussion.

Results and Discussion

Focus group discussion results clearly indicated the importance of tourism in rural development. Rural development concerns that can be addressed through tourism as identified by the focus group participants were poverty, unemployment, food insecurity, inadequate infrastructure, health, and education facilities. The results suggest the following six rural tourism channels as a way of integrating tourism with rural development strategies – community based tourism, agro-tourism, culture and heritage tourism, nature based and adventure tourism, and ecotourism.

Community Based Tourism (CBT)

According to the Kenya Ministry of Tourism, community based tourism is a growing sector globally, which currently accounts for 5% of the global tourism market. This is due to the increasing number of tourists who want to interact with the local communities and to stay in places that positively impact on both the environment and the local population (Viljoen & Naicker, 2000). Focus group participants felt that in order to develop and promote community based tourism, the community involved should be appealing to tourists. It is therefore the responsibility of the local community to strive to make their communities attractive to tourists. However, other participants felt that the local government also had a role to play in this process through such initiatives as beautification campaigns and zoning. Lack of cooperation from local government was seen by participants as a way of creating problems such as unattractive environments making community efforts useless in the long run.

Many participants felt that considerable positive local outcomes and benefits may flow from community involvement through ownership of tourism projects in the area. They proposed provision of land leases as one of the strategies towards tourism project ownership. Participants believed that communities can improve their standard of living through increased revenue obtained from wages, land leases and development funds channelled towards tourism project development. One participant observed that "community members can be employed and trained in the tourism projects and benefit from wages, community development funds and involvement in spin off enterprise." Another felt that by participating in such tourism projects, the local community can build schools, provide safe drinking water and construct health facilities for its people.

Participants opined that the central government must be willing to support community involvement in the various tourism projects in order for the local communities to maximize benefits from tourism activities. Ndlovu and Rogerson (2004), highly recommend government involvement in community support initiatives. One participant said that "there is need for the central government to diversify the tourism product by supporting new and existing ventures, projects and initiatives, and to facilitate sustainable tourism development and enhanced product quality in the rural areas." Another proposed that central government assistance should include identifying, supporting and funding community tourism projects in the rural areas. As one respondent noted, "it is important that water and sewer services appropriate for hotels and restaurants are developed and that proper infrastructure is in place to ensure smooth operation of business and to enhance product quality and experience generated for the tourists." Tourism support facilities, including education and training centres, should be made accessible to the local community to enable maintenance of tourism service quality and high quality customer service delivery. This in turn will ensure sustainability of tourism businesses and therefore long term benefits for the local people.

There was consensus amongst participants that in order to encourage participation of every community member in CBT, special education and training programs should be created to involve older people in the delivery of services. If the older people are involved in the process, this would reduce their over-dependence on support from people living in the urban areas as this could be the means to earn their livelihoods. Through CBT, the participants believed that the local communities may earn income as land managers, entrepreneurs (e.g., handcraft, restaurant owners, hotel and resort owners), service and produce providers (e.g., suppliers of farm produce to the various hotels within the community), and employees in the various tourism facilities established within the community. "Sometimes, part of the tourist income could be set aside for projects which provide benefits to the community as a whole; in this way, everyone in the community can benefit from CBT projects," said one of the participants. In Kenya, the community based tourism concept is just taking root and there is need to harness this product and market it in a more cohesive and systematic manner throughout the entire rural Kenya.

Nature Based Tourism

The World Travel and Tourism Council estimates that 7% of international tourism sales are spent on nature tourism. Nature based tourism can be defined as visitation to natural or near natural areas (Richards & Hall, 2000; Holden, 2000). These include ecotourism and adventure tourism. Ecotourism is a component of nature based tourism, with a focus on education and interpretation of the natural and cultural environment. Ecotourism is an instrument for natural protection and at the same time assures sustainable economic benefits for local people (Hall & Brown, 2000). The concept of ecotourism explains mutual relations established between tourists, environment and culture which not only bring important benefits to the local economy, but also insure the conditions for a long-term development and maximum recreational satisfaction for tourists (Hodur, Leistritz, & Wolfe 2005). According to Strasdas (2002), the main objective of ecotourism is to create high quality tourism, while protecting the environment and stimulating the durable local development, that can be achieved by activating financial resources, realizing the environmental education, and involving local communities.

Discussants outlined several activities related to adventure and nature based tourism that both tourists and local communities can benefit from. While tourists would enjoy the natural scenery in the region, the local community could provide requisite services as tour guides, translators, story-tellers, and in providing food, beverages, and accommodation. Income resulting from these activities will create the possibility of developing the needed infrastructure to develop rural areas of western Kenya and also be directed towards both environment protection and other local developments.

When it comes to this form of tourism, participants from CBOs considered it necessary to involve the local population when organizing tourist activities, not only as beneficiaries of obtained profits, but also as implementers of the tourist developments in their areas. These forms of rural tourism are understood as parts of environmental, sociological and economic categories (Hodur, Leistritz & Wolfe, 2005). As an economic category it crucially contributes to sustainable rural development while at the same time it is a motor of development. As a sociological category, it contributes to higher awareness of the public on the importance of protecting nature, and at the same time, visitors have the impression of protection and maintenance of local communities' social activities. As an economic category these forms of tourism assure promotion and marketing of products from protected areas such as nature, cultural heritage, clean water, fresh air, local authentic products (also from ecological farming).

Cultural and Heritage Tourism

The National Trust for Historic Preservation's (NTHP) defines cultural heritage tourism as travelling to experience the places, artefacts and activities that authentically represent the stories and people of the past and present. It includes cultural, historic and natural resources. Touristic activities associated with cultural and heritage tourism were identified as experiencing cultural environments including landscapes, the visual and performing arts and special lifestyles, values, traditions, and events. Specifically, various activities that could be of interest to tourists include festivals and events, traditional music and dance, village and rural life (e.g. farms, local market activities), gastronomy, visiting/tasting local products, general sightseeing, village buildings and "atmosphere," and visiting historic and religious monuments.

Cultural resources are believed to generate economic vitality by leveraging human capital and culture to generate economic strength through cultural attractions (Newman & Smith, 2000). It was recognized that programs based on cultural resources may restore, revitalize or strengthen a community or neighbourhood by serving as a centrepiece for development and cultural renewal. One participant observed that "the available cultural resources may contribute to an area's 'innovativeness' by making communities in the area more attractive to highly desirable cultural knowledge-based activities and permitting new forms of knowledge intensive production to flourish." Both the NGO and CBO participants thought that rural communities would be well served to begin efforts in developing cultural and heritage tourism using key elements of strategic planning in order to fully understand local conditions and opportunities and to set a strategic direction. They stressed the importance of empowering local individuals and organizations to take leadership in the strategic planning effort in order to develop culture based tourism that benefits the local community. The participants believed that focusing on the cultural and heritage products will support services, public works, education and training, marketing, planning, management and assessment/evaluation and public policy actions.

Participants from the hospitality and tourism business believed that in order to develop and enhance cultural and heritage tourism, it is important for those involved in tourism planning and development to clearly distinguish rural tourism products on offer. They suggested full participation of tourism stakeholders to ensure that products on offer are unique. Two ways were proposed to achieve this – enhancing and renovating historic buildings, monuments, museums, archaeological and historical sites, and developing special events and festivals related to local culture including food, dance, music or economic activities of the region. Developing minority cultural heritage facilities and programs according to some of the respondents would also ensure that the minority groups often overlooked by the government in developmental activities are part and parcel of tourism development in a given rural region. This in turn they believed, would make this group of people feel appreciated and thus more willing to participate in rural development initiatives through tourism. In order to achieve this successfully and throughout all seasons, the quality of the tourism products on offer should be emphasized. High quality of local products on offer would ensure that the region establishes itself as a unique touristic destination.

Government involvement in development of small and medium sized touristic businesses that focus on locally themed items is very important. Government participation, the groups noted, could be through provision of soft loans to the local community involved in such businesses to enable sale of these products as souvenirs to tourists. Other than ensuring employment for the local people, this will encourage a culture of self-dependency and local cultural identity preservation. Participants from the hospitality and tourism industry felt that continued support of businesses such as local restaurants, hotels, and souvenir shops by government, is critical in ensuring sustainability and viability of such businesses in the rural areas. Educating and training local populations in cultural areas such as conservatory, youth and college-level music, arts and crafts programs etc., will also ensure cultural preservation, community support and involvement, and income generation on the part of the local people. Individual organizations should be assisted in developing grant applications for external support for marketing, branding, and promoting rural regions' cultural/heritage sites and events, as well as related tourism services and non-cultural activities.

Participants were of the opinion that the local community can be involved in the development of a tourism master plan such as airport, hotel complex, roads, sports and leisure facilities and cultural activities to encourage medium-stay by tourists. The community could also get involved in the establishment of tourism guidelines for coordinating and cooperating with other stakeholders in creating strategic partnerships (governments, non-profit organization, and private firms). This in turn will provide support for smaller organizations with minimal budgets in achieving some economies of scale and broadening the programs considered to be part of the cultural and heritage tourism activities. In addition, local communities should also participate in negotiating packaging arrangements (itineraries, support services, regional focus) with a variety of arrangements (cultural products of the same type, cultural products of different types such as festivals, cultural and non-cultural products, hotels, resorts, retail areas, sports and outdoor recreation, amusement attractions).

Agricultural Tourism

Agricultural tourism also known as Agri-tourism or Agro-tourism is a combination of agriculture and tourism, referring to the use of agricultural landscapes and rural space to attract tourists (Liu, 2006). t entails agriculture, forestry, animal husbandry, and fisheries as a wide range of agricultural resource-based development of tourism products that provide special service for tourists (Liu, 2006; Ohe, 2006). This form of tourism acts as a link between the local people and the tourism industry, and also supports the broader tourism industry in its entirety. This is because tourists have to eat while away from home and the raw materials for their food are drawn from agricultural produce in the area visited. Despite underdevelopment in Western Kenya, participants believed that this form of tourism could serve as mitigation to some of the challenges facing the local people in rural areas. The government should improve farming conditions and encourage people to employ sustainable methods of agriculture that attract tourists.

By concentrating their efforts on indigenous food farming, the community could supply various hotels and restaurants with indigenous or organic food products while at the same time alleviating food insecurity in the area. For instance, fish farming could serve as tourist attraction while at the same time generating income and providing food for the local community. The figure below summarizes these ideas:

Conclusion

Rural areas are an integral part of the modern tourism experience. In fact, tourism is considered as a tool for revitalization of rural communities and as part of a bigger picture to bring in money and visitors to communities. By understanding that tourism also plays a role in providing exposure to an area that may attract new residents or investment (if they are seen as attractive), then the industry may be seen as an important player of rural development. The above discussion shows that rural tourism is a very important, probably even the most important, factor for economic development in rural areas and it is a solution for lost working places.

Rural development through tourism calls for coordination of all the stakeholders in the tourism industry with the main focus being on the well-being of the local community. Appropriate policies need to be established to support ventures in rural tourism-related activities. It is therefore important for public policy makers to review the various forms of tourism to be sure that they are pragmatic, to allow rural areas develop in a sustainable manner. The basic concept of tourism in rural areas is thus envisaged in the benefits accruing to local community through entrepreneurial opportunities, income generation, employment opportunities, conservation and development of rural cultural heritage investment for infrastructure development and preservation of the environment and heritage.

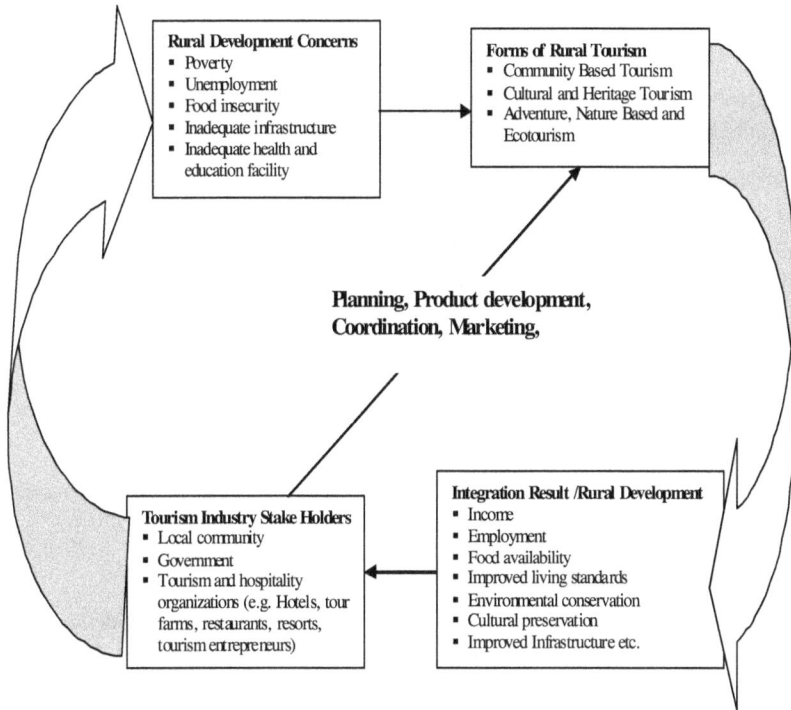

Fig 1: Channels of Tourism Integration with Rural Development

References

Ashley, C. (2000). *The Impacts of Tourism on Rural Livelihoods: Namibia's Experience*. London: Overseas Development Institute.

Barrera, E. and R. Muñoz. (2003). Manual de turismo rural para micro, pequeños y medianos empresarios rurales. Serie de instrumentos técnicos para la microempresa rural. Promerfida, Buenos Aires.

Briedenhann, J., and E. Wickens. (2004). Tourism Routes as a Tool for Economic Development of Rural Areas -Vibrant Hope or Impossible Dream. *Journal of Tourism Management 25:71-79*.

Cabrini, L. (2002). Seminar on Rural tourism in Europe: Experiences and Perspectives, Proceedings of the 2002 Seminar held at Belgrade, World Tourism

Organization. *http://www.world-tourism.org/regional/europe/PDF/rural_en.pdf* (accessed on 29th June 2011)

Equations (2006). From Rural Tourism to Sustainable Rural Tourism History to Current Debates, EQUATIONS, Bangalore, India.

Haghsetan, A., Mahmoudi, B. & Maleki, R. (2011). Investigation of Obstacles and Strategies of Rural Tourism Development Using SWOT Matrix. *Journal of Sustainable Development, Vol. 4, No. 2; April 2011* doi:10.5539/jsd.v4n2p136. Retrieved on 3rd June, 2011 at *http://www.ccsenet.org/jsd*

Hall, D., & Brown, F., (2000). *Tourism In Peripheral Areas*. Clevedon: Channel View.

Hall, C.M., & Page, J.S. (2002). *The Geography of Tourism and Recreation: Environment, Place and Space*. London & New York: Rutledge.

Hodur, N.M., Leistritz, EL. & Wolfe, K.L., (2005). Assessing the economic development potential of nature tourism. *Great Plains Research 15:279-96.*

Holden A., (2000). *"Environment and Tourism"*. London: Routledge.

Jolliffe, L. & MacDonald, R. (2003). Cultural Rural Tourism: Evidence from Canada, *Annals of Tourism Research, Vol.30, No. 2, pp. 307–322*

Kay, C. (2008). Reflections on Rural Development and Development Strategies: Exploring Synergies, Eradicating Poverty. Inaugural Address delivered on 4 December 2008 at the Institute of Social Studies, The Hague, Netherlands.

Kim, H.1., Chen, M.H., & Lang, S.C. (2006). Tourism expansion and economic development: The case of Taiwan. *Journal of Tourism Management 27:925-33.*

Kneafsey, M. (2001). Rural Cultural Economy: Tourism and Social Relations, *Annals of Tourism Research, Vol. 28, No. 3, pp. 762–783*

Liu, C.Z. (2006). *Agro-tourism and Rural Planning,* Paper presented at the Asian Productivity Organization Seminar. June 20 - 27, Taiwan, ROC.

OCDE (1994). *Tourism Strategies and Rural Development: General Distribution.* Organisation for Economic Co-Operation and Development OCDE/GD (94)49, Paris. 013927

Ohe, Y. (2006). *Concept and approaches in the Development of Agro-Tourism.* Paper presented at the Asian Productivity Organization Seminar. June 20 - 27, Taiwan, ROC.

Richards, G., & Hall D., (2000). *"Tourism and Sustainable Community Development"*. New York: Rutledge.

Reeder, R.J., & Brown, D.M. (2005). *Recreation, Tourism,and Rural Well-Being*. Economic Research Report No.7. Washington, DC: USDA, Economic Research Service.

Rogerson, C.M., Visser, G. (2004). *Tourism and Development Issues in Contemporary South Africa*. Pretoria: Africa Institute.

Strasdas, W. (2002). *The Ecotourism Manual for Protected Area Managers*, Germany Foundation for International Development (DSE), Germany.

Tane, N., Thierheimer, W. (2009). *The Connection between Different Rural Tourism Types and Forms*, in the Proceedings of the 4th Aspects and Visions of Applied Economics and Informatics, March 26 - 27. 2009, Debrecen, Hungary.

Viljoen, J. & Tlabela, K. (2007). Rural Tourism Development in South Africa: Trends and Challenges. Human Science Research Council Press, Cape Town, South Africa. Retrieved on 2nd July, 2011 at *http://www.hsrcpress.ac.za*.

World Tourism Organization (2003). Seminar on Rural Tourism: Pathway to Sustainable Development, Proceedings of the Seminar held at Kielce, World Tourism Organization. Available at *http://www.world-tourism.org/regional/europe/pdf/conclusions%20* (Accessed on 13th June 2011).

HIV as a Delimiting Factor for Development in the Lake Basin Region

Introduction

Nyanza region in Kenya continues to lead other regions in HIV prevalence with more than twice the national prevalence rate recorded in Kenya Demographic and Health Survey (2009). This scenario may contribute negatively on the development arena, especially within the context of infant and child mortality rates, wealth quintile, demographic and socio-cultural development. This study explored the visual linkages that exist between HIV prevalence in Nyanza and selected key developmental issues. The study adopted use of secondary data from the latest Kenya Demographic and Health Survey coupled with empirical evidence generated using common search engines to support the visual linkages identified. The results show highly significant proportional differences in HIV prevalence, highest wealth quintile, fertility rates, male circumcision, infant and child mortality rates when Nyanza region proportions are compared to national proportions. The study established bi-directional visual linkages between HIV prevalence and developmental indicators. In conclusion, negative developmental factors such as wife inheritance and low acceptance rate for male circumcision, infant and child mortality rates exist in Nyanza region where HIV prevalence is also high. However, the causal research linking HIV prevalence to selected development indicators are chronically lacking within this region and need to be given a critical thinking.

Despite the fact that Kenya continues to experience a notable decline in HIV prevalence attributed in part to significant behavioral change and increased access to anti-retroviral drugs, Nyanza region continues to lead other regions with more than twice the national prevalence rate, currently. National adult HIV prevalence is estimated to have fallen from 10 percent in the late 1990s to about 5.7 percent in 2010 (Kenya National Bureau of Statistics (KNBS) and ICF Macro, 2010). This prevalence is quite high among women who are also considered to face considerably higher risk of HIV infection than men, and probably experience a shorter life expectancy due to HIV and AIDS. Reasons attributed to this are not clear with a lot of emphasis pointing fingers on socio-cultural factors (e.g. male circumcision and wife inheritance), heath, wealth/poverty, demographic and economic related factors.

One study which focused on wife inheritance and the risk of HIV in Bondo district (Agot *et al.,* 2010) found that when age and level of formal education were adjusted, both widows who were inherited by non-relatives (OR = 2.07; 95% CI 1.49-2.86) and by relatives (OR = 1.34; 95% CI1.07-1.70) for sexual rituals, were more likely to be infected with HIV. This was not the case for widows who were inherited by relatives for companionship (OR = 0.85; 95%CI 0.63-1.14). The implication could be that high risk with regard to wife inheritance also depends on the nature of inheritance. In this paper, wife inheritance is referred to as negative social development, since it is a major risk factor in HIV infection as evident in many studies within the East African region (Luginaah *et al.,* 2005; Oywa, 1995; Malungo, 2001). Some of the studies were conducted among the Luo community in South-West and Northern Uganda (Mabumba *et al.,* 2007; Okeyo and Allen, 1994). Male circumcision is another socio-cultural developmental factor with positive effects on reduction of the prevalence of HIV. Although, a lot of debate surrounds the effectiveness of this practice, scientific evidence has proved its worth by shedding more light on the big debate. Male circumcision is equated to vaccination or increased condom use, which reduces transmission in both directions by 37% (Williams *et al.,* 2006). This position seemed to be agreed upon by some authors (Baeten *et al.,* 2010) who strongly support low risk of HIV among circumcised men. Unfortunately, some authors still express doubt and provide weak support to this positive practice (Templeton *et al.,* 2010).

The second category of developmental issues in relation to HIV in Nyanza region may probably focus on health indicators for development. In this category, mortality rates assume the locus position while HIV prevalence becomes a key factor. Some studies have attempted to link HIV prevalence with increased mortality rate of children (Stanecki *et al.,* 2010; Adazu *et al.,* 2005; Wekesa, 2000) and that of adults (Adazu *et al.,* 2005) in low and middle income countries and more specifically, in Kenya. HIV is seen as a threat to efforts by countries to reduce under-5 mortality rate (Stanecki *et al.,* 2010) which is a key indicator of negative development that needs quick and urgent interventions. Other issues that surround development include nutritional status of children and adults. Undernourishment in children also signifies negative development. HIV is recognized as an independent modifiable risk factor for poor nutritional outcomes with significant contributions to nutritional outcomes at the individual level (Kimani-Murage *et al.,* 2011), and to both direct and mild effect in worsening children's nutritional status (Nalwoga *et al.,* 2010; Sutcliffe *et al.,* 2011). Fertility rate may have an inverse relationship with HIV prevalence with lower fertility rates in HIV-positive than HIV-negative women (Kongnyuy and Wiysonge, 2008). However, cases of higher fertility rates in populations of high HIV prevalence may be due to replacement phenomenon centred on reduced breastfeeding and increased desire for more children to replace the dead ones (Magadi and Agwanda, 2010).

Socio-economic indicators of development also have a link with HIV prevalence. Unequal progress in health Millennium Development Goals (MDGs) in low-income countries appears significantly related to burdens of HIV (Stuckler *et al.,* 2010). However, HIV prevalence in Sub-Saharan Africa does not exhibit the same pattern of association with poverty as most other diseases (Mishra *et al.,* 2007). It is argued that the changing phases of HIV infection indicate that it is no longer poverty that drives the epidemic but wealth and a number of other socio-demographic factors that explain sexual risk-taking behaviour (Awusabo-Asare and Annim, 2008; Parkhurst, 2010). In low-income sub-Saharan African countries, where poverty is widespread, increasing access to resources for women may initially increase risk of HIV or have no effect on risk-taking behaviour (Wojcicki, 2005).

Based on these series of studies which have focused on the links between HIV and potential socio-cultural, health and economic indicators of development, the objective of this paper is to provide critical evidence-based literature to support the analysis of current secondary data on HIV prevalence in Nyanza region and where possible back up existing visual linkages.

Methodology

The methodology adopted for this study involved post-secondary data analysis and existing literature search based on commonly used search engines. Specifically, the researcher reorganized links between HIV prevalence data and selected developmental indicators from Kenya National Bureau of Statistics (KNBS) and ICF Macro (2010) document. Post-secondary analysis included use of test for proportions between the Nyanza region data and national values collected during the same period. Presentations are made in tables and figures for quick visual comparison. Normal search engines including *Pub Med*, *Google scholar* and *Pub Med Central* were used to explore peer reviewed articles, using key words such as "HIV prevalence and wife inheritance", "HIV prevalence and Male Circumcision", "HIV prevalence and Development", "HIV prevalence and Wealth/Poverty", "HIV prevalence and fertility", "HIV prevalence and Mortality rate" and "HIV prevalence and child nutritional status". Information obtained was synthesized to give a strong scientific back up for the visual linkages that would not necessarily imply causation, given that there was no access to raw data for higher level analysis.

Results: HIV Prevalence in the Lake Basin Region

The Lake Basin covers the entire Nyanza region. The prevalence of HIV in this region still stands at 13.9 % (n=1092) for both male and females. Compared to other regions in Kenya, HIV prevalence in Nyanza is significantly higher than other regions. When aggregated by sex the prevalence stood at 16 % (n=599) for females and 11.4 % (n=494) for males (Table 1).

TABLE 1

PREVALENCE OF HIV BY PROVINCES

Region	Women		Men		Total	
	Percent +ve	Sample	Percent +ve	Sample	Percent +ve	Sample
Nairobi	10.8	287	3.4	297	7.0	584
Central	6.2	405	2.6	329	4.6	733
Coast	5.8	284	2.3	231	4.2	515
Eastern	3.8	610	3.0	502	3.5	1,111
Nyanza	16.0	599	11.4	494	13.9	1,092
Rift Valley	6.3	976	2.8	818	4.7	1,794
Western	9.2	394	3.4	334	6.6	728
North Eastern	0.9	86	0.9	63	0.9	149

Source: Kenya National Bureau of Statistics (KNBS) and ICF Macro. 2010

This implies that the female sex is more infected than the male sex (Fig. 1). A test for proportional differences between sexes revealed a significant difference (Z=2.22, P=0.0265) implying serious gender-based differences in prevalence rates with females adversely affected. Ethnicity also reflects significant prevalence differences. Major ethnic groups in the Nyanza region include the *Luo* and *Kisii*. Prevalence rates among the *Luo* community is higher (22.8%, n=470) than that of *Kisii* community (5.1% n=250). The proportional differences between male (Z=5.49, P=0.000) and female (Z=7.42, p=0.000) were significant in both cases and suggested more harmful impact for the *Luo* community. Unfortunately, Nyanza province still leads in prevalence among the youth with the female population being the most affected (Fig. 2; Table 2).

TOWARDS INCLUSIVE DEVELOPMENT IN KENYA

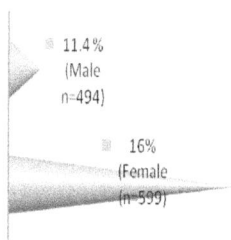

Fig. 1 Prevalence of HIV in Nyanza by Gender

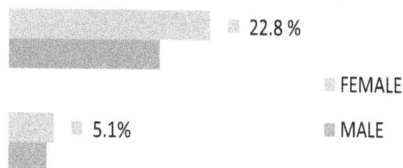

Fig. 2. Prevalence of HIV in Nyanza by Major Ethnic Groups

Source: Kenya National Bureau of Statistics (KNBS) and ICF Macro. 2010

TABLE 2

HIV PREVALENCE OF YOUTH ACROSS PROVINCE

Youth HIV status	Women		Men		Total	
Provinces	% +ve	sample	% +ve	sample	% +ve	sample
Nairobi	5	106	0.2	102	2.6	209
Central	0.7	151	0.8	140	0.8	291
Coast	2.1	124	0	75	1.3	199
Eastern	2.9	225	1.6	263	2.2	488
Nyanza	11.4	287	3.1	255	7.5	542
Rift Valley	2.9	380	0	322	1.6	702
Western	4.5	170	0.3	172	2.4	342
North Eastern	0.8	35	1.2	24	1	59

Source: Kenya National Bureau of Statistics (KNBS) and ICF Macro. 2010

HIV as a Delimiting Factor for Development in the Lake Basin Region   179

Non-causal links between HIV prevalence and selected developmental indicators

Socio-cultural, demographic and economic indicators

The study considered socio-cultural, demographic and economic factors to show the non-causal visual link with HIV prevalence in Nyanza region. Among the factors included were male circumcision, fertility rates, lack of formal education, highest wealth quintile and birth registration (Fig. 4). All these factors are key developmental issues which could have strong visible links with HIV prevalence. The prevalence of HIV among the circumcised men in Nyanza province stood at 5.8% (n=240) while that of uncircumcised men stood at 16.6% (n=282). This implies that majority of HIV infected men were uncircumcised, indicating poor social development and significant difference (Z=4.02, p=0.0001). In addition, Nyanza also recorded lower prevalence of no formal education, highest wealth quintile and birth registration compared to national prevalence levels. Proportional tests revealed significant differences in highest wealth quintile (p<0.001), birth registration (p<0.001), no formal education (p<0.001) but not fertility rate (p>0.5) when Nyanza region prevalence was compared to national prevalence levels (Table 3). Specifically, wealth index based on quintiles was determined by assigning assets a weight (factor score) generated through principal component analysis and the resulting asset scores standardized in relation to a standard normal distribution, with a mean of zero and a standard deviation of one (Gwatkin *et al.*, 2000). In every household each asset was assigned a score and total scores determined in every household based on all assets. Individuals were ranked according to quintiles from one (lowest) to five (highest).

TABLE 3

PROPORTIONAL DIFFERENCES BETWEEN HIV, DEMOGRAPHIC
AND ECONOMIC INDICATORS OF DEVELOPMENT IN NYANZA

	Nyanza	National Prevalence	Z-Score	P-value
HIV Prevalence	13.9 (n=1092)	5.675 (n=6686)	7.58	<0.001
Fertility rate (%)	5.4(n=500)	4.25 (n=4000)	1.08	0.278
No formal education (%)	13.4 (n=2594)	25.11(n=16061)	15.58	<0.001
Highest wealth quintile (%)	12.3 (n=6324)	25.48 (n=38068)	28.07	<0.001
Birth Registration (%)	42.1 (1090)	62.4 (n=5958)	12.51	<0.001

Infant and child mortality rate

Infant and child mortality rates have been used to reflect on the status of development for specific regions in Kenya and in other parts of the world. These mortality rates were categorized into five major groups, including neonatal mortality (NN; probability of dying within the first month of life), post neonatal mortality (PNN; the difference between infant and neonatal mortality), infant mortality (1q0; the probability of dying before the first birthday), child mortality (4q1; the probability of dying between the first and fifth birthday) and Under-five mortality (5q0; the probability of dying between birth and the fifth birthday). Visible results (Fig. 4) show significantly high level mortality rates/1000 live births in Nyanza region compared to national average rates. This implies that so many infants and children were dying for every 1000 live births, which is a clear indication of negative growth of children and a reflection of poor development.

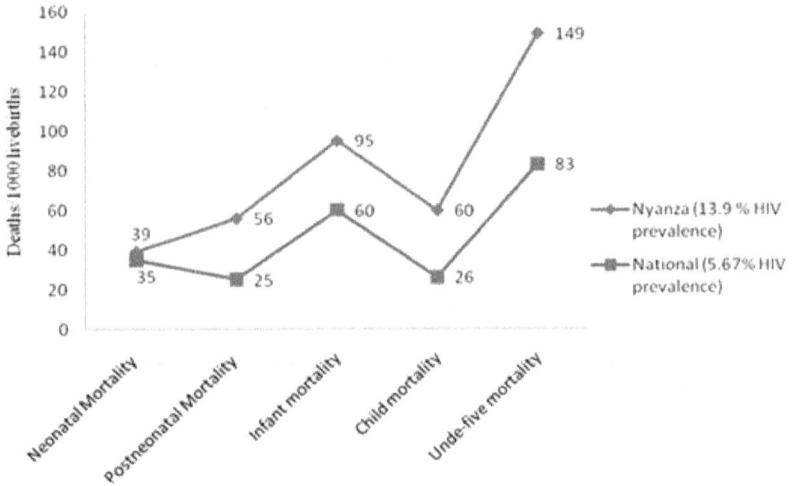

Figure 3: Comparison between infant and child mortality rate in Nyanza and National rates

Nutritional status

Nutritional status is another developmental indicator with high prevalence of global malnutrition reflecting poor development. It was assessed in Nyanza region and values compared with national prevalence levels (Table 4). The results indicated statistically significant ($p < 0.0001$) lower prevalence for wasting, stunting and underweight in Nyanza region compared to national prevalence values. This implies that Nyanza region performed very well in terms of nourishment compared to other regions of Kenya. These developmental indices were based on global acute malnutrition cut-off of -2 z-score values.

TABLE 4

A COMPARISON OF PREVALENCE OF GLOBAL MALNUTRITION
OF UNDER-5 CHILDREN AND WOMEN IN NYANZA WITH
NATIONAL PREVALENCES

Under five nutritional status	Nyanza (HIV prevalence, 13.9% n=991)	National (HIV prevalence, 5.67% n=5470)	z-score	p-value
Wasting (-2 z-score)	3.9	7.69	5.32	<0.001
Stunting (-2 z-score)	30.9	39.21	5.16	<0.001
Underweight (-2 z-score)	10.6	16.16	5.07	<0.001

Discussion

The results displayed in this study have provided a visible HIV prevalence in Nyanza region in relation to some commonly used developmental indicators. Even though it was not possible to establish causal links between HIV and developmental factors, it appears that some visible links indeed exist between these two variables. The prevalence of HIV in Nyanza is far much higher than the national values, indicating potential visible links to socio-cultural, demographic, health and economic development. When the prevalence of HIV is high in a population, developmental related risks such as health burden and economic difficulties may also increase. Again the high prevalence may be due to socio-cultural practices and demographic indicators.

More specifically to this study, it is evident that HIV and Male Circumcision (MC) have a visual linkage in that the prevalence of HIV appears to be high in a non-circumcised population and Nyanza region has a larger percentage of this population. This may be explained by the findings of some empirical studies (Williams *et al.,* 2006; Baeten *et al.,* 2010) which have established true causal associations between MC and HIV risk.

However, this linkage does not imply that MC is a potential cure to HIV infection and should be treated with more caution. Additional cultural related risk factors more closely associated with Nyanza region with regard to HIV is wife inheritance. Even though there were no relevant data to establish this linkage, a study conducted within the region established true causal links between this cultural phenomenon and increased HIV infection risk (Agot *et al.,* 2010) using experimental design. The mystery behind this phenomenon is the high risk associated with wife inheritance for ritual purposes and low risk for companionship. The latter could imply that in such cases the parties would probably agree on mutual grounds and precede with risk reduction behaviors, such as HIV testing.

Highest wealth quintile, formal education, fertility rate and birth registration were some of the socio-demographic and economic aspects of development that the study gave critical consideration. The approach adopted considered that poverty in majority of households falling in the lower wealth quintiles may have a link with increased HIV prevalence. The result has shown a very significantly lower percentage within the highest wealth quintile in Nyanza region compared to national values. This probably would be expected to explain the high prevalence of HIV in Nyanza region. However, this is debatable and would be contrary to the empirical findings which have concluded a non-regular linkage between poverty patterns (Stuckler *et al.,* 2010) and HIV prevalence, and serious risk behaviour leading to increased risk to HIV infection (Awusabo-Asare and Annim, 2008; Parkhurst, 2010). Apparently, wealth should have a positive association with HIV infection if these arguments are true. Fertility rates appeared to be high in Nyanza region implying a highly sexually active region which could also increase HIV infection risk. Some authors have argued that fertility rate in a high prevalence HIV environment may be elevated by replacement phenomenon centred on reduced breastfeeding and increased desire for more children (Magadi and Agwanda, 2010) especially when many infants and children are dying. The percentage of individuals who lack formal education was significantly lower than the national percentage implying a region with formally educated population. Lack of formal education may lead to inadequate knowledge on HIV infection that may also increase the risk to the infection. This seemed not to be the case for Nyanza and probably formal education has no well-established relationship with HIV prevalence in the region. Birth registration appeared very low in the region. Low birth registration would probably interfere with the population estimates also leading to biases in determination of the exact prevalence of HIV infection in the region. Again lack of records could probably deny many children born in the region chances of enjoying quick interventions which could otherwise lower the HIV prevalence rates. However, no proper scientific evidence is available to explain the linkage.

Within the health development indicators, infant and child mortality rates in Nyanza were quite alarming and probably a factor with the strongest linkage to HIV prevalence. It is evident that many children are dying for every 1000 children born alive. If this happens within an HIV prone environment, then chances could be that such deaths may be attributed to HIV prevalence. This kind of relationship may be explained by findings of mortality-HIV links among children (Stanecki *et al.*, 2010; Adazu *et al.*, 2005; Wekesa, 2000) from middle income countries and more specifically, in Kenya. Such deaths may be as a result of opportunistic diseases in cases where preventive measures are not taken up immediately. Nutritional status though expected to deteriorate within the Lake Basin region showed the exact opposite of the expectation. Compared to the national rates, undernourishment (Z-score < -2) of children under five-5 years was much lower than the national prevalence based on the three indicators including wasting, stunting and underweight. Many studies have found HIV to have a significant contribution to nutritional outcomes at the individual level (Kimani-Murage *et al.*, 2011) and both direct and mild effect have serious effects of children's nutritional status (Nalwoga *et al.*, 2010; Sutcliffe *et al.*, 2011). On the contrary, Nyanza region which recorded very high HIV prevalence fortunately had well-nourished children, implying accessibility to appropriate intervention measures.

Conclusion

HIV prevalence in Nyanza has a visible link to negative development exhibited by infant and child mortality rates, socio-cultural factors and to some extent, fertility rates. High HIV prevalence may be the contributor to high level mortality rates in Nyanza region which is a key negative developmental issue. On the converse side, socio-cultural developmental factors including wife inheritance and male circumcision may lead to high HIV prevalence in the region. High level fertility rate may also lead to increased HIV prevalence as it may be a true reflection of high unprotected sexual activity. Other factors such as formal education, wealth quintile and nutritional status still depend on a number of issues which require further causal investigations. However, it should be noted that causal association research is chronically missing within this region and needs to be given critical consideration.

References

Adazu, K., Lindblade, K.A., Rosen, D.H., Odhiambo, F., Ofware, P., Kwach, J., et al. (2005). Health and demographic surveillance in rural western Kenya: a platform for evaluating interventions to reduce morbidity and mortality from infectious diseases. *Am J Trop Med Hyg*. 2005 Dec; 73(6):1151-8.

Agot, K.E., Vander, S.A., Tracy, M., Obare B.A., Bukusi ,E.A., Ndi-Achola, J.O., et al. (2010). Widow inheritance and HIV prevalence in Bondo District, Kenya: baseline results from a prospective cohort study, *PLoS One* Nov 17, 5(11):e14028.

Awusabo-Asare, K., Annim, S.K. (2008). Wealth status and risky sexual behaviour in Ghana and Kenya. *Health Econ Health Policy*. 2008; 6(1):27-39.

Baeten, J.M., Donnell, D., Kapiga, S.H., Ronald, A., John-Stewart, G., Inambao, M., et al. (2010). Male circumcision and risk of male-to-female HIV-1 transmission: a multinational prospective study in African HIV-1-serodiscordant couples. *AIDS*. Mar 13; 24(5):737-44.

Chen, W.J., Walker, N. (2010). Fertility of HIV-infected women: insights from Demographic and Health Surveys. *Transm Infect*. Dec; 86 Suppl 2: ii22-7.

Fox, A.M. (2010). The social determinants of HIV serostatus in sub-Saharan Africa: an inverse relationship between poverty and HIV? *Health Rep*. Jul-Aug; 125 Suppl 4:16-24.

Gray, R.H., Wawer, M.J., Serwadda, D., Sewankambo, N., Li, C., Wabwire-Mangen, F. *et al.* (1998). Population-based study of fertility in women with HIV-1 infection in Uganda. *Lancet*. Jan 10; 351(9096):98-103.

Kimani-Murage, E.W., Norris, S.A., Pettifor, J.M., Tollman, S.M., Klipstein-Grobusch, K., Gómez-Olivé, X.F. *et al.* (2011). Nutritional status and HIV in rural South African children. *BMC Pediatr*. Mar 25; 11:23.

Kongnyuy, E.J. & Wiysonge, C.S. (2008). Association between fertility and HIV status: what implications for HIV estimates? *BMC Public Health.* Sep 11; 8:309.

Lallemant, C., Halembokaka, G., Baty, G., Ngo-Giang-Huong, N., Barin, F., & Le Coeur, S. (2010). Impact of HIV/Aids on Child Mortality before the Highly Active Antiretroviral Therapy Era: A Study in Pointe-Noire, Republic of Congo. *Trop Med.* pii: 897176.

Luginaah, I., Elkins, D., Maticka-Tyndale, E., Landry, T., & Mathui, M. (2005). Challenges of a pandemic: HIV/AIDS-related problems affecting Kenyan widows. *Soc Sci Med.* Mar; 60(6):1219-28.

Mabumba, E.D., Mugyenyi, P., Batwala, V., Mulogo, E.M., Mirembe, J., Khan, F.A., *et al.* (2007). Widow inheritance and HIV/AIDS in rural Uganda. *Trop Doct.* Oct; 37(4):229-31.

Magadi, M.A., Agwanda, A.O. (2010). Investigating the association between HIV/AIDS and recent fertility patterns in Kenya. *Soc Sci Med.* Jul; 71(2):335-44.

Malungo, J.R. (2001). Sexual cleansing (Kusalazya) and levirate marriage (Kunjilila mung'anda) in the era of AIDS: changes in perceptions and practices in Zambia. *Soc Sci Med.* Aug; 53(3):371-82.

Mishra, V., Assche, S.B., Greener, R., Vaessen, M., Hong, R., Ghys, P.D. (2007). HIV infection does not disproportionately affect the poorer in sub-Saharan Africa. *DS.* Nov; 21 Suppl 7:S17-28.

Nalwoga, A., Maher, D., Todd, J., Karabarinde, A., Biraro, S., & Grosskurth, H. (2010). Nutritional status of children living in a community with high HIV prevalence in rural Uganda: a cross-sectional population-based survey. *Med Int Health.* Apr; 15(4):414-22.

Okeyo, T.M. & Allen, A.K. (1994). Influence of widow inheritance on the epidemiology of AIDS in Africa. *Afr J Med Pract.* Mar-Apr; 1(1):20-5.

Oywa, R. (1995). Poverty creates the greatest risk for women in Uganda. Special report: women and HIV. *AIDS Anal Afr.* Aug; 5(4):11.

Parkhurst, J.O. (2010). Understanding the correlations between wealth, poverty and human immunodeficiency virus infection in African countries. *World Health Organ.* Jul 1; 88(7):519-26.

Rujumba, J., Kwiringira, J. (2010). Interface of culture, insecurity and HIV and AIDS: Lessons from displaced communities in Pader District, Northern Uganda. *Confl Health.* Nov 22; 4:18.

Stanecki, K., Daher, J., Stover, J., Akwara, P., Mahy, M. (2010). Under-5 mortality due to HIV: regional levels and 1990-2009 trends. Sex Transm Infect. Dec; 86 Suppl 2:ii56-61.

Stuckler, D., Basu, S., McKee, M. (2010). Drivers of inequality in Millennium Development Goal progress: a statistical analysis. *PLoS Med.* Mar 2; 7(3):e1000241.

Sutcliffe, C.G., van Dijk, J.H., Munsanje, B., Hamangaba, F., Sinywimaanzi, P., Thuma, P.E. (2011). Weight and height z-scores improve after initiating ART among HIV-infected children in rural Zambia: a cohort study. *MC Infect Dis.*Mar 1; 11:54.

Templeton, D.J., Millett, G.A., Grulich, A.E. (2010). Male circumcision to reduce the risk of HIV and sexually transmitted infections among men who have sex with men. *Curr Opin Infect Dis.* Feb; 23(1):45-52.

Wekesa, E. (2000). The impact of HIV / AIDS on child survival and development in Kenya. *IDS Anal Afr.* 2000 Jan; 10(4):12-4.

Williams, B.G., Lloyd-Smith, J.O., Gouws, E., Hankins, C., Getz ,W.M., Hargrove, J., *et al.* (2006). The potential impact of male circumcision on HIV in Sub-Saharan Africa. *PLoS Med.* Jul; 3(7):e262.

Wojcicki, J.M. (2005). Socioeconomic status as a risk factor for HIV infection in women in East, Central and Southern Africa: a systematic review. *Biosoc Sci.* Jan; 37(1):1-36.

Gwatkin, D.R., Rutstein, S.K., Johnson, R., Pande, P., & Wagstaff, A. (2000). *Socio-economic differences in health, nutrition and poverty.* HNP/Poverty Thematic Group of the World Bank.Washington, D.C.: The World Bank.

Promoting Youth Agenda in Nairobi: Benefits Potential of Urban Public Transport in Nairobi

Romanus Opiyo

Introduction

In recent years, the urban agenda has risen steadily as a priority interest for Government and the creation of the Ministry of Nairobi Metropolitan and Development was a clear signal and recognition of the importance of our urban areas to foster development in our national and regional economies and more importantly, the role it plays in improving quality of our individual and collective lives. The realization of this has led to massive public investment in the urban transport sector and several reforms including formation of Kenya Urban Roads Agency (KURA) which is specifically concerned with urban roads infrastructure development, an issue previously addressed as part of crisis management.

This chapter provides an overview of urban public transport in Nairobi and offers arguments regarding how the investment in the sector is likely to benefit the youth. The paper will rely mainly on existing literature on urban transport and specifically analysis of the Government policy documents guiding general development and transportation sector such as the Constitution, Vision 2030, Nairobi Metropolitan Area Bill of 2008, Integrated Transport Policy, and Master Plan for Urban Transport in the Nairobi Metropolitan Area, The Traffic Act (Cap 403) among others.

The outcome of the extensive review is deemed useful in assessing the suitability and relevance of Government and other development partners' thinking in supporting the sector in order to create opportunities for urban areas development and improvement of the livelihoods of the youth in Nairobi. Analysis of the documents will also help in comparing the ideal proposal scenario with the current situation and its challenges to facilitate mapping out of benefits likely to be enjoyed by the youth.

Definition of Key Terms

Urban transportation consists of a family of modes, which range from walking and bicycles to urban freeways, metro and regional rail systems and can be classified into three categories, based on the type of their operation and use. **Private transportation** consists of privately owned vehicles operated by owners for their personal use, usually on public streets. The most common modes of private transportation are pedestrian, bicycle and private car. **Paratransit** or **for-hire transportation** is transportation provided by operators and availed to parties which hire them for individual or multiple trips. Taxi, dial-a-bus and jitney are the most common modes under this category. **Urban transit, mass transit** or **public transportation** includes systems which are available for use by all persons who pay the established fare. These modes, which operate on fixed routes and with fixed schedules, include bus, light rail transit, metro, regional rail and several other systems.

Urban public transportation, strictly defined, includes both transit and paratransit categories, since both are available for public use. However, since public transportation tends to be identified with transit only, inclusion of paratransit is usually specifically identified.

Another classification of travel categorizes transportation as individual or group travel. **Individual transportation** refers to systems in which each vehicle serves a separate party (person or related group) while **group transportation** carries unrelated persons in the same vehicles. The former is predominantly private transportation, the latter is transit, and paratransit encompasses both.

The term **youth**, according to Kenya's constitution means the collectivity of all individuals in the Republic who have attained the age of eighteen years but have not attained the age of thirty-five years.

Premise

In urban areas, mobility needs, whether provided by public or private vehicles, are important in ensuring smooth and efficient movement of people and goods. It has direct economic benefits and enhances productivity of workers. Availability of good and efficient transportation services at affordable costs also enhances the quality of life of residents.

Most cities and urban areas globally are working to improve their public transport service quality. They recognize that public transit plays a critical role in an equitable and efficient transport system by providing basic mobility for non-drivers, efficient mobility on major travel corridors, creating employment opportunities and general support for strategic development. As noted by Sahil *et al* (2003) the poor in developing countries rely on public transport to sustain their livelihoods but these services, whether provided by the public or the private sector, often fail to meet basic needs or to assist them to improve their economic status.

An ideal urban public transport requires high quality, efficient public transport services that are convenient, comfortable, and accommodative including the disabled, reliable and relatively affordable. This is based on the premise that the quality and efficiency of these services affects overall transport system performance and therefore general urban community's livelihoods including the youth's economic productivity and their quality of life.

Zhi Liu (1997) noted that most direct poverty-targeted interventions (schools, health clinics, nutrition programs, and social services) depend on transport system as a complementary input for their effective delivery but their cumulative contribution is mostly ignored. With few exceptions, the distributive impact of transport projects (i.e., how much various social groups such as youth, children etc. gain and lose) and their direct proactive role in assisting them, has generally received little attention.

Cities in Asia and North Africa tend to be more equal than those in other regions and sub-regions. However, in East Africa and North Africa, levels of youth unemployment have risen over the past 10 years and are among the highest in the world. Such inequalities of income, combined with unplanned and rapid growth, have led to a number of related inequalities, including those resulting from spatial patterns of land use and tenure and access to public spaces and transport, as well as social and economic inequalities in terms of decision-making and citizenship, access to health and education, and safety and security (Shaw and Carli, 2011). This shows that inaccessibility to public transport has the potential of excluding youth from gainful activities that may be linked to other opportunities within and without the immediate location.

Borrowing from works attempting to link transportation system with gainful livelihoods, this paper will assess and analyze the potential role of urban public transport in supporting youth, basing its argument on the on-going and proposed reforms targeting Nairobi Metropolitan Area (NMA) transport sector. The primary objective is to establish a sound conceptual framework for identifying, examining, and analyzing the full potential benefits of public transport operations in benefiting the youth.

Urban transport comprises the infrastructure and service components and the adequate functioning of this system is predicated on having an optimal mix of these two. The availability and combination of the two is what makes urban public transport feasible and realistic in hosting a number of stakeholders and eliciting issues dealing with governance, hence its potential in economic empowerment of urban residents. The scope of the discussion will take into consideration the public transport infrastructure that provides basic support under which the urban public transport services operates on.

The paper is conceptualized on the basis of various studies, policies and agenda shaping urban public transport in Kenya and how they are linked to enhance livelihoods, which is further cascaded to benefits targeting the youth in the society.

The challenges faced by Nairobi residents with regard to urban public transport include under-utilization of commuter railway services, inefficient networks of buses and *"matatus"* irrational fare charges, reckless driving, uncouth crew, accidents, and rowdiness, overloading, overlapping, over-charging, un-regulated urban development and land use, and congested mode interchange area (King'ori, 2007; MoNMD, 2011). This problem is not limited only to Nairobi, but also to other comparable cities such as Dar es Salaam and Addis Ababa among others.

The situation facing this sector has led to various initiatives driven by the Kenyan Government and its development partners such as World Bank, Africa Development Bank, JICA and the United Nations agencies. These initiatives are mainly aimed at tackling broader problems facing Nairobi and the entire country such as development initiatives implemented without necessarily linking these efforts with certain segments of society as it is always assumed that the benefits will trickle down to all segments of the society equally. Such initiatives include creation of wealth through employment, meeting Millennium Development Goals (MDGs), addressing the country's Vision 2030 and improving general mobility in Nairobi.

Rationale for Focusing on Youth

Kenya is a young nation, with approximately 75% of its population being under the age of 35 years and 38% between the ages 15 and 35. According to Vision 2030 it is at this age that much of the human capital is formed thus, human development strategies implemented during this transitional period have long-term impact on the structure and quality of human capital. Young people today and in the future, will be the principal stakeholders and beneficiaries of the Vision. Therefore, issues affecting young people will be fully integrated and harmonized into every aspect of public policy and across all ministries and Government agencies.

In Kenya, including urban areas such as Nairobi, a mismatch exists between the aspirations of young people and the opportunities available to them. As noted in Vision 2030, the majority of young Kenyans have high hopes and ambitions. However, poor macroeconomic performance, lack of labour market opportunities and a society that negates the self-expression of young people mean that many young people are unable to translate their aspirations into a productive and fulfilling future. In addition, the potential for disappointing and dimming life prospects leading to frustration and desperation is high among the youth as compared to any other age-groups.

Under Vision 2030, specific policies and interventions will be implemented to fully develop young people's potential as well as prepare and engage them in the socio-economic development of the country. The interventions will cover the following fundamental areas: building capacity and empowerment to equip youth to engage in productive activities, creating employment opportunities, providing the youth with the necessary support (e.g., financial and market linkages) supporting initiatives that mould character, strengthening programmes to advance youth health and well-being and, giving the youth a voice to articulate their issues as well as participate in decision making (GoK, 2008). The Kenya constitution also recognizes the role of youth in development and they are now treated as respectable partners in the development agenda. Chapter 4 of the Constitution clearly spells out that "The State shall take measures, including affirmative action programmes, to ensure that the youth have opportunities to associate, be represented and participate in political, social, economic and other spheres of life".

This paper therefore will seek to analyze opportunities likely to emanate as a result of reforming public transport and see how the youth can position themselves in order to fully benefit from the various proposed projects. The paper will not limit itself to the already existing peripheral and unstructured benefits like '*Kamjeshi*'[1] but look at more fulfilling and rewarding roles as investors and managers of the sector by seizing the available opportunities.

Policies and Plans Shaping Urban Public Transport in Kenya

The problem of urban public transport in Kenya presents significant challenges in respect of its ability to ensure adequate mobility for the people. In addition, the poorly functioning urban transport network has implications on the efficiency of the private sector to produce and create jobs. A further danger of the malfunctioning urban transport network is the "marginalization" of vulnerable segments of society. In an era of limited resources, it is critical that investment in urban transport be focused at achieving optimal functionality of the urban areas and ensuring supportive dynamic linkages with their hinterlands, while at the same time taking critical account of the urban poor (Aligula, *et al,* 2005).

Urban transport system is a major contributor to the inefficiencies or otherwise, of the wider national economy. Therefore, providing solutions to the same would impact positively on the efficiency of the urban system in Kenya and therefore economic growth. It would also facilitate efforts aimed at wealth creation and poverty alleviation (GoK, 2010). Associating urban transport with development has led to various initiatives driven by the GoK and development partners since early 1990s, including some notable ones such as the World Bank funded Sub Sahara Africa Transport Policy (SSATP), Kenya Urban Transport Infrastructure Programme (KUTIP) and development of policies and plans to improve urban public transport system. These have also encouraged the Government to develop policies and plans aimed at enhancing the performance of the sector as a development and growth catalyst.

Government Policies and Initiatives

This section highlights the policy and regulatory framework guiding transportation sector in the country as these are supposed to shape the sector's performance and mode of operations.

The Constitution of Kenya has re-organized the administrative levels of the country into 47 counties. In general, it indicates that the guiding philosophy, spirit and principle is a fair devolvement of functions and powers between the national government and county governments, and that the county governments are autonomous as regards the functions allotted to them under the Fourth Schedule.

These levels of governance – in relation to the Bill of Rights which gives youth opportunities to associate, be represented and participate in political, social, economic and other spheres of life – improves visibility of youth agenda both in national and local politics, since it provides nomination of youth in Parliament, membership of Senate and County assembly. This is salient in articulating issues relating to public transport both within Nairobi and also urban areas, including developing and moving bills and agenda which are likely to give urban youth opportunities to play a critical role in investing and managing of the sector.

The constitution also provides for formulation of not more than 22 ministries at the central level. Considering the prospective size and importance of Nairobi and general urban development, management and governance, it is the right time to establish a Ministry of Metropolitan Development at the Central Government level to harness and harmonize development of key sectors including urban public transport.

However, the new Constitution does not recognize "Urban Public Transport" as a distinct function, despite the growth of the sector and anticipated benefits accruing for citizens especially youth, which includes ability to make governance simple, transparent, accountable and responsive.

Since independence, the first Policy on transportation was launched in 2003 by the then Minister of Transport, Hon. John Michuki, who formed a National Transport Policy Committee with the sole mandate of formulating an Integrated National Transport Policy (INTP). Development of this latter policy was a result of the Government's realization that the transport sector is one of the critical enablers in achieving Vision 2030. The policy aims at enhancing Kenya's development in terms of integrating production, marketing and population centres, hence facilitating mobility in rural and urban areas, national and regional integration, trade promotions, improving the overall welfare of the people and Kenya's competitiveness.

The report "Integrated National Transport Policy: Moving a Working Nation", identified a number of challenges inhibiting the transport sector from performing its facilitative role in respect of national and regional economies. The challenges included inappropriate modal split, unexploited regional role of the transport system, the transport system not being fully integrated, urban environmental pollution, lack of an urban/rural transport policy, institutional deficiencies, inadequate human resource capacity, and lack of a vision for the transport sector (GoK, 2009).

In addressing the challenges associated with the transport sector, the policy document proposed several measures that are deemed useful in making the transport sector more organized and vibrant. The issue of management of the transport sector was given high profile and the framework developed proposed establishment of the Directorate of Transport, consolidation of transport functions under one Ministry, and separation of policy making, regulatory and service provision functions, enhancing the role of the private sector in transport infrastructure development and management, integration of non-motorised and intermediate means of transport into the transport systems, and consolidation of urban public transport (GoK, 2009).

The INTP takes into account the inefficiency of urban transport due to poor infrastructure, high transport costs for both passengers and goods. It links this with the majority of low-income urban workers who find public transport costly and financially inaccessible and hence meet most of their transport needs through walking and head loading, despite lack of appropriate support infrastructure such as footpaths and cycle paths for such users, hence risking their lives by utilizing non-motorized and intermediate means of transport (NMIMTs). About 50 per cent of the country's total GDP is generated in the urban areas, thus the adverse consequences of the above scenario on worker's efficiency and productivity, fuel consumption, education, health and the environment cannot be overemphasized. The major challenge still facing the country is lack of an urban transport policy which can cascade issues highlighted and proposed in the national policy to a focused urban transport guide, more so in linking urban public transport with the wider urban development agenda.

In discussing the roles of various stakeholders as proposed in the national transport policy, the document notes that public policy making is undertaken at various levels of government. As such, transport institutional policy needs to address arrangements for relationships at various levels of government and among various statutory bodies and the private sector. The respective roles are listed in the table below.

Table 1: Summary of Stakeholders Role as Proposed in the National Transport Policy

Stakeholder	Roles
1. CENTRAL GOVERNMENT	a. focus on policy and strategy formulation
	b. retain its regulatory role to ensure unbiased regulation of safety and quality in general,
	c. regulate market access for transport operators where this is necessary and discourage excessive tariffs in case of monopolies.
	d. facilitate competition, private sector participation and will be the custodian of environmental and social interests
2. LOCAL GOVERNMENT	a. involve improvement of local finances including utilization of Local Authority Transfer Fund (LATF) and cess
	b. in collaboration with the relevant government agencies and stakeholders, focus on development and management of transport infrastructure as appropriate,
	c. implementation of urban policy
	d. development of local transport plans and integrating these with overall urban land use planning
	e. environmental management, enforcement and local traffic management.
3. PRIVATE SECTOR	a. encouraged to participate in the provision and financing of transport infrastructure and services
	b. the government will ensure that a minimum of 30% of the total shareholding in privatised transport entities is reserved to Kenyans.
4. NON-GOVERNMENT BODIES	a. encouraged to participate in and lead efforts aimed at creating public awareness on relevant transport issues
	b. consumer protection
	c. transport research and lobbying.
5. CITIZENS	a. Increased use of mass public transport

Source: GoK, 2010

From the analysis of the roles of various stakeholders, it is assumed that there will be opportunity for youthful entrepreneurs to invest and participate in the sector and at the same time, for the commuters to get protection from the Government by discouraging excessive tariff charges.

Other national Initiatives and Regulations Linked with the Transport Sector Growth

A list of other initiatives have also led to changes in the sector, some of them are listed and summarized in the table below.

Initiative	Focus	Comment
1. Vision 2030	The Kenya Vision 2030 is a vehicle for accelerating transformation of Kenya into a rapidly industrializing middle-income nation by the year 2030.	Transport sector is seen as an accelerator of meting benchmarks set in the Vision 2030
2. Economic Recovery Strategy for Wealth and Employment Creation (2003-2007)	Creating 500,000 jobs annually, mostly from the informal sector	The youths were the main target
3. Development of Physical Infrastructure and Services	- Building and maintaining durable quality "standard roads with emphasis on safe and efficient transportation - Privatizing Kenya railways by offering a unitary concession to a private operator	Enhancement of the productivity and reliability of public transport
4. Traffic Act Cap 403	An Act of Parliament to consolidate the law relating to traffic on the roads	Give immense power to the Minister in charge of transportation to prescribe devices to be fitted to any class or type of vehicle for restricting their speed, the number of passengers etc. Revolutionized Public Passenger transportation (Michuki rules)
5. Physical Planning Act Cap 286	An Act of Parliament to provide for the preparation and implementation of physical development plans and for connected purposes	The act is suppose to control urban land use development, hence has impact on the urban form, which directs the urban transportation landscape
6. Local Government Act Cap 265	Guides the operations of all Local Authorities	The Minister shall, before he gives any approval required under this section, consult the Minister responsible for the licensing of public service vehicles.

Nairobi Oriented Policies and Plans

Nairobi is the capital city and the hub of economic, commercial and political activities in Kenya. According to a report by Ministry of Nairobi Metropolitan and Development, the share of GRDP of Nairobi Metropolitan Region (NMR) is estimated to be more than 50% of GDP of Kenya (GoK, 2010). Nairobi is dominant in employment generation in Kenya for both the informal and formal sectors and accounted for 35% of the total wage employment in Kenya in 2009. Nairobi City had an urban informal sector employment rate of 65% accounting for 25% of the total informal sector employment in the same year. The major employment challenges include high youth unemployment, a rapidly growing labour force, underemployment, the problem of the working poor, and gender inequality in employment (GoK, 2011).

Given this primary function and visibility, various initiatives driven by the Government and development partners have been mooted with the aim of improving service delivery and making it competitive in the region. The transport sector is one of the major beneficiaries of this goodwill as indicated by the number of projects and volume of funds allocated to improve the general performance of the sector.

The Study on Master Plan for Urban Transport in the Nairobi Metropolitan Area

This master plan was prepared in 2006 through funding from JICA and has been used to guide transport projects in the Nairobi Metropolitan Area (NMA) resulting in various projects including upgrading and expansion of roads such as Thika Road, Uhuru Highway and small but very important Non-Motorised Transport Infrastructure retrofitting projects along Nairobi's major corridors of Jogoo, Mbagathi, and Ngong Roads among others. Other issues raised in the Master Plan with regard to public transport in Nairobi include inefficient network of buses and *matatus*, non-incentives to private sector, under-utilization of railway services, inadequate and non-functional mode interchange area, and congestion of the CBD (Katahira, 2006).

The report gives a comprehensive analysis of transport sector in Nairobi Metropolitan Area. In highlighting the Nairobi transport modal split, the report shows that 47% of Nairobians walk, 29% use *matatus*, 3.7% use buses and 3.1% use school or college buses to their preferred destinations.

In addressing the challenges mentioned above and solving transportation mismatch between demand and supply of public transport services within Nairobi Metropolis, key proposals are made in the plan. To increase efficiency of the network of buses and *matatus* there is need to develop bus oriented policies e.g. exclusive bus lanes along the major public transport corridors and for *matatus* to be operated along feeder routes. In addition, a re-organization of existing mode interchange areas such as the bus station and railway station is critical as is upgrading of existing railway lines e.g. Nairobi to Thika route, Nairobi to Athi River, Nairobi to Embakasi and Nairobi to Limuru and the introduction of a new railway (Light Rail Transit) to optimize on the use of railway services (Katahira, 2006).

Spatial Planning Concept for Nairobi Metropolitan Region

This is a regional plan and a technical report on the conditions, resources and facilities of the area, combined with statement of policies and proposals in regard to allocation of resources and the locations of development within Nairobi Metropolitan area. The plan aims at providing for the proper physical development of land, securing the suitable provision of infrastructure and services, and orderly organization of human developmental activities such as commerce, trade, industry, education, etc *(GoK, 2011)*.

This report is a progressive step in the implementation of the Nairobi Metropolitan Area Transport Master Plan where it is reported that there was no corresponding comprehensive land use plan at that time to guide provision of transport infrastructure for the growing metropolitan population and its expansive sub-urban area.

Issues Highlighted by the Spatial Plan Document with regard to Public Transport are listed below.

- Bus companies compete for the same traffic with *matatus* in the same route
- Profitability margins are very thin
- Utilization of vehicles is below par due to the congestion on roads
- Bus fleet maintenance is poor and
- Low productivity
- Limited number of routes and services for Commuter Trains
- Inadequate Inter-modal transfer facilities

- Lack of safety
- Lack of comfort and
- Long walking distance between the railway station and places of work.

In relation to improving public transport in Nairobi the report proposes the introduction of Bus Rapid Transit (BRT) which is a road based system comprising high capacity buses with dedicated lanes either at median or at kerb side. The cost of initial investment for BRT is less than that of a rail based system. A BRT system can carry passengers from 5000 Peak hour peak direction traffic (phpdt) to 12000 phpdt. Another initiative would be introduction of Light Rail Transit (LRT) which is a rail based public transport system. It is an energy efficient, high speed and high comfort system. The capacity of LRT is higher than BRT system and can carry passengers from 12000 phpdt upto 30000 phpdt.

The implementation of the above proposal will reduce travel time for most commuters and since it will create employment opportunities either directly or through other associated subsidiary services associated with such services, there will be room to absorb youth and more citizens within this improved system.

Urban Public Transport Development and Nairobi Youth Benefits

The discussion of various policy documents and proposals in relation to expected reforms in urban public transport in Nairobi can be listed as follows:

a) Improved urban transport service levels – this will create direct employment and access to employment opportunities within Nairobi due to increase in the number of goods and services moved from one point to another.

b) Reduced living costs – The proposals made e.g. Bus Rapid Transit which is based on moving voluminous passengers at an improved speed will enable young people to live in far-flung areas paying cheaper house rent

c) Room for investment – With the new constitution empowering youth in running of the affairs both at local and national level, the youth can use the opportunity to negotiate for investment packages and subsidies that can help them be included in the investment and management of the public transport. The youth can negotiate for a certain percentage e.g. 15% of public transport investments to be reserved for future youth projects.

d) Provision of public transport support services within the proposed modern Inter-modal Change opportunity also will create room for employment and investment in services such as shopping, catering, internet, recreational facilities and massage facilities and services, among others

e) The youth and general citizens are going to play a critical role in the sustainable development of public transport sector as provided for by the new constitution and this is important for making leaders accountable and honest.

f) Provision of various modes of transport through development of diverse infrastructure options such as footpaths and upgrading of railways also will give youth viable options of enjoying facilities without necessarily going deep into their pockets

g) Reduction in highway congestion lessening travel time

h) Reduction in the number of accidents leading to increased life expectancy due to proper accommodation of various modes of transport through integrating all modes of transportation

i) Increase in volume of passengers, goods and general economic activities in the area

j) Sound investment guided by proper development control of Nairobi as proposed in the spatial plan which helps in proper linkage of transport infrastructure and facilities with other land uses such as commercial, agricultural, residential, among others.

Notes

[1] Corrupted word for self proclaimed stage managers or commanders who demand payment from public transport crew and owners for protection fee

References

GoK (2011). Spatial Planning Concept for Nairobi Metropolitan Region, accessed from the Ministry of Nairobi Metropolitan and Development Website

GoK (2010). Sessional Paper on Integrated National Transport Policy, Ministry of Transport

GoK (2009). Integrated National Transport Policy: "Moving a Working Nation", Ministry of Transport

Katahira (2006). The Study on Master Plan for Urban Transport in the Nairobi Metropolitan Area In the Republic of Kenya

Knowles, J. & Behrans, J. (2005). The Economic Returns to Investing in Youth in Developing Countries, A review of the Literature. *http:// siteresources.worldbank.org/HealthNutritionandPopulation/Resources/281627- 1095698140167/KnowlesEconInvestYouth.pdf*

Shaw, M. & Carli, V. (2011). Practical Approaches to Crime Prevention

Urban Transport and Poverty Reduction. *http://www.gtkp.com/assets/uploads/ 20091127-173521-7792-Chapter3.pdf*

Our Youth, Our Future: Moving Forward to Address Youth Development in Kenya. *http://siteresources.worldbank.org/Intunitfessd/Resources/ Chapter6_Edited_MCMay30_.pdf*

Investing in Knowledge Economy: Opportunities and Challenges for Youth in Rift Valley, Kenya

Alexander Luchetu Likaka

"What struck me so forcefully was how small the planet had become during my decades in prison.... [ICT] had shrunk the world, and had in the process become a great weapon for eradicating ignorance and promoting democracy." (Nelson Mandela, *Long Walk to Freedom, 1994, (pp, 30).*

Introduction

This chapter discusses opportunities and challenges for youth in knowledge, technology and innovation for economic growth. It offers some of the best practices on the use of information and communications technologies (ICT) to generate youth employment in the Rift Valley (RV) region. The main focus is on the big shift of our understanding of economic growth exemplified by emergence of terms such as "knowledge based economy", "ICT revolution" and "innovation", which although not an entirely new issue, has not received much attention. Particular emphasis is placed on youth for the new micro-enterprise on innovation and the knowledge based economy for Kenya under the Vision 2030 flagship. Best practice principles include promoting youth entrepreneurship, promoting public-private partnerships, targeting vulnerable groups of young people, bridging the gap between the digital economy and the informal sector and placing young people in charge. The chapter shows that the success of the national economy can be partially attributed to its ability to absorb and adapt globally advanced technology, huge flows of foreign investment, its large pool of knowledge and talent, and its enactment of a policy framework that provides incentives to domestic and foreign firms towards innovation. A summary of challenges facing ICT's future growth and sustainability is made. Finally, we offer recommendations aimed at promoting ICT-related opportunities for young people. The digital divide is real and prospects for ICT-generated employment for young people in Kenya are explored. This paper seeks to balance optimism about ICT's potential with an awareness of the constraints that obviously exist in Kenya as a developing country.

The last decades of the 20th century have represented a turning point in the global development process. It is knowledge that has become the engine for social, economic and cultural development in today's world. Knowledge-intensive economic activities are now a factor of production of strategic importance in the leading countries. They have also become the main indicators of the level of development and the readiness of every country for further economic and cultural growth in the 21st century. The emerging knowledge-based economy has affected other areas of societal activity in every country, including institutional and innovation systems, human resources development, and vice versa. It has also become an engine of progress in most countries, and in many cases, developed countries have an advanced knowledge-based economy. Where a country is considered less developed, this component constitutes just a small fraction of its economy.

To assist in addressing youth's skill training and employment problems, this paper scrutinizes useful international practices, policies, initiatives and programs targeting the former problem, particularly in ICTs. National government and County authorities in Kenya could consider implementing similar initiatives and strategies to address some of the youth employment issues. The broader aim of this paper is to investigate the successful practice and strategies for the information and communication related income generation opportunities for young people as noted in Vision 2030.

The rest of this paper is organised in five parts. First, the paper provides an overview of the literature on Youth and Post-election Violence in Rift Valley and on the knowledge economy, skill, education, and training issues. Secondly, it reviews the role of Information & Communication Technology (ICTs) for vocational skill development and employability for youth in Rift valley. Thirdly, it discusses the issues surrounding the development of the digital divide. Fourthly, the paper underlines types and the importance of developing ICT initiatives targeting young people, and initiatives from both developed and developing countries that offer opportunities to young people for learning, skill development and employment. Then the paper concludes by providing useful generalised recommendations for the authorities and youth in Rift Valley in advocating possible opportunities for ICT generated employment for young people, and discussing how ICT policies could be modified and adopted to meet young people's needs.

Communication in the broadest sense has developed to an unprecedented degree. ICT is but one aspect of the technological revolution that has taken place. However, ICT is not, as yet, a major priority for many developing countries notwithstanding the fact that a knowledge based economy will be the future motivating force in production and competitiveness. Consequently, awareness of the power of ICT is not always reflected in the policies and development programmes of the less developed countries. The challenge facing the international community is not limited to bridging the "digital gap", but in preventing this from getting wider. Otherwise, the developing countries will become, more and more marginalized. A number of global changes taking place at present have prompted many to herald the onset of the twenty-first century as marking the birth of the "knowledge society". Knowledge Economy (KE) is a system of consumption and production that is based on intellectual capital and this commonly makes up a large share of all economic activity in developed countries. In a knowledge economy, a significant part of a company's value may consist of intangible assets, such as the value of its workers' knowledge (intellectual capital).

It is a paradox of globalisation that young people in developed countries, which are now experiencing unprecedented levels of extended economic growth, face less competition for jobs, compared with the situation facing young people elsewhere. This suggests that young people in developed countries are not only benefiting from the greater opportunities available in fast growing economies. They are also in a more favourable position when compared to earlier age cohorts as there are fewer young people chasing the new jobs being created. However, in the least developed economies, the share of young people to the total population is over a third of the population as in the case of Kenya (Semboja, 2005). This suggests that these young people face not only more limited economic opportunities, but also increasing competition for the fewer jobs and other limited economic opportunities that are available due to the greater absolute numbers of young people in these economies.

The starting point for this paper is the recognition that no country can afford to ignore ICT as an employment generator, whatever their stage of development. Although this technology may not be of decisive importance to the poorest countries, it still exerts a major influence on their ability to acquire knowledge and tap into global networks. A recent report on 75 countries' access to ICT has noted:

> ICTs have yet to be adopted or used by most of the world, but it is those people who have not yet used the Internet or spoken on a telephone who perhaps have the most to gain from the potential of ICTs. *Richard Curtain, Youth Employment Summit* (15 June 2002)

ICT can be broadly defined as a set of activities that facilitate, by electronic means, the capturing, storage, processing, transmission, and display and feedback mechanisms of information. This paper uses the term ICT to encompass the production of both computer hardware and software as well as the means of transferring the information in digital form. It also includes low cost forms of communication such as radios.

Another term commonly used to describe the changes produced by information technology is the digital economy. This expression emphasises the new opportunities created by transforming information into a binary digital code. The digital economy refers to more than the boom and bust cycle of many new ventures aiming to tap the potential of the Internet for commercial purposes. The more profound effect of ICT is likely to be in improving the efficiency and reach of the mainstream production of goods and services, in both the public and private sectors of the economy.

ICT may also be defined as computer hardware and software and telecommunications technology. ICT is the world's fastest growing economic activity; the sector has turned the globe into an increasingly interconnected network of individuals, firms, schools and governments communicating and interacting with each other through a variety of channels and providing economic opportunities transcending borders, languages and cultures. ICT has opened new channels for service delivery in areas such as e-government, education, and e-health and information dissemination. Rapid development of ICT accompanied by the convergence of telecommunications, broadcasting and computer technologies is creating new products and services, as well as new ways of learning, entertainment and doing business. At the same time, more commercial, social and professional opportunities are being created through the unique opportunity provided by ICT. As a result, the world is undergoing a fundamental transformation as the industrial society that marked the 20th century rapidly gives way to the information society of the 21st century. The new society promises a fundamental change in all aspects of our lives, including knowledge dissemination, social interaction, economic and business practices and political engagement.

In most African countries, including Kenya, unemployment, under-employment and poverty levels have continued to rise and have remained at extremely high levels despite considerable efforts to promote sustainable development by national governments and international development agencies, (Economic Commission for Africa-ECA, 2002). In recent years, there has been increased concern over the tragic waste of human potential, particularly for the youth as most are either unemployed or underemployed. On the other hand, they can also be overworked in conditions lacking the core labour standards.

The proportion of young women in poverty is still greater than that of men, standing at 51.2% against 48.8% for men in Kenya (KNSB, 2010), although women assume the chief roles in maintaining the family. They work more in the agricultural and informal economy, occupying jobs in low profitability activities and earning low incomes. This is one of the main economic reasons for the feminization of poverty in Kenya. The challenge therefore is to design integrated employment-generating macroeconomic policies that create decent opportunities for young women and men, who represent a majority of the population and in the labour force, (Semboja, 2005).

The centrality of youth employment has long been recognized by the East Africa countries as one of the major means to alleviate poverty and empower people to be part of the social, economic and political processes. Regional intergovernmental organizations and global development partners are now also gradually taking a similar position. The East African Community was established as the regional intergovernmental organization of the Republics of Kenya, Uganda, Rwanda, Burundi and Tanzania with the goal of enhancing co-operation and integration in all sectors for the mutual benefit of the partner states. In order to reach this goal, a Customs Union has been established as the first phase to be followed by a Common Market, then a Monetary Union and ultimately a political federation of the East Africa States. One of the preliminary strategic moves is the regional integration of the labour market, with the goal of facilitating free movement of factors of production, including the youth labour power.

Youth population in developing countries is increasing as a result of rapid advancement in medicine and this situation brings with it a large number of social and economic problems as well as opportunities. For instance, the impacts of job and training availability and the physical, social and cultural quality of urban environment on young people are enormous, and affect their health, life-styles, and well-being (Gleeson and Sipe 2006). Besides this, globalization and technological developments are affecting youth in urban areas in all parts of the world, both positively and negatively (Robertson 1995). The rapidly advancing information and communications technologies (ICTs) help in addressing social and economic problems caused by the rapid growth of urban youth populations in developing countries. ICTs opportunities have a downside: young people in many developing countries lack broad access to these new technologies, they are vulnerable to global market changes, and ICTs link them into global cultures which promote consumerism, potentially eroding local cultures and community values (Manacorda and Petrongolo 1999). However we believe that the positives outweigh such negatives.

Currently, at the beginning of the 21stcentury, the world's young population is higher than ever before. There are over a billion young people between the ages of 15 and 24, with 85 % of them living in developing countries and mainly in urban environments. Many of these young people are in the process of making, or have already made the transition from school to work. During the last two decades all around the world, these young people as new workers have faced a number of challenges associated with globalization and technological advances on labour markets (United Nations 2004). The continuous decrease in employment opportunities within manufacturing industries has made many of the young people face three options: getting jobs in the informal economy associated with insecurity, poor wages and working conditions; getting jobs in the low-tier service industries; or developing their vocational skills to benefit from new opportunities in the professional and advanced technical/knowledge sectors. Moreover, in developing countries a large portion of young people are not even lucky enough to choose among any of these options, thus becoming highly vulnerable.

The United Nations' World Youth Employment report (2004) indicates that in almost all countries, females tend to be far more vulnerable than males in terms of long-term unemployment, and secondly, young people who have advanced academic qualifications are far less likely to experience long-term unemployment than others. In the limited opportunities of the formal labour market, those with limited vocational skills resort to forced entrepreneurship and self-employment in the informal economy, often working for low pay under hazardous conditions, with only few prospects for the future (United Nations 2005a).

Unemployment and lack of economic prospects of the urban youth are pushing many of them into criminal acts, excessive alcohol use, substance addiction, and in many cases resulting in processes of social or political violence (Fernandez-Maldonado 2004; United Nations 2005a). Long-term unemployment leads young people into a process of marginalization and social exclusion (United Nations 2004). The sustained high rates of long-term youth unemployment have a number of negative effects on societies. First, it results in countries failing to take advantage of the human resources to increase their productive potential at a time of transition to a globalized world that inexorably demands such leaps in productive capacity. Second, it reinforces the intergenerational transmission of poverty. Third, owing to the discrepancy between more education and exposure to the mass media and fewer employment opportunities, this may encourage the spread of disruptive behaviours as witnessed in the 2008 post election violence, recourse to illegal alternatives for generating income and the loss of basic societal values, all of which erode public safety and social capital. Fourth, it may trigger violent and intractable political conflicts. And lastly, lack of opportunity and meritocracy in a system that favours adults who have less formal education and training but more wealth, power and job stability (Hopenhayn 2002).

Youth and Post-election Violence in Rift Valley

In the aftermath of the 2007/2008 post-election violence, youth were both victims and perpetrators of violent and criminal acts. The marginalization of youth in Kenyan society is neither coincidence nor conspiracy. Kenyan youth are excluded from viable economic livelihoods and positive citizen engagement in policies that affect them. Youth, defined by the Kenya

Government as people between 15 and 30 years old, constitute 32% of Kenya's 36 million people. It is important to note some of the insights into the social, political, economic and community dynamics facing youth in Kenya and particularly in Rift Valley.

First, the population of youth is expected to increase to 16 million by 2012. This high population growth is accompanied by rapid urbanization. A very high proportion of urban growth has been attributed to youth migrating from the rural areas in search of better livelihoods. Almost two million youth are out of school, and the great majority of these have no regular work or income, making them particularly vulnerable to recruitment, for pay, into political campaigns and criminal gangs (Maupeu, 2008).

Second, the Kenyan youth face a complex reality: on one hand, they have a relatively high level of basic education, with a literacy rate of over 90%, and more than half of those who are out of school have completed some or all of secondary schooling. However, 75% of the out-of-school youth do not have regular, full-time employment. As many as 40,000 of these youth are entering the labour force each year with tertiary education, and facing an employment market that has only created 150,000 new formal sector jobs in the past six years. This is reflected in increasing levels of youth who are on the street and highly vulnerable to recruitment into petty crime, gangs and prostitution.

Third, youth frustrations and failed expectations, and their lack of opportunity for regular employment, fuelled but did not drive the widespread chaos that spread throughout the Nairobi, Central, Rift Valley, and Western regions in the post-election violence four years ago. Rift valley was indeed the epicentre of violence. It is true that almost 80% of those who were direct perpetrators and victims were youth, but they were the ammunition and the targets — not the gun or the trigger (Calas, 2008). In Kenya, the political culture has increasingly used youth as a central tool for gaining and holding power. Enlisting and paying youth is a relatively cheap and effective way to mobilize for political rallies, to gather votes through persuasion or threat, and to intimidate the opposition. Politicians also mobilize youth and communities by highlighting historical grievances, particularly the allocation and control of land, and ethnic demonization. This is not an isolated phenomenon, but rather systematic and widespread, that is well documented and understood by youth, the general public, and by politicians.

Fourth, youth are vulnerable due to multiple and complex reasons, with historical roots in the colonial and post-colonial Kenyan experience. On one hand, there is an education system that is designed to be highly individualistic and competitive, in which "paper" examinations determine one's life opportunities, and the majority "fail" before attaining qualifications that are needed for formal sector employment. On the other hand, the education system raises expectations, leading school leavers to disdain agricultural work, without providing the knowledge, skills, and disposition to seek livelihood through enterprise and self-employment. Yet youth who are not from wealthy, and well-connected families have little opportunity for wage employment in the formal sector.

Fifth, the evolution of political life in Kenya has increasingly led to the enlistment of youth to support politicians' partisan and ethno-centric agendas. Politicians have fuelled inter-ethnic hostility, citing historical injustices and grievances. Rampant corruption in land allocations, the bias in national resource allocations, and the distortions in public service appointments, including ethnic bias in hiring for the security forces, are viewed through ethnic lenses, so that it is perceived to be the tribe that gains or losses politically. The widespread abuse of government authority and lack of accountability has resulted in a pervasive corruption of public affairs, notably in the police force.

Last, the great majority of youth have lost trust in the integrity of Kenya's political and social institutions and leaders, resulting in alienation and, without other means of support, a high level of involvement in petty crime such as drugs and prostitution, and for some, militias and gangs. Many youth lack a stable community with leadership that guides their own social, economic, cultural, and spiritual development. Youth are looking for such leadership and say that, if they cannot get it from elected politicians and community leadership, they will create it themselves. These points to the devastations by this group and thus need for attention and creation of opportunities.

Opportunities and Prospects for Youth in Rift Valley

Innovation is the amalgamation of invention and creativity that leads to the generation of social and economic value. It is a key driver for economic growth, global competitiveness and the integration of national level economy into the global knowledge economy, as well as an essential aspect of good governance. Moreover, the level of innovation within a society generally correlates with a nation's gross economic development. Kenya today boasts of highly developed ICT infrastructures, with multiple access channels to the Internet and Web services, whether through personal computers (PCs), community centres, mobile devices, kiosks, etc. compared to her neighbours. Proper utilization of knowledge, information and ICTs, then, is the greatest opportunity and challenge too. While entertainment usage, such as chatting and gaming, is prevalent among youth, it is possible to turn this to the educational, creative and research aspects of the Internet.

Knowledge Economy, Skill, Education and Training

Countries worldwide face the prospect of major transformation in the 21st century as the world moves towards a global information order (Castells 2000). In this new era, which is already upon us, urban economies are being radically altered by dynamic processes of economic and spatial restructuring (Graham and Marvin 1996). For the last two centuries social production has been primarily understood and shaped by neo-classical economy thought that recognises only three factors of production: land, labour and capital. Neo-classical economics consider knowledge, education and intellectual capacity as secondary, if not incidental, parameters of production (Knight 1995) – that is, human capital is assumed to be either embedded in labour or just one of numerous categories of capital. In the last decades, however, it has become apparent that knowledge in and of itself is sufficiently important to deserve recognition as a fourth factor of post-modern production.

The knowledge economy is an economy that can apply its rapidly increasing knowledge effectively in work and social situations to increase productivity and general well-being, and to create and apply new knowledge. It values cross-cultural skills for global trade and other cross-cultural exchange (Victorian Government 2002). At the centre of the move from an industrial to an information or knowledge-based economy is lesser importance placed on capital, labour and land as compared to knowledge, technology and innovativeness. The divergence, which is occurring between nations and between socio--demographic groups within economies, is as much to do with differences in the knowledge and skills base as with available technology.

In the knowledge economy, human capital is any country's greatest asset and nations need to take time to invest by benefiting their people from new technological opportunities through educational or employment programs. The shift to knowledge economy and skill-biased technological progress is increasing the relative demand for skilled labour at the expenses of the less-skilled (Manacorda and Petrongola 1999). Unarguably an important factor with regard to much of the structural unemployment in developed countries has been the mismatch between skills and newly created jobs (Jones, 1995). Perhaps the key issue is that ICT based work tends to require lower levels of traditional skills and greater abstract and synthetic reasoning skills (Mansell 1998).

In the knowledge era, criteria for employability are getting higher and higher every day, and more advanced skill requirement is becoming a prerequisite for employment. Most important, knowledge workers or the creative class have already gained mobility, that is to say, there exists tough global competition for high-skilled jobs (Florida 2000; 2002). Hence, providing education, vocational training and advanced skill development to young people for their labour force participation have never been that significant before.

A strategic investment in the youth through the deployment of information technologies either in vocational training or educational activities, provide opportunities for a "catch up" in human capital development. This is particularly important in Kenya where decades of the unequal distribution of national resources including education facilities, created an educational gap among different groups which consequently stifled human capital development in the country. This should also be viewed against the opportunity cost in time lost by many young people in Kenya as they engage in social vices such as youth pregnancy, insurgency and prostitution.

As observed by James Knowles and Jere Behrman (2006), the private and social rate of returns to different investments in youth depends on the context of such investments. The use of ICTs such as mobile telephone, computers and the internet system to leverage development is gaining popularity in rural and urban communities in the developing world. For instance, the rapid diffusion of mobile phone technology in sub-Saharan Africa has exceeded any single technological innovation in the region in recent times. The region has the world's fastest growth in mobile phone ownership and this technology is playing an important role in reducing poverty (Development Magazine, 2006). This has no doubt affected the lives of people in the region in a positive way.

At its simplest, a mobile phone allows farmers and fishermen to find out the prices in various markets, and allows a handyman to travel to nearby villages only when he receives communication (via) phone that there is a job available. In Kenya and Tanzania mobile phones are improving healthcare provision, where doctors use them to diagnose patients living in remote communities. (The Development Magazine, 2006, p.8).

The rate of returns to the deployment of information and communication technologies for educational and vocational training for the youth can be understood within the context of the level of technology adoption in social and economic activities in Rift Valley. The application of modern communication technologies such as computers, the Internet (including Web 2.0 technologies), Personal Digital Assistant (PDA) devices and mobile phones in the country have reached a critical mass given that these technologies have become part of everyday life in both rural and urban part of Rift Valley, Kenya.

In the same vein, the use of other modern technologies, albeit slow, has offered some glimmer of hope to the poor in secondary education sub-sector in Rift Valley. The right to quality education for the youth is always considered the responsibility of the government. Although effective educational policy and regulatory framework remains the responsibility of the government, it must be acknowledged that the large and complex nature of education and knowledge acquisition in today's world, particularly in a low-income region such as Africa, can no longer be left to the government alone. Rather, the enrichment of secondary education and youth development depend on a sustained collaborative partnership between African governments and social entrepreneurs from within and outside Africa. The ability to harness the benefits of ICT provides tremendous opportunities for developing the potential of African youths through education and training. Such collaborative partnerships and the enabling environment provided by good policy frameworks are essential in stimulating a broad scale application of ICTs in youth and community development in Kenya.

Role of ICT in Vocational Skill Development

The production and use of ICTs have become the driving force of change in the modern world (Mobbs 2002). ICTs have dramatically reshaped labour markets around the world. The increasing importance of knowledge to economic development and the greater capacity to codify information and knowledge are rapidly increasing the movement in service work to the locations with the cheapest or most capable workers around the world (OECD 2001; 1997; 1999; Morris 2000a). Consequently, social inequality within and between countries has increased and young men and women have tended to bear the brunt of this. The number of unskilled, semi-skilled and entry level jobs in a wide variety of sectors have declined and the demand for skilled workers has increased with these positions being filled by qualified workers from abroad. Large organizations in both the public and private sectors have shed millions of low-skill previous positions. For young people this has resulted in stubbornly high unemployment levels and in most countries these are locked in at many times above national unemployment rates (Morris 2000b).

ICTs are playing a pivotal role in revolutionising the ways in which most of the traditional services are produced, traded and delivered, as well as offering opportunities for the generation of new activities and employment in many service industries (Petit 1995; Andersen *et al.* 2000). The emergence and widespread diffusion of ICTs have an impact on employment in the service sector through three main channels, that is by expanding final demand or shifting its composition from tangible goods to intangible, information and knowledge intensive services by changing the composition of intermediate demand both in services and manufacturing towards information and knowledge based inputs and processes; and by increasing labour productivity in some of the service activities traditionally affected by the so-called cost-disease or productivity-bias (Evangelista and Savona 2003:452).

Non Governmental Organizations (NGOs) have been working on a wide range of ICT initiatives to close the ever growing digital divide. These initiatives include but are not limited to, providing public ICT access through libraries and community centres, offering ICT skill training programs, providing ICT access and training to disadvantaged target groups including people with disability and their carers, distributing free computer training resources through libraries, shop-fronts and community centres, and establishing computer reuse schemes to provide affordable refurbished computers to people on a low income and non-profit community groups (Yigitcanlar and Baum 2006).

While the globalization of the knowledge economy is increasingly intensified in the 21st century, the links and relations between countries, regions, cities and their residents have become much more advanced. The widening digital divide issue has aroused a concern all around the world. For the balanced and sustained development, countries and cities started to establish aforementioned initiatives and understand their responsibilities with respect to information resource sharing and narrowing the digital divide. The continuum of these initiatives and policies will likely be able to change the digital divide into a digital opportunity. The labour market for young people has changed significantly over the past two decades under the combined impact of globalization, market liberalization and the adoption of ICTs into work places. ICTs are playing an essential role in providing new training and employment opportunities for the youth. There are a number of successful initiatives from both developed and developing countries that endeavour to provide support for young people in developing skills and employment opportunities. Some of these opportunities and prospects are examined below with reference to their application in the Rift Valley region.

Providing ICT and Skill Training

ICT training could offer particular advantages to young people starting a business (i.e. SMEs) in Rift Valley. One of these advantages is that ICTs offer potentially low cost forms. Another one is the greater range of opportunities the application of new communication based technologies can offer for servicing the needs of disadvantaged people and marginalized communities in the Rift Valley who occupy remote areas and have poor infrastructure.

Education through ICT

ICTs are increasingly being used to support alternative advanced education to improve the efficiency, accessibility and quality of the learning process in developing countries. One of the most clearly demonstrated applications is distance education (or e-learning). Distance education has been a particularly successful model in developing countries where affordability and geography have been real barriers to access. To date, distance education has mainly been applied to tertiary education where the motivation and commitment of students are high. The six largest distance education universities in the world are located in developing countries: Turkey, Indonesia, China, India, Thailand and Korea and closer home the UNISA in South Africa– all of which offer expanding virtual campuses. In the case of primary and secondary education, distance education is not as common as tertiary education. However in recent years this has gained momentum particularly for servicing remote rural areas and could be considered for the expansive Rift Valley region.

Narrowing the Digital Divide

ICT initiatives targeting digital divide and disadvantaged people's skill development have a huge potential role to play in providing help in achieving universal skill training and education through reducing physical and social barriers to education, promoting efficiency in education, and improving the quality of teaching and learning (Guttman 2003). Among many initiatives targeting to narrow the digital divide are two American NGOs' – AmeriCorps and NetDay. AmeriCorps is a network of American national service programs that engage more than 50,000 Americans each year in intensive service to meet critical needs in education, public safety, health, and the environment. AmeriCorps members, in partnership with technology firms and non-profit organizations, are bringing technology support to schools and community organizations across America. Serving as program facilitators in schools located in low-income communities, AmeriCorps members interface with teachers and students, teaching technology-based programs during school hours and in after-school programs. NetDay is an American national non-profit organization whose mission is to connect every child to a brighter future by helping educators meet educational goals through the effective use of technology. NetDay provides AmeriCorps members with technical training and support, as well as orientation on community service. NetDay-AmeriCorps Bridge Program model has potential for socio-economic development of the region if replicated in Rift Valley to reach the young, low income, people with disabilities, and those in remote areas.

ICT Employment Generation through Entrepreneurship

Young entrepreneurs have been closely identified with ventures associated with the knowledge economy, particularly in Japan, China, India and

Singapore. The entrepreneurial activities include young people as information intermediaries, opportunities for e-commerce-based entrepreneurship, tele-centres as income generation for young people, and income generation through cable television. The widespread use of English on the world-wide-web has created a need for local content and applications to enable utilization by non-English speakers. This provides an opportunity for young people with language and ICT skills to work as information intermediaries (Curtain 2003).

Young people in Rift Valley can also make a living through developing websites in local languages to facilitate communication between people and organizations (e.g. local websites of international NGOs). Providing an e-commerce prospect to local communities would promote employment for youth. A good example would be the global e-commerce project that is based on marketing local culture artefacts. Youth in Rift Valley could form organizations to promote and market local cultural products (e.g. music, art, handicrafts) of the region by building sustainable community centres for people to gather and display their products as well as advertise and sell them via e-commerce websites.

Promoting Public-Private Partnership to Generate Employment

Public-private partnerships have the potential to enable governments to increase public infrastructure or public services while using fewer of their own resources and maintaining or even improving the quality of the standards offered. Public-private partnerships are particularly suited to ICT-related development programs because the private sector partner is in a good position to not only provide funding, but also assist with the knowledge and expertise required to operate ICT facilities. Rift Valley region has the highest number of counties and this provides an opportunity for youth in ICT to promote public-private co-operation for economic growth. Call centres, technical support services, help-lines, data conversion centres could be established through public and private partnerships.

ICT-Based Employment Opportunities for Disadvantaged Youth

The creation of ICT-based employment opportunities to assist the most vulnerable among young people is another opportunity for youth in Rift Valley. This can be achieved through young people utilizing acquired ICT skills to assist local development agencies and operators to deliver services to those most in need. For example, the use of low-cost ICT in the health system (such as internet and GIS) creates a demand for young people with ICT skills. This group could use relatively simple internet-based data management systems to exchange information such as patient records between healthcare professionals. Geographical information systems (GIS) are another common method for reaching the poor and isolated.

Knowledge Economy and the Informal Sector

This could target to bridge the gap between the knowledge economy and the informal sector by creating opportunities for youth to provide informal sector workers easy access to internet through tele-centres to enable them obtain information on markets or administrative procedures, and to publicise their services to a wider customer (Curtin 2003). In Rift Valley, the informal economy predominates as a livelihood activity for poorer people and ICT provides an opportunity here as it is of particular importance for people in poor urban and rural areas, women and farmers, thus the youth could bridge this gap.

Putting Young People in the Lead

The last group of initiatives intends to put young people in charge. As was argued at the United Nations' World Youth Forum in August 2001, young people and youth NGOs are the best agents for delivering change for other young people. Therefore, young people's participation in the design and implementation of ICT-based initiatives are essential.

ICTs have been extremely important in generating three strongly diverging forces for the world's young workers. First, they have contributed to the automation of processes making some workers redundant and closing off jobs many young people could have expected to begin their careers with. Secondly, they have changed the economics of many sectors reducing the importance of scale, facilitating an upsurge in employment in small and medium enterprises (SMEs), and third, they have created new skilled employment opportunities through a number of ICT training initiatives (Morris 2000b). Whereas young people, with the benefit of a good education and training foundation, could have once expected to have a job for life, this is no longer the case. In the knowledge era, continuous education and training is the only way for job security. Especially if the education and training is in ICT-related skills, and if they demonstrate enterprise and resourcefulness, there are vast opportunities for the young people. Equitable access to information, knowledge (or know-how) and education is one of the most vital principles in the emerging global knowledge economy. ICTs are practical tools in narrowing knowledge gaps between countries, regions and also people, by providing new frontiers in the areas of information exchange, intellectual freedom and online education. ICT can make a tremendous contribution to human development, but only for those that have access (Haldon 2001; Walsh et al. 2001). ICT access and usage differs mainly by socio-economic status, and not because of personal preferences, and because many crucial social and economic benefits may accrue from greater access to and usage of communication technologies (Kozma *et al.* 2004).

The rapid pace of technological development in the new knowledge economy has created increasingly more powerful ICTs and increasing demand on workers with advanced (ICT) skills. However, just because the technology is available does not mean everyone can get the training and develop skills in it. Those who cannot access necessary information and training, and cannot keep up with technological revolution will be left behind and vulnerable as the knowledge economy has already wreaked havoc in unskilled and semi-skilled employment (Hull 2003).

This rapid technological development has caused the digital divide where it is generally understood as a multidimensional phenomenon encompassing three distinct aspects. The 'global divide' refers to the divergence of ICT access between developed and developing societies. The 'social divide' concerns the gap between information rich and poor in each nation. And lastly within the online community, the 'democratic divide' signifies the difference between those who do, and do not, use the panoply of digital resources and ICT to engage, mobilise and participate in social, cultural and economic aspects of life (Norris 2001).

Challenges

The rapid and continuing growth and development of information and communications technologies (ICTs) is transforming the ways in which we live and work. The role of ICTs in transforming national as well as global development has been recognized the world over. To achieve regional human development, for example, Rift Valley has to exploit the ability of ICT to deliver information for strategic decision-making in the county governments, trade, agriculture, manufacturing, social services and other sectors. It is acceptable that access to communication services will empower rural communities to participate and contribute to regional socio-economic development. However, youth in Rift Valley are faced with numerous challenges.

Rift valley is an expansive region bordering Ethiopia and South Sudan to the north, Uganda to the North West and Tanzania to the south. It is faced with limited availability or distribution of various communication services, especially in the rural areas. There are reduced fixed telephone connections despite increase in exchange capacity. The region has also faced closure of several postal outlets due to the limited commercial viability in rural areas and lack of incentives for operators to invest in the rural areas. Majority of the populace lack access to communication services due to low reliability of infrastructure occasioned by the frequent breakdown of communication links and inadequate infrastructure as a result of the limited bandwidth of Telkom Kenya's *Jambonet*. Furthermore, the roll-out obligations in operators' licenses and other reform initiatives by the government in the last five years have not had much impact on availing communication services to the rural areas.

The high costs of providing various communication services in the rural areas within Rift Valley, such as, backhaul links, frequency spectrum and communication facilities pose a great challenge for youth entrepreneurs. Meantime, for potential service providers, processes of application for frequency, obtaining frequency spectrum and type approval are long and tedious, with complex licence forms and lacking transparency. Computers are still expensive in Kenya. While second hand computers cost as little as $150, branded new computers are sold at $500 or higher. In a country with a GDP of $1600, majority of individuals and educational institutions cannot afford to buy a computer and consider it as a luxury item, which is more expensive than a TV.

There is no institutional framework for Universal Access to support young and upcoming entrepreneurs. Lack of sustainability of rural communications and a stringent licensing framework do not favour rural operators. ICT is an emerging sector that has yet to develop a workable policy and strategy that addresses access to ICT by a majority of its citizens, especially citizens in the rural areas. It is important that a mechanism be developed to enable the rural population access affordable benefits of communication services since the majority of the Rift Valley's population, as in many other regions in Kenya, reside in rural areas.

Majority of rural homes, schools and training institutions in Rift Valley are still not connected to electricity. Kenya being a developing country, the government has not been able to connect all parts of the country to the national electricity grid. Consequently, those institutions which are supposed to spur technological development that are located in such areas are left handicapped and may not be able to offer computer studies which are fundamental for knowledge economy.

The provision of communication services is skewed towards urban areas, especially towards towns and district headquarters. There is therefore a need to ensure widespread access by rural people, of basic communication services of acceptable quality and at affordable prices. This need is made even more urgent by the fact that there are huge disparities in socio-economic development between rural and urban areas. Most institutions and schools are not able to connect to the World Wide Web due to the high costs involved in accessing high speed connectivity. On average, it may cost approximately $120 per month to connect to about 15 computers on a bandwidth of 128/64kbps. This is considered very expensive for such slow speed.

The entire Rift Valley has high levels of illiteracy, as most of its occupants are pastoralists whose nomadic lifestyle is a major hindrance to accessing quality education. The few decision makers within the area have limited awareness and knowledge of the importance of ICT. Community leaders charged with looking after the interests of the community do not perceive the need to purchase and install computers in their community as a priority. Socio-cultural practices which peg livelihoods and status to livestock keeping for majority of Rift Valley residents have negatively affected adoption and utilization of ICT. They consider the focus on provision of health care, water, education and other basic human needs amenities as having resulted in ignoring the supportive role of ICTs in these initiatives. This has led to inadequate utilization and harnessing of ICT potential and inability to cope with fast changing technologies. Consequently, there is lack of ICT training and support capacity in most rural areas. Rural populations are not aware of communication services available and their impact, and do not have the basic skills and knowledge to exploit communication facilities, thus posing a challenge to development of knowledge economy for this region.

Apparently, the dilemma which arises in providing educational technology stems from inadequate financial resources and a limited distributive capacity. In addition, many institutions have not been able to employ teachers, and provide other requisite resources to keep up with this demand. This brings about compromised quality of education. Further, many local schools are unable to carry out necessary comprehensive educational expansion programmes that could support economic development of the area.

Rift Valley, like the rest of the nation, lacks enough qualified ICT teachers in schools. The demand for ICT learning has been tremendous and the number of trained teachers cannot meet the demand. There are more students willing to be taught computing skills than there are teachers to transfer the skills. Moreover, computers are still very expensive and despite spirited efforts by government agencies, NGOs, corporate bodies and individuals to donate computers to as many schools as possible, a greater percentage of the schools still remain unable to provide computers for use by their pupils.

The Kenyan system of education which focuses on creating a generation of "producers" rather than "users" is another challenge. Archaic teaching and learning methods often hamper the spirit of innovation and stifle creativity. Despite the recognition that the arts can promote capabilities and skills that are beneficial to other areas of study and learning, and in spite of efforts to make curricula more student-centred, teaching remains textbook-driven and pedagogical. Moreover, school curricula tend not to factor in job market demands, thereby hindering the next generation's chances of employment. This is a national problem and not necessarily specific to Rift Valley region.

ICT in Rift Valley could play a significant role in equalizing opportunities for marginalized groups and communities. But the paradox is that for those groups that are unable to cross the technology divide, ICT is yet another means to further marginalize them. Education has a major role to play in resolving this problem. Thus, unless ICT becomes part of both the delivery and content of education, the disadvantage will deepen and development will suffer.

The failure to use ICT is itself a result of the digital and knowledge divides that exist, and their causes are deeply embedded in the complex historical and socio-cultural context of the region. Fortunately, with the Vision 2030 goals, the national government has begun to implement strategies that will address these paradoxes. Further, it has been accepted that access to communication services will empower rural communities economically and enable them participate and contribute to the national socio-economic development. This will also help to address the huge socio-economic divide mentioned above. The rapid growth of mobile telephony in the country demonstrates the tremendous capacity and potential for communications development, including other sectorial development in rural areas.

ICT Entrepreneurship Support Programs

Entrepreneurship is not an easy option and is best suited to those with the necessary skills and acumen. Some of these skills can be acquired, even via the Internet. However, some skills such as risk taking and self-confidence may be more socially oriented. Young people starting their own businesses are likely to experience a range of problems many of which could apply to anyone starting a new enterprise but some are specifically related to the youthful age of the entrepreneur. Young people are likely to have more limited business networks and contacts, fewer financial resources as they have had less time to accumulate personal savings or acquire property, and may also experience age discrimination from customers, suppliers or finance lenders. One fundamental problem is the inability to secure start-up funds leading to under capitalisation (starting a business without enough funds).Other problems commonly encountered are managing cash flow, particularly dealing with bad debts and late payments, and coping with stress especially without the support of friends who understand the demands of self-employment. Once under way, problems can arise with managing the expansion of the business such as working out how to employ the right staff and managing other people for the first time.

Governments, the private sector, non-government agencies and local communities can each in their own way promote efforts to support young people starting up enterprises based on ICT. However, enterprise support programs run by governments or international agencies have often had high failure rates due to insufficient financial resources and staff, and overly rigid and inappropriate procedures.

Moreover, taking advantage of the digital revolution while maintaining a society's ethical and cultural codes is a delicate balancing act. Awareness and online child protection campaigns are vital to protecting people from harmful or offensive content. However, overly prohibitive measures such as fully blocking multimedia sharing platforms can greatly restrict the development of a culture of creativity and innovation which Rift Valley is in dire need of to spur economic development based on intellectual capital.

Enterprise-based employment programs for young people need to have several key features. First, external assistance provided by governments or NGOs needs to have a commercial orientation. This means acknowledging that the venture being assisted has the productive capacity to create profit, re-pay loans and expand to employ others. Second, the assistance needs to help young people manage risk more effectively. Third, the assistance needs to be tailored to meet the needs of individuals in terms of their skills, work experience, aspirations and capacity to obtain resources. Finally, the enterprise support program needs to be cost-effective and not rely on a single source of external support, be it technical, organizational or financial.

Conclusion

The Rift Valley economy like the national economy is in the process of a profound transformation, spurred by globalization and supported by the rapid development of ICTs that accelerate the transmission and use of information and knowledge. Intangible resources such as knowledge, know-how and social capital are the coal, oil, and diamonds of the twenty-first century for developed, developing and emerging economies (Carayannis et al. 2006). Therefore, in the 21st century solutions for promoting youth employment in Rift Valley are clustered around successful policy implementations on education and training, towards the knowledge economy.

Promoting youth employment and employability requires important integrated effort that includes actions in the areas of education, skills development, job supply and support for young low-income entrepreneurs, particularly in the knowledge intensive sectors. All international best practices, as well as the successful examples and cases discussed in this paper, need to be reviewed and considered by the authorities of the region. However it is important to modify these initiatives by considering social, cultural and economic differences of the region. To be successful, the initiatives must provide participation by various stakeholders, from state to private entrepreneurs, international and national NGOs, local authorities, youth leaders, the media, and the public.

While it is clear that there is extensive potential for ICTs to generate employment for young people, this potential will not be realized unless the region has a range of supporting strategies in place, including an enabling environment. This enabling environment includes opportunity and resources to engage in skills training in technology, access to data and information, and high quality work and training environments.

ICTs offer youth in Rift Valley the opportunity to close the gap with developed countries and narrow the global digital divide. Applying ICTs in education is paramount in enabling young people acquire ICT skills. Therefore governments need to ensure that they provide quality education to all with ICTs as integral components of education planning and school curricula.

The participation of young people in the development and implementation of initiatives involving the use of ICTs to generate employment is a key factor in the success of such initiatives. ICTs are also beneficiary tools to support young people's participation in decision-making processes.

Mentor support for starting ICT-related enterprises is a key service that central government, NGOs, corporate bodies or county authorities could organize to provide advice and guidance to young entrepreneurs. The mentor program may also include providing incentives such as tax exemptions, grants or micro-finance facilities to encourage young people and their SMEs undertake business. Partnership with national and international organizations such as United Nations and its agencies may help those implementing new best practices in building global, national and county networks of partnership. Lastly, investing only on technology is not the solution to the young population's problems, investing on social and human capital makes a more sustainable change. As Mansell and When (1998) indicated, investing in mere technology and not human capital will only lead to increase in energy consumption and not in economic growth and employment opportunities for young people.

A culture of innovation within society can lead to sustained economic growth, greater global competitiveness, enhanced employment and entrepreneurship opportunities, and a more inclusive society for youth.

ICT and the Internet have been repeatedly identified as key drivers for promoting innovation among youth, and for cultivating a more innovative society as a whole, and youth in Rift Valley cannot afford to be overtaken by this development.

References

Andersen, B., Howells, J., Hull, R., Miles, I. and Roberts, J. (2000). (Eds.), *Knowledge and Innovation in the New Service Economy*. Cheltenham: Edward Elgar.

Calas, B. (2008). From rigging to violence. Lafargue, J. (Ed.). *The general elections in Kenya*, 2007. (pp. 165-185). Dar es Salaam: Mkuki na Nyota Publishers Ltd.

Castells, M. (2000). *End of the Millennium: The information age economy, society and culture*. Volume 3. Oxford: Blackwell.

Curtain, R. (2000). Identifying the basis for a youth employment strategy aimed at transitional and developing countries. Report commissioned by the United Nations Social Development Division.

Curtain, R. (2003). Creating more opportunities for young people using information and communications technology. The World Summit on Information Societies, Geneva, 12-14 December 2003. Services: Firm and sectoral evidence. *Structural Change and Economic Dynamics*. 14(2003): 449-474.

Fernandez-Maldonado (2004). *ICT-related transformations in Latin American metropolises*. Delft, the Netherlands: Delft University Press.

Galanouli, D, Murphy, C. and Gardner, J. (2004). Teacher's perceptions of the effectiveness of ICT-competence training. *Computers and Education*. 43(2004): 63-79.

Gleeson, B. and Sipe, N. (2006). *Creating child friendly cities: reinstating kids in the city*. (Eds.) New York: Routledge.

Government of Kenya (2010). *2009 Population and Housing Census,* Available at *http://www.knbs.or.ke* accessed on 29/10/2011.

Graham, S. and Marvin, S. (1996). *Telecommunications and the city: Electronic spaces, urban places*. London: Routledge.

Guttman, C. (2003). Education in and for the Information Society. Paris: United Nations Educational, Scientific and Cultural Organization.

Haddon, L. (2001). Social exclusion and information and communication technologies. *New Media and Society*, 2(4): 387–406.

Jones, B. (1995). *Sleepers Wake: Technology and the Future of Work* 4th Edition. Oxford: Oxford University Press.

Manacorda, M. & Petrongolo, B. (1999). Skill mismatch and unemployment in OECD countries. *Economica*. 66: 181-207. *technology and sustainable development*. Oxford: Oxford University Press.

Maupeu, H. (2008). Revisiting post-election violence. Lafargue, J. (Ed.). *The general elections in Kenya, 2007*. (pp. 187-223). Dar es Salaam: Mkuki na Nyota Publishers Ltd.

McGuirk, J. (2001). Youth at risk: Is technology the answer? *Literacy and Numeracy Studies*. 11(1): 53-66.

Mobbs, P. (2002). Glossary and Cross-Reference Index. Green Net Civil Society Internet Rights Project. Accessed on 6 November 2010 from www.internetrights.org.uk.

Morris, P. (2000a). World Wide Work: Knowledge-intensive Globally Distributed Work. Department of Industry Science and Resources, Canberra.

Morris, P. (2000b). A survey of the implications of information and communication technologies on youth employment. An Issues Paper prepared for the International Labour Organisation.

Norris, P. (2001). *Digital divide?: Civic engagement, information poverty, and the Internet worldwide, Communication, society, and politics*. Cambridge: Cambridge University Press.

OECD (2001). *Putting the Young in Business: Policy Challenges for Entrepreneurship*. Organisation for Economic Development & Cooperation, Paris.

Hopenhayn, M. (2002). Youth and Employment in Latin America and the Caribbean: Problems, Prospects and Options. The Youth Employment Summit, Alexandria, Egypt, 7-11 September 2002.

Hull, B. (2003). ICT and social exclusion: The role of libraries. *Telematics and Informatics*. 20(2003): 131-142. *Youth*. Geneva: ILO.

Knight, R. (1995). Knowledge–based development: Policy and planning implications for cities. *Urban Studies*. 32(2): 225–260.

Kozma, R., McGhee, R., Quellmalz, E. and Zalles, D. (2004). Closing the digital divide: evaluation of the World Links program. *International Journal of Educational Development*. 24(2004): 361–381.

Lever, W. (2002). Correlating the knowledge–base of cities with economic growth. *Urban Studies*. 39(5/6): 859–870.

OECD (1996). International Trade in Professional Services: Assessing barriers and encouraging reform. Organisation for Economic Co-operation and Development, Paris.

Robertson, J. (1995). Electronics, environment and employment: Harnessing private gain to the common good. *Futures*. 27(5): 487-504.

Semboja H.H. (2005). A Concept Paper on Promoting Opportunities for Youth Employment in East Africa, Prepared for the ILO regional Office and presented at the EAC Meeting of Labour Commissioners, Silver Springs Hotel, Nairobi, Kenya, December 2005.

United Nations (2001a). *Youth Participation Manual*. Human Resources Development Section, Social Development Division. New York: United Nations Publication.

United Nations Development Programme (2001). *Creating a Development Dynamic*. Final Report of the Digital Opportunity Initiative. United Nations Development Programme. June, 2001.

Yigitcanlar, T. and Baum, S. (2006). Bridging the Digital Divide through E-government. In M. Khosrow-Pour (Ed.) *Encyclopaedia of E-Commerce, E-Government and Mobile Commerce: Concepts, Trends and Challenges*. 353-358. Hershey, PA: Idea Group Publishing.

Notes on Contributors

Alexander Luchetu Likaka is the founder of the Centre for Ageing and Rural Development (CARD) Kenya and a lecturer at the Department of Sociology at Egerton University.

David Omondi Okeyo teaches in the School of Public Health and Community Development, Department of Nutrition and Health, Maseno University.

Easter Achieng is the Executive Director & Programs Coordinator, Kenya Female Advisory Organization (KEFEADO).

Erick Victor Onyango Fwaya is a Lecturer, School of Business & Economics, Narok University College.

Felix Ngunzo Kioli is a Lecturer at the Department of Sociology and Anthropology. Maseno University.

Frederick Kang'ethe Iraki is an Associate Professor, United States International University (USIU).

George Otieno Obonyo is a Graduate Assistant, Department of Eco-Tourism, Hotel and Institution Management, Maseno University.

Hamadi Iddi Boga is the Principal, Jomo Kenyatta University of Agriculture and Technology-Taita Taveta Campus .

Kīmani Njogu is a cultural analyst and Director of Twaweza Communications.

Lusweti Sellah is a Lecturer at the Department of Foreign Languages and Social Sciences, Pwani University.

Margaret G. Gecaga is a Senior Lecturer and Chairperson of the Department of Philosophy and Religious Studies, Kenyatta University.

Mohamed Mraja is a Lecturer at the Department of Philosophy & Religious Studies Moi University.

Musambayi Katumanga is a Senior Lecturer in the Department of Political Science and Public Administration, University of Nairobi.

Rocha Chimerah is a Professor of Kiswahili at Pwani University.

Romanus Opiyo is an Assistant Lecturer, Department of Urban and Regional Planning, University of Nairobi.

Shauri Halimu is an Associate Professor and Chairman Department of Social Sciences, Pwani University.

www.ingramcontent.com/pod-product-compliance
Lightning Source LLC
Chambersburg PA
CBHW032129020426
42334CB00016B/1095